Proverbs

A Devotional Commentary
Volume One

Chapters 1-6

PTLB
PRINCIPLES
TO LIVE BY
LIFE IS RELATIONSHIPS

Gil Stieglitz

Proverbs: A Devotional Commentary
Volume One
Chapters 1-6

Published by Principles to Live By, Roseville CA 95661
www.ptlb.com

Cover by John Chase

All Scripture verses are from the New American Standard Bible unless otherwise indicated.
New American Standard Bible: 1995 update.
1995 La Habra, CA: The Lockman Foundation.

ISBN 978-0-9838602-8-0
Commentary

Printed in the United States of America

Dedication

This book is dedicated

to the *Stieglitz* family

and to those who are
or will be a part of my family
through faith.

Table of Contents

Preface

This small little project which was originally meant to help my girls – Jenessa, Abbey, and Grace as they grew up and raised families of their own – has turned into a 2400+ page behemoth which just scratches the surface of God's wisdom through the pen of Solomon. I feel very privileged that these devotional thoughts on God's wisdom through Solomon have been spread around the world through email. I have received many encouragements to collect these thoughts into a commentary so people can easily go to any verse in the Proverbs and understand the depth of what Solomon is saying. The fact that many have been filled with God's wisdom to act differently than they would in themselves means that my comments have helped Solomon achieve the original purpose for the Proverbs.

I must give thanks to a number of crucial people who without their efforts these volumes would not exist. Sandy Johnson who has read these comments over and over to edit them, you are invaluable. Debbie Purvis is a true God-send as she has seamlessly made the material in this book ready for publication and arranged with all the appropriate people to make these volumes happen.

I must give thanks to my Hebrew professor Dr. Tom Finley from Talbot School of Theology who made me memorize many sections of Scripture in Hebrew and understand the Hebrew grammatical structures until I grasped at least some level of Hebraic thinking. What you taught gave me the opportunity to dig deeper than the average reader of the proverbs.

I must also give thanks to Richard K. Hum who was at one time my youth pastor and instilled in me a deep love of the Scriptures. He put into me the incredible value of digging deep in Scripture in order to understand it and then the value of meditating upon it to initiate a more lasting change. I can remember countless times when he initiated my memorizing Scripture and quizzed me about the lessons that that Scripture should have on my life if I really took it seriously.

How can I not thank my wonderful wife, Dana? Every day she asks me what God said in my quiet time. What verses from the Proverbs did God highlight to you last night? What insights did God give you about our situation through the Scriptures? What do you think God wants you to do? Her rapt attention and desire to live in the will of God completely is another constant joy to me.

I must thank the Lord God Almighty who is willing to meet with me about my petty issues and pour out wisdom to me personally so that I will be wiser. It is a wonderful grace that He gives. The wonder of my interaction with God through the pages of the Scriptures and often through Proverbs is my daily highlight. Almost every night I enjoy a deep interaction with God about my day, the state of our world, my concerns, meetings I have planned in the future, and things I hope to accomplish. I am thrilled to say that the answers to my questions to God pour out from the Scriptures. It is wonderful to know that I can ask God a question and He will answer. More often than not His answers to my personal questions come through the proverbs. He explains how my natural reaction is not correct and that there is a better way to handle the situation. He helps me dig for a higher level of wisdom than I would pursue on my own. He helps me classify a person's tendency and understand how to treat that type of behavior.

Prepare to be amazed by the insights from a man who lived 1,000 years before Jesus Christ. What you wanted to know about how to handle the people in your life is in this book; don't miss it.

Introduction

King David kept saying to his young son Solomon that the key to life was to *Acquiring Wisdom* and *Acquiring Understanding*. In other words if Solomon was going to be successful in life, he was going to need both of these crucial qualities in increasing amounts: Wisdom and Understanding. David boiled success in life down to these two things for his young son, Solomon: If you get these, my son, then you will be guaranteed a great life. What was David trying to pound into Solomon's head as the keys to a great life? Wisdom in the proverbs means to know how to find and make the triple-win choice. Wisdom is the choice that would honor God, benefit others, and be a win for the individual. Wisdom is the practical application of information and people in such a way as God is glorified, righteous people are benefited, and the individual also wins. Understanding in the book of Proverbs means that the individual sees the connections between people, events, situations, and reactions. Seeing both the public and hidden connections changes how one acts, speaks, and plans. We see in the book of Proverbs that Solomon got his father's message – even more than David could have imagined.

God inspired Solomon, the King of Israel, to record incredibly insightful wisdom on human relations. This book was penned 3,000 years ago, and it is still weighty, profound, and insightful about making our way through life. Let me give you an abbreviated list of the wisdom in this book. There are in this book the secrets of leadership. There are comparisons throughout this book that bring us to our senses before we get lost in a stupid pursuit or perspective. There is in this book the ways to deal with 63 different kinds of fools that will come into your life at various times. There are in these pithy sayings the rules of money that will allow you to gain all you need without being corrupted by it. There are crucial insights for marriage. This book contains the answers on how to conduct your life so you stop yourself from being stupid or destructive. In reality, the secrets of having a great relational life are recorded in the powerful statements in the book of Proverbs. It is amazing. Too often a person waits till they have experience before they know what to do. The Book of Proverbs is God's way of saying: here is wisdom so you don't have to learn the hard way what is the wise path. There is not a day that goes by that I do not consult the book of Proverbs for God's answers to the specific issues and problems I am facing. This book is a collection of my comments about Solomon's insights into life and people.

Take a look at the genesis of the book of Proverbs. Solomon did not start out as the smartest man to ever walk the planet (just like all of us). He started as an overwhelmed, young man who inherited a job that was too big for him. He knew it and the people knew it. He cried out to God for wisdom and insight to be able to rule the people he had been put over. God's answer to Solomon's prayer clearly came true.

> 1 Kings 1:3:5 - In Gibeon the Lord appeared to Solomon in a dream at night; and God said, "Ask what you wish Me to give you." Then Solomon said, "You have shown great loving kindness to your servant David my father according as he walked before you in truth and righteousness and uprightness of heart toward You; and you have reserved for him this great loving kindness that You have given him a son to sit on his throne, as it is this day. Now, O Lord my God, You have made Your servant king in place of my father David, yet I am but a little child; I do not know how to go out or come in. Your servant is in the midst of Your people which You have chosen, a great people who are too many to be numbered or counted. So give your Servant an understanding heart to judge Your people to discern between good and evil. For who is able to judge this great people of Yours?"

It was pleasing in the sight of the Lord that Solomon had asked this thing. God said to him, "Because you have asked this thing and have not asked for yourself long life, nor have asked riches for yourself, nor have you asked for the life of your enemies, but have asked for yourself discernment to understand justice, behold, I have done according to your words. Behold, I have given you a wise and discerning heart, so that there has been no one like you before you, nor shall one like you arise after you. I have also given you what you have not asked, both riches and honor, so that there will not be any among the kings like you all your days. If you walk in My ways, keeping My statutes and commandments as your father David walked, then I will prolong your days."

Aren't you glad that Solomon wrote down some of the insights that God gave him so that we could benefit from the wisdom that he received? I believe that if you cry out to God for wisdom rather than riches and power, God will give you wisdom. I believe He will direct you to the book of Proverbs and the wisdom He gave Solomon. My prayer is that you will grow and behave differently because of the explanations and understandings that come from this devotional commentary on Proverbs.

Proverbs 1

PROVERBS 1:1 - *The proverbs of Solomon the son of David, king of Israel:*

The word *proverb* is the word *masa*l, which means to become like or to be comparable to. The idea seems to be that a proverb is a way of declaring or seeing a truth by comparing it with something else. It is the comparison that brings a truth to full view.

In the book of Proverbs, all types of comparisons are used to bring the truth of life with other humans to light. It is amazing how many people want life to work like they want it to work. It doesn't; it works like God structured it. Working with other humans has rules. When you follow those rules, things go much better.

Notice that these proverbs are the proverbs of Solomon, the son of David and the king of Israel, which suggests that he wrote these before he himself became king of Israel, which would make these writings before the book of Ecclesiastes.

God inspired Solomon's insights into life: One, by giving him the wisdom to see them in the first place. Two, by allowing him to see the right comparison to bring out the truth. Three, by breathing into Solomon during those writing sessions only those truths that needed to be recorded and not writing those that did not need to be recorded.

One of the other things about this book is that it follows a Hebraic form with thought rhymes and not word rhymes. The ideas are connected by thoughts that are similar which gives them the context. They are hooked one to another until there is an obvious break in the thought. We are not used to thinking in this way, but it is the basis of the book.

Are you willing to listen to the wisdom of the wisest man who ever walked the planet? Are you willing to adjust your life when you find that you are at odds with that wisdom? Incline your ear for you will find great truth and helpful actions to avoid many of the common problems that derail others.

PROVERBS 1:2 - *To know wisdom and instruction, to discern the sayings of understanding,*

to know

The word *know* is interesting in that it is the Hebrew word *yada* which is expressed in all the different verb forms in the Old Testament but is always a form of knowing that involves that which comes through the senses – experiential knowledge; almost Aristotelian knowing, growing out of sense experience or other's sense experience. Solomon does not want to give us theories about how to live life, but he wants to pass on what really works and how to make the best choices. He wants us to know that this way that does not seem right to us is the best way – the wise way. Because of the experience we have had in watching others, hearing his words, observing life, He does not want us to have to wait until we have experienced the negative consequences of being a fool.

There are three crucial tasks in this verse that Solomon lets us know this inspired book is designed to accomplish.

Wisdom is the first and the foremost. It is often defined as the application of knowledge in a proper or ethical way. While this is true, it is a much broader, richer term in this Hebraic understanding. Wisdom throughout the book is that action or choice or speech which is difficult to find – not instinctual – that causes God to win or be glorified, others to win, and us to win. There is a choice or action in every situation which is the wise one. It may cost us in the short term, but it will pay off in the long term. Consistent actions of wisdom – finding the triple-win choice or action consistently is a rich life. It will have setbacks and difficulties, but there is much protection and reward. This book, inspired by the Holy Spirit and penned through the writing of King Solomon, is the distillation of how to find and live the triple-win choice or wisdom.

The second thing that this book is designed to accomplish is that it is it self-instruction – not in the simple sense of a set of instructions but in terms of training. If the plans and actions of this book are followed, it is the training manual for an unbelievable life. You will not just intellectually know the right thing to do, but you will be trained to respond that way in the various situations of life. Constant attention to this book and its sayings will train your mind to perceive what you do not perceive at present and to react and act in a way that now you find impossible. This is the course on people dynamics and applied moral ethics. It is this book that will form the role-playing manual for a new way of living.

instruction

To know instruction is to know how others would rebuke you if they had the chance. The idea of instruction is education in what you don't know or don't see or don't want to see. To become a wise person is to be willing to look at yourself honestly and work where the work is needed, not just where you want to work. The wise person seeks instruction and seeks realistic views of himself or herself. An interesting question to ask yourself is: If God were to openly rebuke me right now for three things, what would they be?

The third aim of this book is an ability to perceive the sayings of understanding. This phrase is lost to modern hearers because we do not see its incredible power or claim. The word *understanding* is the word *bina*. It carries a relational connotation with it. It carries a sense of interconnectedness – how this relates to that in ways we don't suspect. This book is claiming that you will be able to see the hidden relationships between saying this and this other thing happening in your life. Why when this happen, friends come or flee. When you do this, it strengthens your marriage or destroys it. There are invisible strings or webs of relationships between things that we would not normally perceive or see, but biblical understanding means seeing these cause-and-effect devices. The book of Proverbs consistently tries to open peoples' eyes between seemingly independent actions and choices.

The book of Proverbs is worth spending great time in – over and over again – because it offers to help us find the triple-win choice or action in every situation. It offers to train us so that our natural reaction is no longer going to subvert our way; and it offers to show us the invisible connections between actions, relationships, and choices that cause everything to change on the chessboard of life with a single move.

PROVERBS 1:3 ~ *To receive instruction in wise behavior, Righteousness, Justice and Equity;*

receive instruction

Notice that one has to receive instruction in wise behavior. It takes learning, concentration, and new information. We don't come equipped since the fall with this orientation. Since the fall of man in Adam, even though we may know the right thing to do, we are oriented toward the selfish thing.

The Hebrew word translated instruction is the word *musar* which means instruct, chasten, train, discipline. Therefore the idea is that one must come to the place where one is ready to enter into a training course to become a person who acts wisely. Wisdom does not automatically flow from us; in fact, we are automatically oriented toward self.

This suggests a picture of a learned master beginning a rigorous training process with a young disciple who wants to learn to be wise. The youngster has heard and watched the actions of the master and presents himself to be schooled so that he will not longer make life-killing, foolish decisions. The book of Proverbs is the ancient manual of that old master. It is Solomon's textbook for the school of wisdom.

In fact, I write these devotional comments for my grandchildren and great-grandchildren that have not even been conceived yet so that they would be willing to enter into the school of God's wisdom. I want them to know that I was thinking about them years and decades before they were ever around. And that God knew everything about them before the world ever began. God had Solomon write this book so that in God's grace each of us could overcome our natural bent towards selfishness. Young men and young women, realize that wisdom is a rich treasure that must be learned.

So many times we must admit that we have acted foolishly and could wish that we had thought through what we did with greater insight – that is what this book is for. It helps us realize that what feels right at a given moment is not necessarily the right or wise thing to do.

When a person who has learned wisdom has finished their life, they sit in their chair surrounded by people who love them preparing to go home to meet face to face the Supreme Being who they have been relating to for a long time.

Never forget that the ultimate goal of wisdom is living out the two great commandments: *Thou shalt Love the Lord your God with all your heart, soul, mind and strength and your neighbor as yourself.* Life is relationships and wise people build them.

wise behavior

The word wise here is the word *sakal* which is close to the word understanding in the Hebrew. It emphasizes the intelligent understanding of what certain behaviors will do and what others won't do. It is sometimes translated insight (Jeremiah 3:15). It is clear that the goal of Proverbs is for one to look past his/her own urges or cultural impulses and examine all the potential actions in any given situation and choose the one that will result in God being honored, others being benefitted, and the individual being blessed. Wisdom looks for this action, and it is not ready to move until it finds that action.

Wise behavior always promotes relationships. It deepens and strengthens connections between people. Unwise behavior is selfish behavior. If unwise behavior were known, it would immediately weaken connection and bring disconnection between people.

The term "wise behavior" is broken into three sub terms in this opening lecture in the inspired school of wisdom. Wisdom's component parts are righteousness, justice, and equity.

righteousness

This is the first of the words that describe the larger term "wise behavior." This is the clearest moral action term. That which is right. The straight measuring rod. The commandments of God are the definitions of righteousness and the individual would be wise in working them out in his/her life. The Lord is described as righteous in all His ways and holy in all His works. What is interesting is that at times it is difficult to discern how God is being righteous in a particular action, so righteousness is at times a complex and daunting behavior. But the book of Proverbs is the training device for the task.

That which is right or righteous is not just inside the boundaries of the Ten Commandments; it is the opposite of the violation of the Ten Commandments. Look at each of the Commandments and go to the core of that command – or in most cases its opposite – and you find that which is truly righteous.

- No other gods. True full-hearted worship of the Almighty.
- No graven Images. Awesome reverence for the boundaries of God. He cannot be contained or explained by anything in the three-dimensional, space-time world.
- No taking the Lord's name in vain. Powerful and positive verbal worship on a regular basis.
- Remember the Sabbath Day to keep it holy. A day set aside to pursue God and His demands and commands – desires and person.
- Honor your Father and your Mother. Adding true value to your parents through your conduct, interaction, and speech.
- No murder. True love of your fellow man. A commitment to improving the lot of your fellow man, not just not destroying a person.
- No adultery. True faithfulness. Deep committed love to one spouse all your life, creating an environment of committed love.
- No stealing. Generosity of spirit. Hard work and saving in order to give to others.
- No bearing false witness. Truthing in love.
- No coveting. Contentment with God's provision and desire to fulfill the full measure of your lot in life, not someone else's.

Each of these are expressions describe what it means to be truly righteous. Righteous can never be a negation or defined as what one doesn't do. It is a positive in even a greater sense than wickedness is positive action in an evil direction.

justice

This is the second of the descriptors of "wise behavior" stated above. The word is the Hebrew word *sapat* which means to lead or exercise the power of governance. In the ancient world there was not a separation of the powers of government into three branches, but instead there was the leader. When the Proverbs speak, it is designed to help the leader make the type of decisions that will be right. The Proverbs are a course in how to be a righteous king or a leader with integrity.

Thus the ability to govern or be a leader is critical to this discussion. That is why the Proverbs are full of references to the king. This is the supreme leader within an Old Testament setting. If a person understands how to deal with a king and how to act like a wise king, then they will be a great leader. We would say that the book of Proverbs is a course in leadership. Notice that the book refers to leadership and to comparisons: This is better than that; that is worse than this. It is in part in these comparisons that the foundations for wise decisions are made.

The book of Proverbs is designed to be a course in leadership development. How to rule well. How to be a good and wise leader. If one can see the truths of the book of Proverb being lived out, then it will begin to be true for you in your life. The book of Proverb was designed to be a course on how to be a great leader.

equity

Each one of these words is a partial definition of wise behavior that is stated as the goal. This word *equity* carries with it the idea of moral uprightness. How to fully follow the Lord's commands. To be upright in every situation. The word comes from the idea to go straight ahead or to proceed on a level place. To apply uniformly or smoothly. Some have suggested that this is the idea of fairness. What is equitable is what is fair or balanced. The fact that this word is associated with leadership and governance would suggest that there will be some very difficult calls in leadership. That there will be times when two good things are demanded that seem to be in opposition to one another. Other times it will seem that the only choices are evil choices. But the book of Proverbs guides us around and through these conundrums towards the correct course even if it takes a while to see that course of action. Enter into this unique training program that was instituted over 3,000 years ago with the official stamp of God's breath. Begin growing in wise behavior so that you will enjoy all the life that God has for you.

PROVERBS 1:4 - *To give prudence to the naive, to the youth knowledge and discretion,*

to give prudence to the naive

prudence

The word translated *prudence* is the Hebrew word *arom* which has both a positive and negative meaning. When used negatively, it means a crafty schemer – one who plans out destructive, sinful things. When used positively, it means prudence. The English dictionary definition of the word prudence is a quality which allows a person to always choose the sensible path. This is not what the average person today thinks of when they hear the word prudence. The Hebrew word carries the idea of thoughtful planning to a good end with an ability to choose that good end. Perhaps the word should be translated: planning ahead or preparedness. It is the ability to realize that if I want this thing over there, then there are a number of steps that I have to take to get there.

It could be thought of as planning or goal-setting or preparation. In order to achieve anything in life, there is more planning than the naive is usually willing to realize. Things don't just come together at the last minute. Sometimes the plans take a decade to come together. In fact, one of the things about successful people is that they are always planning for the next ten or twenty years into the future. What education, investments, relationships, and experiences do you need this ten years to prepare you for the decade?

One of the greatest things that a young person could realize is – what kind of planning do we need to do this thing we want to do?

Recently my wife and I started putting a whole new level of prudence into our vacations, and the quality of the vacation has shot through the roof. We have started planning for a year or more for each trip we take. How much money will it take? What could we do? Where could we go? What is there to do at the various places? In fact as, I write this, I am enjoying a little trip with the family to Carmel, California, having ridden horses on the beach and kayaked in the ocean all because of prudence. Things go better with prudence.

We all like to be spontaneous and it can serve you well, but prudence or planning and goal-setting allows a much richer life. God prompted me when I was nineteen to lay out a basic plan for my life: what I wanted to accomplish, things I wanted to do, relationships I wanted to have, places to see, etc. That then allowed me to think through what kind of education I would need; when it might be appropriate to get married, have children, do various things. Through this general plan God has been able to guide me and prepare me to be more maximally useable for Him. I am more alert to opportunities and possibilities that are little pathways to accomplish much larger goals. I know what to look for and alert to information I might need later. The plan keeps developing and I try and update it every ten years. This process of prudence has suited me extremely well and given me a general map for my life as well as clarity about when to deviate and when not to. I am deeply enjoying life because of God's gracious direction in providence. When I turned fifty a few years ago, I updated it for the next twenty to fifty years – what I hope will be the most productive years of life.

I have noticed that the more impulsive I get, the less wise I get. Now spontaneity is wonderful within the boundaries of a good plan.

Take a few minutes at the beginning of the week to plan. Take a few minutes at the beginning of the day to plan. Take a day at the beginning of the year to plan. Look into the future and ask God, "What is possible?" Then begin planning how to get there.

naïve

The quality of naïveté is simple-minded; taking things always at face value; only engaging in things that are right now in their pay-off; being simplistic in your understanding or planning. It means only thinking about today or the section of the day that you are presently living in. "Are we having fun yet?" is the motto of these folks. It is all about the "right now." The Hebrew word *peti* comes from the idea of open or spacious. It is consistently translated simple or even foolish for the naive person is too open to the dangers and seductive allurements of the world.

In our day and age those who are open to the pressure of advertising are completely in debt. Those who are open to the suggestions of others get taken advantage of and lured into sin.

The one thing that the naive or simple person needs is a plan and the realization that not everyone or everything is as it seems. There are people who will take advantage of you. There are products and companies and groups that do not have your best at heart.

It is interesting that God wrote a book to make sure His people are not naïve, and yet many Christians have done this to their children by not training their children in the importance of prudence and by not helping them realize that there are selfish people out there who will use and abuse them. In fact, it is almost considered axiomatic that Christian kids will be naive about the ways of the world. The Scripture wants us to be as harmless as doves but as wise as serpents. We must learn to plan ahead and not be duped by the selfishness of others.

to the youth knowledge and discretion

youth

This is the Hebrew word *naar* which means boy or young maiden. It usually refers to a person who has not reached full maturity. In a girl it referred to a young maiden who was not married and, therefore, not into full adulthood. We would call this person the teenager.

knowledge

This is the Hebrew word *daat* which is knowledge, information, perception, skill. One of the things that young people need is information that they don't have and the development of skills that will allow them to live a good life. The proverb declares if young people will pay attention to the inspired words in this book, they will gain two things they desperately need: information about the way the world really is and skills that will allow them to develop a great life.

It is a shame when kids do not grow up in these two crucial areas. They need information about the real world, not the world of the pre-adult. They also need life skills: how to get along with people; what kind of people to avoid; what must be done to succeed at life. All these skills and much more are taught in this book.

discretion

This is the Hebrew word *mezimma* which means purpose, plot, goal, aim. It is used on a number of occasions for the goal or aim of a project. It does also carry with it the idea of planning or a plan. So in this way it is not that different from the word translated prudence. But its focus is more on the goal than the plan.

It seems clear that what Solomon is saying is that the two things that young people need desperately are information/skills and goals. Without these two things they will not have a successful life. They will instead, most likely, fall into the impulsive wanderings of a fool – selfish, impulsive, rebellious.

Don't fall into that trap. Gain the information that you need. Take the tests you need to take to discover what God-given talents, abilities, and gifts He has given you. Then chart a course to utilize those abilities.

An awful lot of trouble has come because a young person had no goal for the weekend or the summer or afternoon. Build this quality of being purpose-directed rather than just aimlessly wandering through life, waiting and hoping that something interesting or exciting will come along. Commit to good things. I know that some other good thing may come along, but more joy will be created by developing goals and plans than if you just sit and wait.

That means volunteer at the church or charitable organization. That means to sign up to work. That means to agree to go to a particular place even though something better might come up. There will always be a next time if it is a good thing.

PROVERBS 1:5 - *A wise man will hear and increase in learning, a man of understanding will acquire wise counsel,*

The message in this verse is that the person who is already recognized as a person who makes right choices and does not selfishly hew to his own way can gain enormous value from reading and absorbing the information in these divinely inspired passages.

There are experiences and observations and situations that are beyond what any one person can have experienced. These truths and insights can make a person more ready for whatever life throws at us.

There is another interesting point made in the first phrase of this fifth verse. If you are wise, then reading the Proverbs will make you wiser; but if you do not get anything out of the Proverbs, then you are not as wise as you suppose. No matter how wise you are or suppose yourself to be, there is always another level or series of insights waiting for you in this God-breathed book.

PROVERBS 1:6 - *To understand a proverb and a figure, the words of the wise and their riddles.*

Solomon begins this first chapter by explaining what the whole of the book is for. If someone will pay attention to the comparisons, the riddles, and the ideas that are mentioned here in the book of Proverbs, they will become wise and avoid lots of the problems of normal life.

to understand

The Hebrew word translated *to understand* is the word *bin*. It means to perceive, to embrace the information contained in what was said or the situation; but it also means that one grasps the connections between things. If a person is going to be wise, they must see that things are connected to each other. Solomon has included over 700 observations about human nature in these proverbs. Each one of the proverbs is pregnant with meaning in all kinds of directions. Solomon wants us to look beneath the surface and see all the ways that a particular proverb could apply to your life. He wants us to know that there are levels of meaning in each proverb. Don't just read a proverb – seek to understand its core idea and watch as that core idea connects to all different parts of your life.

These are not just Solomon's observations on life. They are also God's approved observations on life. Solomon made many observations on life that we do not have a record of, but these that are included in Scripture are the ones that God wanted us to have because they were the truth at a deep level. The fact that they are in the Scriptures speaks to the inspiration that God breathed into them. These human relationship principles have stood the test of time because they were penned by the wisest person who ever lived, and they were approved as accurate by the superintending Holy Spirit. Long before there were any people skill books, there were Solomon's insights on how to deal with people recorded in the book of Proverbs. We can have confidence that the insight that is shared in a particular proverb is true on many levels. And we can have confidence that spending the time to dig out the meaning and application for our lives is worth it on relational, spiritual, emotional, and mental levels.

I find myself going back to the proverbs again and again. I see new application and new depth in these timeless proverbs just as Solomon and God knew that I would. Seek to understand the complexity and simplicity of the comparisons, the riddles, and the ideas that are recorded here. The thoughts in this book are designed to be helpful ways of taking these insights into your daily interactions with people. I do find that the more that I can see my people interactions and relationships through the lenses of the proverbs, the more wise I look to others.

a proverb

The Hebrew word that is translated *proverb* here in this verse is the word *masal*. It can mean anything from a short pithy saying to an extended story. Jesus used the extended form when He was teaching His parables in the New Testament. He encased deep truth in a simple story. People could enjoy the story but ignore the point. They could enjoy the story and get the point. They could enjoy the story, get the point, and keep pushing for the deeper applications of the story for themselves. The same is true for the proverbs that are recorded here by Solomon. The insights that Solomon packs into the phrases and comparisons that he uses are weightier than most people skill platitudes. These are suitcases out of which we can pull truths and projects that don't seem to fit in such a few words.

When you are praying over the proverbs and God seems to highlight a particular proverb for you that day or in a particular situation, spend the time to unpack that proverb and grasp its connection with your situation. Sometimes I have spent an hour working through how a particular proverb could be connected to my situation. One time, recently, I thought I had unpacked why God had highlighted a particular proverb to me after three hours only to find that six hours later in the middle of the night a whole new perspective on that proverb and my life opened up.

a figure

The Hebrew word for *figure* is the word *melisah*. which means an elusive saying or a figure or a proverb. It often is associated with scorn or satire which suggests that this was a way of saying something that made you see an issue from a completely different angle. In our day this could be comparing the fact that Americans spend ten times more on cosmetics than they do on mental health. This is shown in the book of Proverbs where Solomon hyperbolizes a comparison: "It is better to live in a desert land than with a contentious woman." "It is better to be unknown and have a servant than to be well known but be a self-promoter."

As you read through the proverbs you will read of Solomon making crazy comparisons or crazy statements to jolt you into realizing a truth. God is goading us through Solomon's figure of speech to notice a deeper truth. Dig for understanding and how this truth relates to life. Each proverb or figure relates to real life and can help us be wise, avoid a foolish decision, deal with a foolish person, and chart a course of decisions that will develop a great life. But too often the big things of life are hidden by our culture, and we just blindly move forward making the same decisions as all of the people around us. This results in the same consequences as everybody else. What we really need to look at is whether we should choose some different choice because it really does make more sense if we just stop and look at it.

Wise people do not throw their pearls around for everyone to misuse or misappropriate. Wise people hide their wisdom in riddles and mysteries so that their insights will only be revealed to the person who looks with intensity or pursues the truth with tenacity. In the book of Proverbs you will find a wealth of people knowledge. There are sixty-three different types of fools that are described with the appropriate responses to them. You will find the eight friends of wisdom and how to use them to find wisdom and a great life. You will find some of the most amazing leadership advice so you can accomplish the purposes that God put in you. I often find myself asking God, through the book of Proverbs, how to handle a leadership situation I am facing by looking at every verse that talks about the king. I often prayerfully ask God to guide me through working with a person who is driving me sideways because of particular trait. I will look up their version of foolishness (arrogance, anger, laziness, sexuality, violence, etc.) and pay special attention to what Solomon says to do with this kind of person.

PROVERBS 1:7 - *The fear of the Lord is the beginning of knowledge; Fools despise wisdom and instruction.*

This proverb is about how to avoid being a fool. A fool is one who is self-focused and selfish. The fool doesn't want to learn the facts because they have made up their mind. The fool wants what they want and they are bent on getting what they want or the world is an unfair place. But God is playing a different game. God is playing the wisdom game. In wisdom, everyone gets a win but it may not be the big personal win that the selfish person has in mind. God may maneuver you into a situation where many more people than you win. Your win may be a much different win than the one that you always wanted (getting the girl, the big promotion, the pile of money).

The foolish person despises wisdom and instruction because they want what they want. They don't want to hear about how God can get glory or lots of other people can win if they would just accept this other type of win. Remember a fool is self-focused. God may be offering you a great win but it is not the one you wanted. If you cannot see the wisdom or want to learn what He may be up to then you are confirming your self-focused and selfish orientation. Grow up and focus on the fact that God is in charge and you are not. He has a great plan for you but it may not involve playing center field for the Boston Red Sox or singing lead for the Beatles. Learn to reverence the Lord God and try and understand what God may be up to. It is always bigger than your self-focused concerns. Cooperate with God by being wise and embracing the triple win.

Let's take a deeper look at this......

The first piece of data that should go into the one who wants wisdom is the fear of the Lord – Reverence, Awe, Wonder, and Fear at the Almighty – a healthy respect for the person and boundaries of the Lord. The moral boundaries of the Lord are not physical limits but instead are universal, personal and moral limits on behavior. It is here one must fear moving beyond the will of the Lord. There is freedom in every direction in the will of the Lord except when one presses up against one of the moral boundaries of the Lord. Too often in our society there is no thought of God and His opinion before an action is taken or a word is spoken. The constant attention to the person and boundaries of the Lord is a key piece to insert in the life of a person seeking wisdom, leadership, maturity, and a blest life.

fear

The Hebrew word for *fear* is *yare*. In this discussion, biblical usages of yāreʾ are divided into five general categories: 1) the emotion of fear, 2) the intellectual anticipation of evil without emphasis upon the emotional reaction, 3) reverence or awe, 4) righteous behavior or piety, and 5) formal religious worship. Theological Wordbook of the Old Testament

Lord is the personal name for God; the name that He gave Himself when He specifically revealed it to Moses. There is clearly a note here to begin a personal relationship of reverence, awe, wonder, and even fear with the one personal Supreme Being, Yahweh, who knows all and is capable of guiding you through this life to the reward on the other side. If you are going to really begin gaining wisdom, you must understand that there is a personal God who set up the rules and whom you will be offending by foolish and sinful behavior. Too many people believe that either they are making up the rules to the game of life or that they are impersonal rules that have no connection to a real being who can be offended by our conduct on this planet.

beginning

This is the Hebrew word first or head. It is the word for first fruits or the first of something. Solomon is not saying that some of the first bits of information that you need to have in your wisdom data bank is a reverence for God. He is saying that the first bit of knowledge – in fact the operating system which will organize all the other bits of knowledge – must be reverence, awe, wonder, and fear for the Supreme Being who is the personal God, Yahweh. If this information is not first and in that sense functioning as your operating system, then all the other information will float as randomized bits of knowledge without the proper relation to each other and to the source.

knowledge

This is the Hebrew word for information and skills. It will be used throughout the Proverbs for information that must be acquired and for skills that must be gained. This proverb deals with the first set of information and skills that must be gained to get started on the wisdom journey. It is interesting that it is a personal relationship with the personal God who has revealed himself in the Bible. If you do not have this personal relationship, then you cannot really gain true wisdom and the pieces of the puzzle will not fit together.

fools

This is the word for the natural state of sinful man – selfish, rebellious, imperfect. This is the first instance of the main contrast to the wise person. It does not mean mentally slow or stupid, but instead it is the word for morally inept and lacking in moral sense. The fool absolutely does not like the win-win scenario. Instead the fool wants the pure selfish win. They maximize their personal win at the expense of others. This shortsighted approach fits their moral bankruptcy. They just do not see the point of waiting, digging, and finding the choice that allows everybody to win. They despise the triple-win and new information that may turn them away from their selfish direction.

despise

This is the Hebrew word for disregard, hold as insignificant, even holding in contempt. The fool does not see any wisdom in looking for the triple-win: God, others, then yourself. In fact, they see the search for this wise choice as a stupid, insignificant, and even a contemptuous quest for the ridiculous. The only choice they are interested in is the one that most quickly and purely benefits themselves. They also fail to see that each time they make this selfish choice, how it impoverishes them.

wisdom and instruction

These are the words for the basic goals of a godly life and the training method to get there. Wisdom is the triple-win: God, others, and yourself. The word for *instruction* is the word to bind or to straighten through pressure that which is crooked. Both wisdom and instruction must be embraced as the normal part of the life of godly righteousness. There are many times that we do not realize that we are being foolish and seeking our own way, and God must bind us to a course of life that will manifest our basic selfishness.

A fool does not want to look for the triple-win solution or the area where their life does not measure up. They do not want to pass by the selfish choice and embrace the triple-win choice and get excited about being rebuked. But this is exactly what the wise person does.

PROVERBS 1:8 - *Hear, my son, your father's instruction and do not forsake your mother's teaching;*

This is an interesting proverb for it helps us understand a way of thinking biblically that we are not given to consider. The biblical idea of father and mother is one of protection, instruction, nurture, and help. This idea extends to all those who rightly exercise authority over us. Therefore, in the biblical mindset those who would be a boss or government official are extensions of our natural father and mother. They are governmental fathers and vocational fathers. There are also spiritual fathers and mothers who offer protection, instruction, and nurture for us as we live our life.

It is this role of spiritual father that Solomon is assuming in this first section of the Proverbs. He is setting down the information that those who would be willing to be mentored by him will need to know to avoid the pitfalls of living.

One of the consistent things that I find in ministry is that many people need to be re-parented in many areas of their lives. They may not know how to handle money. They may not know how to be disciplined with their time. They may not understand how to be warm and grateful to other people. They may not know how to make friends. They may be ignorant when it comes to how to relate to God. All these and many others could or maybe should come from our mothers and fathers as we are growing up. But God has structured, in a well-ordered society, that we will have many fathers and mothers who will "parent" us. There is no perfect parent and, therefore, everyone in this fallen world could criticize their parents for not instructing them in some needed wisdom for life. But we are not limited by the knowledge or skill of our natural parents. God has placed throughout our lives those who know more than us and those who are in authority over us who will offer protection, instruction, and nurture. He has also given us the inspired Scriptures to act as a further parent for us.

We are never too old or too smart to not need a number of fathers and mothers in our life. Solomon is offering to become a spiritual father to us, teaching us wisdom to live life in a deeply enjoyable way.

Do not become proud and refuse to receive instruction from these fathers and mothers all around you.

I have watched as people have become bitter over what their parents did or did not teach them, when there are people all around them at the present – as they are spouting bitterness and anger – who would re-parent them if they were only willing to listen. God has not left you without the protection, instruction, and nurture you need even if your parents were far less than perfect. Too often though we enjoy our bitterness and refuse instruction because we are too proud.

Who are the fathers and mothers that God has placed in your life right now? Are you listening to their instruction? Are you growing by their wisdom? Do you accept their protection or push away at their restrictions? Rejoice in that God is our father and has mediated his protection, instruction, and nurture through a myriad of people in your life so that you are not alone.

Allow yourself to be re-parented and grow and learn. In our day and age it is called leadership development and mentoring, but we must allow ourselves to learn and listen and respond to those who have authority over us and those who have greater spiritual insight.

In fact, while my wife and I are parenting our children, we are always on the lookout for mentors, instructors, and role models who can parent our children through a period of their life in ways that we cannot.

There will be times when you will be parented by an author or by a tape series or by a professor or a friend. Those men and women who offer sound advice to you are to be respected and honored and listened to. It is even helpful to ask these people in your life for their advice. Don't make them force their opinions and wisdom on you. Ask.

In this particular case you are being parented by Solomon and his considerable wisdom filtered through and prompted by the inspiration of God. This is a good parent.

PROVERBS 1:9 - *Indeed they are a graceful wreath to your head and ornaments about your neck.*

graceful wreath

The word *graceful* is the Hebrew word *hen* which means grace or favor. The word *wreath* is the Hebrew word *liwya* which only occurs twice in the Old Testament. In that day when a person wanted to show that you were a favored person because you had done something significant or you were deeply loved or valued, they would present you with a wreath made out of various materials. We are used to this idea from the Olympic wreath bestowed in the Olympic Games. The presence of this wreath meant that you were important or significant in some way.

What is interesting here is that Solomon is offering to be a father to us and to put a wreath of favor, significance, and blessing on our head by teaching us about how to make our way in the world. It is tragic that there are many children who did not grow up in homes where their parents really blessed them with wisdom, knowledge, safety, security, and love. But here God is offering to become your parent; to make up for what your parents may or may not have given you and to place on your head a wreath of significance for all to see: THIS IS A FAVORED CHILD OF MINE. In the New Testament, God offers the ultimate wreath of favor: salvation through Jesus Christ. While I would urge each and every one of you to accept the wreath of salvation in Jesus Christ by accepting His death for your sins and becoming His follower, I would also beg you to accept the wreath of significance and success that God offers through this book of Proverbs. Allow God to favor you with the way to live life on a different plain.

I know that many of you who will be reading this did not have happy and loving childhoods. It is all right. While the scars will remain, God is now offering to teach you the lessons of life that you didn't learn from your parents. It does not matter how old you are as you read this – 15 or 95 – the principles of wisdom that God wants to teach you will place on your head a sign for all to see that this person has been favored by God or all these good things would not be happening to them. Will you sit at God's feet and learn how to live wisely rather than making decisions that seem right to you?

Does your life say to those around you: God has favored this one? Then this book of Proverbs is for you. God wants to warn you how to avoid the pitfalls of life. He wants to direct you towards the rewards of life. He doesn't want you to toil 30 years at a job only to have missed the real rewards in life. He does not want you to unknowingly classify yourself as a person who cannot be trusted or who is unwilling to be prompted. I have countless numbers of people who have been upset at their life and who refuse to realize that it is their own behavior that dooms them to constantly be passed over for promotions; to be missed out when the opportunities are present.

In all of our lives there are areas where we need the wisdom of God as our parent. Even the best parenting job done by the best parent can use the supplement of God's wisdom. I believe that I had some of the best parents a person could have; they did an awesome job. And yet, obviously, when I submit to the fatherhood of God in my life, He hangs a "wreath of favored one" on my life for all to see and that gives Him glory.

necklace

In Judges 8:26 and Ezekiel 16:11 we see the practice of honoring a person of significance with necklaces. God tells us through Solomon that He will hang obvious honor on your life if you will submit to the lessons in this book. There will be rebukes and encouragement; love and discipline in this book. You must be willing to be corrected; you will have times when you need to be encouraged and just wait. There will be times when you will have to abandon what seems to you like the right way. If you are willing to submit to the insights and life lessons in this book, then a huge necklace of honor will appear on your life. In our day we might say a huge ring or an expensive suit of clothes or a very nice car. The necklace was the way and the place to display high levels of honor and status.

I don't know about you, but I want to be a trophy of honor and blessing in God's trophy case. I want Him to be able to point to me as one of His children who follows His ways and avoids many of the common pitfalls that are a part of the process called life.

What has He been warning you about that you want to do anyway because it seems right to you?

PROVERBS 1:10 - *My son, if sinners entice you, do not consent.*

This Proverb is crucial advice and insight for every young person. It is also important for everyone at every life stage.

You will be enticed to join sinners; do not go with them. You will be offered an opportunity to be with some "in" group if you will just watch or participate in their sinful behavior.

The lure of acceptance; the seduction of participation; the joy of sin – is a strong magnet. But we must realize that it is like being a fish and lured towards a worm on a hook; in the end, sin always has a hook in it.

When a person is young, the sins that are the most enticing are lust, power, and acceptance by those who are older. When we are older, the sins that are the most alluring are money, ease, and acceptance by those who are younger. At every stage and place we will hear the siren song of those who are near to us who want us to join them in a lifestyle of sin.

The word *sinners* is the Hebrew word *hatta* which means to miss the mark. It is like the word *hamartia* in the New Testament. We might call these the sins of omission – things we should have done but failed to do. This is not so much a willful breaking of God's commandments but instead a failure to do what God has clearly prescribed. What is the positive that God would have you do in various situations? The sinner is the one who does not do these things and usually will do something very selfish instead – even law breaking.

The word *entice* is the Hebrew word *pata* which means entice, deceive, persuade. The root verbal idea is to be open, wide, spacious toward a person or thing. It clearly became to entice in that one is open towards a person in a deceptive manner to lure them into a situation.

The idea here seems to be that those who do not live up to God's standards are being open and inviting towards you. They are seeming to accept you and offer connection and all you need to do is participate in their sinfulness.

Solomon is saying that this form of enticement or lure or acceptance will come, and each young person must be ready for it. I have watched many a teen give in to the actions of sin because they felt the peer pressure of acceptance. Hold out for something more significant than acceptance by those who disregard God and righteous authority.

These people will be coming after your children. Have you prepared them? Are you personally prepared for this type of temptation to come at you? What if a classmate asks you to join them in cheating on a test? What if a colleague at work asks you to join them in stealing stuff from work?

Right now is there a group of people who are offering you acceptance with just a little bending of the rules?

Do not give in to their desire to have you come along even just to watch. It is not appropriate and will expose you to stuff that will bring you to the place of living outside of the boundaries of God's will.

PROVERBS 1:11 - *If they say, "Come with us, let us lie in wait for blood, let us ambush the innocent without cause;"*

This is the talk of gangs. This is the temptation that reaches out to young men and wants them to prove their toughness. This is the type of seduction that relies on violence. While this may seem like a silly temptation to many who are reading this, it does not seem silly to many young men who are feeling their manhood and are looking for a place to belong. This would include gangs, mob connections, outcast teens, boys looking for "fun." Young men need to be taught and trained that gaining through violence is not the answer. It is a street that you can take and it seems like it is paved with riches when you first get started, but it doesn't pay off in the end. There aren't many old, violent men. Those that are still around are broken down and or bitter. Young men need to be told this. We cannot just assume that they see this.

Just as Solomon predicted, there is a large percentage of the population where success through violence is a reasonable option. These young men must be taught, trained, and redirected or we will even be more afraid in our own homes and afraid to walk the streets. When violent young men take over the neighborhoods, no one is safe. All young men must be told repeatedly that violence is not the way to get ahead.

Notice that he says that the young man will be tempted to help ambush the innocent without a cause – just because you can – just because it's fun – just because it's profitable. This is a dead-end road. A few years on this violent path and you will not make it off.

It is amazing that Solomon lunges after this wrong road first as he deals with young men. He spends a lot of time – ten verses – on this subject of gangs and violence and its seductive quality for young men. Men must learn how to control their urges. Parents who are raising boys must teach them how to control their urges. If boys are not given a high level of impulse control, it will be disaster for society as a whole, them personally, and their family. We cannot throw boys away to this problem of violence. If a boy is allowed to get what he wants because he is violent, intimidating, or angry, it teaches that young man to succeed in the wrong way. This must be opposed by parents, teachers, clergy, friends, police, society, etc. Everyone must, together, help shape young men to not use their aggressiveness, brawn, and violence to get their way.

PROVERBS 1:12 - *"Let us swallow them alive like Sheol, even whole, as those who go down to the pit;"*

There are two basic ethical principles for those who embrace wickedness and violence. Who benefits from the actions you do? Does your action harm others?

The way of the fool always violates one or both of these questions. Either the only one benefited by the action is oneself and/or others are or will be significantly damaged by the foolish action.

Solomon is screaming at us to notice the kinds of language and goals that the gang or thieves pursue. It is open foolishness masquerading as a focus of life.

This whole section deals with the lure of easy money and power through gangs, violence, and theft. Solomon is trying to get young men to turn away from the most destructive forms of foolishness: violence, gangs, and intimidation. This lure is so destructive and changes one's whole life so that there is no going back. These kinds of choices continually come up in life – choices to take the fool's road through life or to take the harder, more disciplined, patient way called wisdom.

Yes, there are times when wisdom seems like the stupid choice, but selfishness and harm are always the wrong direction no matter the short-term payoff. Right now you might be facing this kind of choice – in business, in relationships, in government, in family. This is how the temptation comes. "If you just up your power and intimidation factor, you will win." "This is war and they need to lose big time so that you can win." "It is either them or you. Go for the win."

If your plan involves the destruction of others (with the exception of those who are immoral in their behavior and you are the approved instrument of justice), then it is the fool's path. Don't go that way. Find a way for everybody to win. There is a way.

PROVERBS 1:13 - *"We will find all kinds of precious wealth, we will fill our houses with spoil;"*

It is a goal of wisdom and everyone to have a storehouse full of treasure so that they can pull it out and live off of it. This is a reasonable goal for everyone. It is the wicked who pursue it through violence and immorality. It is the foolish who pursue it through impulse and get-rich-quick schemes. It is the righteous that pursue it through diligence and time.

Do not be tempted to profit by destroying the lives of others. Do not be tempted to try and gain all the wealth you will need to live off quickly in one deal. It doesn't work that way.

Notice that Solomon refers to precious wealth of all different kinds. The idea of precious wealth is those things that everyone wants and holds personally dear – the things that a person will protect and value. The path of wisdom receives these as a result of hard work, wisdom, and as gifts from God's hand. The fool tries to claim them quickly and without working through stealing, scheming, violence, or the like. The very precious things that they desire will not have the same taste because of how they are obtained.

PROVERBS 1:14 - *Throw in your lot with us, we shall all have one purse,*

One of the typical con games of those who are swindlers is that they advance a little to those they are trying to con and this convinces the gullible person that they are in on the take; and then the masters begin to milk the unsuspecting person either of money, work, time, expertise, access, or some other valuable commodity. All the while the person believes that they are sharing everything equally.

lot

This is the Hebrew word *goral* which means lot or portion or allotted portion. It could be land or money or some possession. In this instance it seems to be some amount of money that the rebel has and that the thieves want to have their hands in. They convince the person with some money to share their money with the whole group because the whole group will share everything with them when they have some funds.

The difficulty of everyone having one purse is that there is always an unequal distribution of goods collected. There is also always an uneven amount of work accomplished. There will always be inequities with this system. It sounds good in principle, but it does not work in practice.

Take the lot that God gave you and make it bloom for the glory of God through wisdom, hard work, and good planning.

PROVERBS 1:15 - *My son, do not walk in the way with them. Keep your feet from their path,*

This is the crucial item of protection for the young person. Do not think that you can hang with people who live a wicked lifestyle and not get sucked in yourself. If you hang around with those who do drugs, steal, beat people up, are sexually active, you will eventually embrace this activity.

Notice that Solomon is talking to us as our spiritual father and telling us what we need to hear even though we may not want to hear it.

There are people who are very accepting and even kind towards new people in order to have a new person involved with their activities. I have noticed that in the teen years there is always a group of druggies and bad kids who are always willing to accept the outcast teen. Eventually those people become your friends and you start doing stuff with them.

The only way to save yourself from all the pain that their lifestyle will cause you is to not be with them. Period. There is no super-strengthening process that will allow you to be with them and not eventually fall to their way of life. You have to get away from them. Choose different friends.

The proverbs will go on to detail the consequences of a sinful and selfish life, but let me just outline a few things. It will begin to have a negative impact on your relationships with your other friends. You will begin to get in trouble with authority: parents, school officials, teachers, police, others. Your potential for the future is diminished because you no longer put in the time to study and pursue those opportunities. You will limit what you can do to earn a living and limit the amount you can make. There will be some people who will heed the advice of this verse and begin to stay away from you. All this begins to happen just because you do not remove yourself from the group of people who are doing evil things.

You can and should pray for them, but you should not walk in the way with them.

PROVERBS 1:16 ~ *For their feet run to evil and they hasten to shed blood.*

For the young, what gangs and criminals have to offer can sound so enticing and exhilarating: getting money easily; acquiring things, activities, and relationships through cheating and raw power. But young people must come to understand: it will redirect the course of your life towards evil. Your destiny will be different.

feet run to evil

The word *evil* is the Hebrew word *ra* which means bad or evil. The expanded meaning is that which violates God's rules for the boundaries of selfishness in society. There is a certain amount of selfishness that a society can permit and still sustain itself with damage to the innocent, but there are forms of selfishness that immediately threaten the innocent and the well-being of the society as a whole. These places are where God has told us to make laws and enforce those laws. If people are allowed to cross these lines to high levels of selfishness without correction, societal shame, punishment, or significant consequences, then widows, orphans, the oppressed, the poor, and other innocent people at the margins of society will be damaged. If this goes on long enough and spreads throughout the society deep enough, then everyone is threatened by this pervasive selfishness. The lines where all this begins to happen is laid down in broad brush strokes in the Ten Commandments. Beyond the Ten is the biblical definition of the evil.

Solomon is trying to get young people to recognize the enticement of unrighteous friends and acquaintances through what they are suggesting: EVIL. What they are suggesting is enticing and easy because it is evil and because it makes others lose so that you can gain. Don't be fooled with how easy it is, with how exhilarating it is, with how harmless it seems. If it is beyond the Ten Commandments, it is the wrong place and the wrong direction.

hasten to shed blood

The word *blood* is the Hebrew word *dam* which means blood guiltiness or the shedding of blood. It is the idea of murder or physical violence. It is a focus on power, violence, and intimidation. Young people – and young men especially – are enamored with raw physical power and the impact of violence. They feel the raging of impulses and the desire to force others to give them what they want and to have others embrace this philosophy that feels so right. It can begin through involvement in protection rackets. It can begin through bullying at school or in the neighborhood. Solomon is talking openly about what young people will be tempted to embrace: "might is right." He screams: Do not be taken in by this path of life! It will not be the liberation you think it is. It will not be the unlimited leverage to the good life that it feels like it is when you are young.

It is crucial that young men get a handle on their anger at an early age. They should be trained how to be angry but not explode in rage or use their anger for selfish advantage. They should be taught how to have more flexible expectations. They should not be allowed to have great success through the use of anger, or it will become a pattern their whole life. Allowing anger to express itself is a choice. If this idea is trained into young men at an early age, it will save them a lot of trouble.

Parents need to talk to their children about this temptation to use violence for selfish purposes. They need to talk about the fact that boys will be exposed to others who make a life out of intimidating, hurting, hitting, and even murdering people who do not do what they want.

PROVERBS 1:17 - *Indeed it is useless to spread the baited net in the sight of any bird;*

Solomon is incredulous over the willingness of the fools to walk into a trap they know was set. The believer has three enemies: the world, the flesh, and the Devil. Each of these sets different traps in order to capture, incapacitate, damage, or destroy the person in their living for Jesus Christ. We know what the traps will be and yet each week people walk right into them and do great damage to themselves.

useless

This is the Hebrew word *hinnam* which means out of favor, useless, in vain. In this case Solomon is pointing out that if you show birds where the nets are, they will fly around them even if they have some lures in them. It doesn't do any good to set traps that the prey knows about, but this is not the same for the selfish person. They want what they want when they want it. They will walk right into a trap that will destroy their life, just to get the selfish pleasure they want. People in Solomon's day – and in our day – want money, sex, power, and fame; and they will walk right into a trap to get it. Even though they see what happens to people who gain these things, they still go after them somehow ignoring the consequences or thinking that this won't happen to them.

We know that being famous creates a prison in which you can't go out in public and do not have the freedom of a normal person and yet people still seek this.

We know that sexual unfaithfulness allows all kinds of diseases, emotional pain, guilt, and even unwanted pregnancies and yet people still dive right in pursuing it.

We know that drug use shortens your life span, destroys relationships, leads to criminal behaviors, destroys potential, damages your body and brain, and yet people still do it even though they know it is a trap.

We know that absolute power corrupts absolutely and causes people to compromise their values, lie, wound, participate in many unethical practices, and yet people claw and scratch and fight to have more power.

bird

This is the Hebrew word *kanaph* which means wing. Clearly Solomon has in mind a bird, and he uses the bird to be a symbol of the freedom that it has and the intelligence it has to not get caught. It doesn't want to get caught, so it avoids places with nets.

in the sight of

This is the Hebrew word *ayin* which means eye, before, before the eyes, sight. The idea is that the bird is not so stupid to go into a trap that it knows is there.

Solomon gives us a picture of how gullible our selfish desires make us. He is pleading with us to be wise. Don't be lead around by the nose like some trained circus animal just waiting for the next morsel doled out by your handler. Be wise – don't get sucked into the traps of selfishness. Sure, selfish pleasure is enjoyable; but it will put you in a slave labor camp eventually working for your selfish pleasure instead of the other way around.

Realize that God wants you to enjoy life and will crown your life with the very things that you could selfishly pursue near the beginning of life, but He will do it in a way that does not wound you or anyone else. He will give you honor, wealth, and intimate relationships within the boundaries of righteousness if you would just learn wisdom.

PROVERBS 1:18 - *But they lie in wait for their own blood; they ambush their own lives.*

This proverb highlights one of the key ideas of wisdom and life: The choices you make will make or break your life. Sure there are things that happen to you, but largely the life you will live is a result of the choices that you make. Many people, in their shortcuts to get what they want, chose to destroy their own lives.

Think about the person who makes a decision in their teen years to begin stealing to get what they want. Or what about the person who in the teen years decides to get what they want through bullying or violence? Think about how that changes the trajectory of their lives. Think about the people who begin to commit adultery to get what they want; it messes with the rest of their lives. This particular proverb specifically deals with the issues of violence and robbery, but the principle of willful choice lies just beneath the surface. You can mess up your life with a few ill-timed choices.

Notice that Solomon is forcing young people to see that the gain they think they are having is coming out of the potential of their own lives. They lie in wait for their own lives. Only a fool would be selfish enough for the present to destroy the future to have a little trinket or pleasure now. And yet this temptation to gain by violence or any temptation to live beyond the boundaries of the Ten Commandments reaches out and consumes a part of your potential life. It destroys your future. Aesop wrote in his fables about the dog who had the piece of steak in his mouth and while walking over the bridge he saw his reflection in the water. Another dog with a steak in its mouth, he thought, so he snapped at the dog to get its steak and lost the steak in his mouth.

As you are reading this, you are facing temptations to be selfish and to gain or move forward in all kinds of ways. Those ways that require that you break one or more of the Ten Commandments are not wise. They will consume far more than you gain by employing them.

It is fashionable these days for young women to delve into witchcraft and other religions to get power, so they can get what they want. This is a foolish choice. Breaking the first commandment is not wise.

There is a new interest in bowing down to and praying to statues and rocks and pictures to get what you want; again this is not a wise choice. Breaking the second commandment is a foolish choice even if you gain a few things in the process.

Teens often feel tempted to use swear words and curse words to feel more adult. This does not profit you but begins a pattern of not being able to control your tongue. Breaking the third commandment willfully to gain prestige is a fool's choice

More and more people are saying that they don't need church to feel close to God, so they give up the regular assembly of Christians and the habit of church is lost. Jesus Christ is the Sabbath for Christians, and He does not want you to give Him one day in seven but every day. It is not a wise choice to say, "I don't need Jesus for I can handle the stuff this day."

Many young people are tempted to begin a life of rebellion to get what they want. It almost always starts with rebellion from parents; a refusal to honor them but instead to put them down and identify more strongly with friends than parents. This is the fool's profit. A life of rebellion is like riding a picket fence.

Young men learn in their early years that they can gain through anger, violence, intimidation, and physicality. If they choose the path of violence in order to get their own way, then they will ambush their own lives this proverb says.

Young men and women are super-charged sexually and they face the temptation whether they will keep their sexuality reserved for their future mate, or they will use it as a tool or weapon to get what they want. If they imbed sexuality as a means to an end, then they will suffer a myriad of consequences for their short-sightedness.

As stated earlier, young people are tempted to steal to get what they want. Don't cross that line. If you do, then repent.

Everyone is tempted to gain through lying. It is very crucial that you do not build your life on a lie or even a distortion of the truth. The little that you gain by telling a lie will come around to haunt you.

All people are tempted to build a fantasy world in which they have every relationship; gain their enemies' possessions and take their employees, etc. But if you live too long in the world of coveting others' things, you will not be making progress on the future you could be building. It is a shame to watch people focus their skills and abilities on trying to take other people's stuff rather than building their own.

This proverb is so powerful. Don't destroy your own life. Make the right choices. Live in the Ten box full of love for God and others. It is a much better life.

PROVERBS 1:19 ~ *So are the ways of everyone who gains by violence; it takes away the life of its possessors.*

This is a summation statement regarding this whole section. Solomon does not want his new students to miss the point of the first lesson.

gains

This is the same word that is used for violence. In fact, in this instance Solomon uses the same word *basa basa*. The idea is to cut off or gaining almost always in a bad sense. The word means to cut off or cut away and so involves a level of gaining but also a level of violence.

violence

This is the Hebrew word *basa* which means to cut off, gain, covetous. The idea seems to come from cutting a piece of cloth free from the loom that it was woven on. It also is used of cutting away profits or goods from their rightful owner; i.e., covetousness. The King James Version puts the emphasis on being greedy or covetous. The NASB translators put the emphasis on the violence or ripping away of the goods. The Septuagint puts the emphasis on stealing or trying to complete oneself through lawlessness.

life

This is the Hebrew word *nephesh* which means life, soul, creature. Its original meaning seems to be the idea to breathe. It is the word that God used when He breathed into Adam his breath of life and he became a living soul.

The clear idea is that you may gain the item that you are looking for or the relationship you want, but you get something else with it. You get a flesh-eating, soul-eating disease. When one gains in this way, it begins to eat away at the life of the one who wanted to add to their life through breaking something away from its rightful owners.

Notice the parallelism in the summation statement. A person cuts away something they really want to add to their life, but it takes away their life to have someone else's goods in their possession.

PROVERBS 1:20 - *Wisdom shouts in the street, she lifts her voice in the square;*

This is a bold statement – that the triple-win solution is an open secret. It is shouted to those who have ears to hear. It is available to all. It will just not sound right to the foolish and the wicked.

This proverb tells us that God has not hidden His wisdom, but it is hidden because of our selfishness.

Later in this section we are told of three types of people who do not get the wisdom that is being shouted: those who are simple or naïve, those who are scoffers, and those who are fools. Each has its own way of avoiding or misperceiving the wisdom that God is laying before them.

Naive people refuse to believe or embrace solutions that take a number of steps. It must be instant and one step, or it is rejected as no solution. They want instant solutions to their own complex money problems; their own convoluted relational problems. Wisdom tells them what to do next, but they can't see how that will solve everything immediately so they don't try it or they try it and refuse to seek out wisdom for the next choice.

Scoffers delight in being critical and contrary. They can find the flaws with any really wise plan. What if this happens? What if that happens? How are you going to handle that or this? They can throw cold water even on that which is brilliantly wise.

Fools are selfish, rebellious, and impulsive people who already have their mind made up about why things happened and how to get out of the difficulty, so they will not listen to the facts of the case. They don't want facts; they have their opinions.

You have to really want wisdom to hear it, receive it, and stick with it until it completes the solution. Wisdom is never hidden but at times it is complicated, doesn't have all the answers, and is open to new ideas and real facts.

PROVERBS 1:21 - *At the head of the noisy streets she cries out; at the entrance of the gates in the city she utters her sayings:*

This is a recurrent theme in Proverbs. Wisdom is not hidden; it is shouting for people to pay attention but few turn aside to look. Wisdom is often portrayed as being at the head of the street or the gates of the city.

gates of the city

This was where the elders of the city decided the business of the city. Usually the businessmen who had become successful were at leisure from doing business every day and could attend to the business of the city. Therefore Solomon could talk confidently that the wisest people would be found at the gates of the city. These people were not politicians; they were people who had actually accomplished something in their life and had lived long enough to know wisdom from folly. Usually the elders of the town were some of the oldest residents, but it was not because of their age that they were at the gates – it was because of their results. They had demonstrated an ability to work hard, to show kindness, to avoid destructive temptations, to handle money without letting it handle them, to keep confidences, to hire, to plan, to build something instead of just criticizing other's work. It is these types of qualities that Solomon says are essential for wisdom.

Some have suggested that it is not that these men at the gates have all wisdom; it is that wisdom is shouting by what they did. They acted wisely to be where they are, but sometimes they don't themselves really understand the wisdom that they displayed.

There is also the suggestion in 2 Chronicles 17:7-9 that the priest and teachers of the law gathered people at the gates of the city to instruct them as to God's law for ultimately it is God's direction that will bring about wisdom in the heart of man.

PROVERBS 1:22 - *How long, O naive ones, will you love being simple-minded? And scoffers delight themselves in scoffing and fools hate knowledge?*

The implication of this proverb is that it has been too long that these various kinds of people have indulged their particular problems. They need to see that things are not getting better following the plan they are following:

> According to God's assessment

> The naive cling to simple explanation when something is very complex

> Scoffers find great delight in being critical and pessimistic

> Selfish people do not want new information that would force them to change their perspective

Make sure that you do not fall into any of these categories, clinging to a way of being and acting that keeps you from enjoying the life God gave you.

In what areas do you continue to embrace a simple explanation for a complex process: Government, Church, God, Marriage, Family, Work, etc? In order to grow in wisdom, one has to acknowledge complexity. The world is a complex interplay of things, and it is important to not lock onto a simplistic explanation of why things happened or how things work when a multitude of factors may be present.

In what areas are you cynical and pessimistic? While this may make you look – from the surface – smart and sophisticated, it does not really help. Only when a person begins to offer positive solutions and get on the solution side of the equation does your contribution help. Penetrating analysis of the problem with the intention of helping solve the problem is a good thing. A critical, fault-finding, and it-will-never-work attitude is rarely helpful. It also dooms the person who adopts this attitude to an isolated life.

In what areas have you shut the door to new information because you have the conclusion you want to be true? Be careful of an unwillingness to consider other perspectives and new discoveries. It is a frightful thing when people close their mind. It means that they have become selfish and are ready to move ahead with their destructive plan.

PROVERBS 1:23 - *Turn to my reproof, behold, I will pour out my spirit on you; I will make my words known to you.*

This little proverb tucked near the end of the first chapter could be considered the key to the whole book of Proverbs. God is alive and will have conversations with you throughout your life when you wander off the path of life. He will converse with you through the difficulties, problems, obstacles, rebukes, and turmoil of your life. He wants to show you that He loves you by caring enough to discipline you. He desperately wants you to listen so that you will not ride the picket fence of difficulties that He has placed on the boundaries of acceptable behaviors. We want to call Him unloving because these rebukes are there. He wants us to know that He placed them there because He loves us.

This verse opened my eyes to what life is really all about and how it works. This verse is sooooooo important to living a blessed life. You will mess up. You will make mistakes. God will have to rebuke you, but His rebuke is an evidence of His love; and if you respond correctly, then even this rebuke will be a wonderful blessing.

reproof

This is the Hebrew word *tokeha* which means reproof or rebuke. What is clear from this section of Proverbs and from the Scriptures is that God has built the universe to respond to a certain way of living. If you do not live that way, then you will receive regular shocks or rebukes or "red flags" which are trying to warn you to stop and go in a different direction and try something else. God's rebukes – which are designed for our benefit – come from all different places. It could be the circumstances; it could be finances; it could be authorities; it could be colleagues; it could be internally either emotionally or physically.

The consistent testimony of the Scriptures is that God is still in the business of telling people when they are moving beyond His will for them. We have, however, turned a deaf ear to His reproofs and then proclaim that He doesn't send any.

He rebukes us with a lack of money. He rebukes us with a failed relationship. He rebukes us with guilt. He rebukes us with a deal that falls apart. He rebukes us with a troubled spot in our marriage. He rebukes us with a child that begins to rebel. Each of these rebukes is designed to get our attention and cause us to stop and examine why this thing has happened.

We have embraced a naturalistic-chance universe and, therefore, are unable to see or understand His rebukes. We do not connect the difficulties that we are having with any type of lesson the Lord may be teaching.

It is true that some in the past went overboard with this way of thinking and have seen a message from God in every fallen leaf or bark of a dog. This is ridiculous, but it is naive to deny a larger message and issue behind some of the difficulties and problems we are facing.

At times we might call these the natural consequences of our actions, but they are a part of God's rebuke. If one person doesn't want to be your friend, then it may just not have worked out; but if no one wants to be your friend, then it might be you need to learn something about how to make friends.

turn into my rebuke

Listen to what God is saying. These four words are so important and crucial to living a great life. God orders us to do the very thing that we don't want to do. When something difficult is happening, we naturally want to get away from it. But when we had some part of the cause, then we should turn into it and learn from it.

How often have we seen the teenager who is not listening to the reprimand from their parents. They are turning their head or refusing to listen. They want to do what they want to do, and they don't want anyone to tell them they shouldn't or that bad things will happen to them if they don't stop.

We are just like this. It is, however, absolutely crucial that you and I listen to God when He is rebuking us. What is He saying we should do different? What is He saying we should stop doing? What is He saying that we should learn?

I have watched so many people who have rebelled from this wise advice. They destroy their first marriage and blame their spouse and then begin the same patterns and behaviors in their second marriage. They have been repeatedly fired from jobs, always blaming the boss for the firing and never listening to why they got fired or changing their behavior. They have been overbearing with their children, driving them away; and then at a moment of tenderness in their grown children's life, they again are overbearing and condemning. They rebel from their parents, not wanting anyone to tell them how they should live; and then they continue this pattern of selfish independence in their jobs, marriages, and friendships.

pour out

God promises that if you would be willing to listen to what He wants to teach through all these rebukes, He would pour out His Spirit on you. This is such a wonderful promise and so powerfully true. When the alcoholic finally stops, hits bottom, and faces the wound they have been running from and the drink they been using to hide, they receive a new level of God's Spirit to walk in wisdom and wholeness. When the teen stops being so selfish and rebellious and listens to the things that their parents are saying, then God will give a new measure of His Spirit to understand how to embrace that information.

This verse is very New Testament in its promise of a pouring out of the Spirit of the Living God. God will pour out His Spirit on any true seeker and will guide them into a great level of connection and love. God wants to pour out a new measure of His Spirit on those who already have a relationship with Him but are in need of more help in one of the areas of life.

PROVERBS 1:24 - *Because I called and you refused, I stretched out my hand and no one paid attention;*

It is an amazing thing that God can stretch out His hand to people and they can ignore it; they can pretend that they don't need His help. God is calling through the voice of wisdom, and yet we have such a natural affinity to selfishness that we don't want to hear the sound reason of the triple-win. All we hear screaming at us is "go for the maximum win for yourself." What do you want?

What we should do in any given situation that is available to us; we often just don't want to pay attention. I am amazed at the number of times I have asked people, "What do you think you ought to do in the situation you are facing if you were to really do what you think God might want?" and they come with the right idea. But that is not what they will do because it doesn't feel right to them; or because it is too hard; or because it takes too long; or because they have a few people telling them that they deserve to get what they want. So they ignore wisdom for some reason and happily go down the fool's path of selfishness.

When you are at those choice points this coming week or in your life, realize that wisdom is there somewhere seeking to give you God's direction and the best possible course of action for the long run. But you have to want it. You have to pay attention.

This verse in the first proverb is the turning point to understand the warnings and consequences of foolishness. Solomon wants you to know that it is not penalty-free if you ignore wisdom. It is not that you don't get the benefits of wisdom, you get the calamity and difficulty and penalties of foolishness. God, through wisdom, is saying "I was there trying to guide you but you didn't want any of my wisdom; you only wanted your self-focused wisdom." And so for that reason all kinds of problems and difficulties will come to you. The fool's road is not just less beneficial than the wise road; it is full of land mines, sharp cliffs, and whirlwinds.

When you look back at the replay of your life, the Lord Jesus will be pointing out those choices that you made that swung your life and aimed it down the drain. Will Jesus point to the decisions that you make this week as good decisions or bad decisions? The choice is yours. Wisdom is stretching out its hand.

PROVERBS 1:25 - *And you neglected all my counsel and did not want my reproof;*

Solomon continues to paint a picture of what happens to those who do not listen to the advice that wisdom gives.

When life goes bad, in many cases it is possible to go back and see where wisdom was rejected and selfishness was embraced. Many times we want to see life as fickle and arbitrary, but really our choices and the choices of those around us send us down the road we are on.

neglected

This is the Hebrew word *para* which means to let go, to let alone, to draw away, to neglect.

The idea that Solomon is trying to get across is that wisdom was there when you made the decisions and yet you were far more interested in what was selfish, quick, or the rebel way. And for those reasons you let the guidance of wisdom sit there.

I am amazed, in counseling, at the number of times when I ask people, "What do you think you should have done other than what you did?" They will consistently come up with the right decision. "Why didn't you do that?" "I didn't want to at that time." In many cases people can figure out what is the wise thing to do, but they do not want to do it. In many cases the wise thing is not a big enough win for them or an obvious loss for their rival. So they drudge down the path of the fool, inviting the consequences of selfishness, impulsiveness, or rebellion. This could be called stupid tax.

counsel

This is the Hebrew word *etsah* which means counsel or advice. This is the information and suggestions that wisdom gives. It will result in getting through a problem. It will result in an everyone-wins scenario. It will involve in moving away from sinful activities. It will involve planning and strategy. It will require that you slow down the decision-making process until you can really see what you are doing.

In most cases it is the counsel that you come up with when you ask the question. What do you think you ought to do in this situation? It is also the counsel that comes from asking what Jesus would do in this situation.

reproof

This is the Hebrew word *tokechah* which means rebuke or correction. Many times wisdom's counsel comes in the form of a previous rebuke or a person who corrects you when you are just about to do something foolish. But we often reject this counsel because it is from a person we don't like or it comes from a authority or it comes with a bad attitude or with a cynical edge. We often reject wisdom's voice because it doesn't come from a sweet, encouraging voice.

We must realize that God is going to get you the wisdom that you need if you are at all open to it. But it may not show up wrapped in angels' wings, singing sweet songs to you. But it will be wisdom.

We are about to see what happens to those who foolishly ignore what they should do and instead push ahead with what they selfishly want to do. It changes the course of their lives, and often they do not recover the full potential or possibilities that were available to them. Choices count. What you decide makes a real difference in the life you lead. Choose wisely.

PROVERBS 1:26 - *I will also laugh at your calamity; I will mock when your dread comes,*

This is the interesting reaction of wisdom personified to the troubles that those who are selfish, impulsive, and rebellious bring on themselves. In a sense, wisdom is saying when you choose the selfish choices that would give you immediate satisfaction with no thought for tomorrow, I allowed it knowing that you would end up here in these troubles and difficulties. The judgment here is strong and follows the theme of the whole Bible: a person will receive in accordance with His deeds.

laugh

This is the Hebrew word *sachaq* which means to laugh. It is translated amuse, celebrate, laugh, joke. In a sense, wisdom is saying, "You thought you were getting ahead, but look at where your impulsive selfishness has landed you." You and I cannot sin against wisdom and get away with it. Selfishness brings consequences – either physical, mental, emotional, relational, or spiritual; but there will be consequences for selfish behavior. The universe that God made is wired to have this cause-and-effect relationship. If you choose wisely, then you will be moving toward life. If you choose foolishness, shortcuts, and impulsiveness, then you will be moving toward calamity.

calamity

This is the Hebrew word *ed* which means calamity, destruction, ruin, disaster, distress, vengeance, trouble, misfortune, doom. It is clearly the negative consequences of the choices that you have made. The consequences of your choices will find you whether they are good or bad. Solomon is trying to get us to pay attention to the fact that you cannot escape the consequences of your choices. If you make poor ones because they are easy, then you will receive the results of those choices.

Really, the message is that we are responsible for the life we live. Even if bad and horrible things happen to us that we have no control over, we will be given choices after those things happen. We are responsible for those choices. Our culture is a victim culture that seems to refuse to take responsibility for the choices it makes. It is always someone else's fault. But it isn't. We cannot always control what happens to us, but we can control how we react and respond to it. If we choose wisdom rather than foolishness, everybody wins rather than just ourselves; and we will receive a completely different "win" in our life than the short-term gain we were tempted to go after.

Wisdom means that we work hard to make the right people win in the right way. This brings a great result.

mock

This is the Hebrew word *laag* which means mock or deride. It is interesting that Solomon uses this word to describe the behavior of wisdom. One would not expect wisdom to have this sarcastic tone. This is a "you made your bed, now lie in it." This is a "you are getting what you deserve."

Our culture right now majors on looking compassionate and caring rather than helping people see that because of one's choices they are where they are. So we do not embrace the idea of wisdom which allows people to suffer the consequences of their choices. We, as a culture, do not believe in shame. We are afraid to expose people to shame and/or the natural consequences of their own decisions. God says that wisdom laughs and mocks at the results of foolishness. This is "You made your bed; now lie in it."

I have watched as families have tried everything to help the wayward son and brother who embraces drugs, stealing, parties, and yet finally has to emotionally disown the homeless bum who lives a few miles away and will not break away from his selfish, proud choices.

I have watched as the families have tried to talk the selfish husband or wife out of their adulterous, drunken ways but they will not listen. They will cheat this rule of reaping and sowing. Then a few years later to see those same loving family members be openly disgusted with their former loved one, appalled at where this person's choices have taken them.

Nobody cheats the law of sowing and reaping. What you sow, you will also reap. If you sow a crop of selfishness, pride, impulsiveness; you will reap destruction to your soul and body.

Solomon is trying to scream at us: You are responsible for your choices. Make good ones. Dig for the everybody-wins choices.

dread

This is the Hebrew word *pahad* which means dread or fear. When someone makes selfish choices, they usually are aware of the things that they are trying to cheat their way out of or around. It is those things catching up with them or the fearful results of what they are doing that is catching up with them.

The idea of dread is the fear that you will be caught. This is not the calamity or the actual problem, but it is the fear of the bad that could happen. In some cases, it is this emotional problem that haunts the person who is selfish. They worry constantly about what will happen if so and so really finds out or if the truth comes out.

When we are in the midst of the cutting corners or the selfish actions, we don't think about this fear that will grip us; but it will come. So don't do things that cannot bear the scrutiny of the light of day.

PROVERBS 1:27 - *When your dread comes like a storm and your calamity comes like a whirlwind, when distress and anguish come upon you.*

This proverb uses four terms to describe the unexpected consequences of foolish behavior. Solomon is having wisdom talk here. Wisdom is pointing out that following your own selfish, impulsive, rebellious ways will go along fine for a while but then there will be a reckoning. The results of your behavior will begin to pour into your life, and it will not be good. You can only pursue a selfish, impulsive, rebellious course so long before the results of those choices come crashing back into your life.

dread

This is the Hebrew word *pahad* which means dread. It refers to a strong feeling of fear over an impending or potential situation.

calamity

This is the Hebrew word *ed* which means calamity, distress, destruction, ruin. The idea is clearly that foolish behavior sets up the conditions for consequences to come and sweep you away. You did a few things illegal. You ticked off the wrong people. You cheated the wrong person. You selfishly pursued your own interests at the expense of others. If any or all of these are true, then you are waiting until you are found out and the whirlwind lands on your head.

The reason Solomon is saying this in this way is to make us realize that we should abandon these foolish ways before the consequences come. There is a way out of where we are; we don't just have to keep going. If you recognize yourself in these verses, then repent of your selfishness and embrace wisdom. There is a way to pursue the triple-win – no matter how dark your world has become.

distress

This is the Hebrew word *sara* which means distress, difficult straits. The idea is something that is narrow and confining. You are boxed in

73

and cannot maneuver and be free. Your choices or circumstances are limited.

anguish

This is the Hebrew word *suqa* which means distress or pressure. This word deals with the pressure of confining circumstances and situations much like the word above. It is an intensification of the idea of the confining and pressurized situation.

Solomon is saying that if you do not get off of the foolish track, it will end in a confining pressurized situation of which there will be little freedom and no escape. One thinks of prison, but Solomon did not have prisons so this was not in his mind. This is more that your opportunities are gone; your skills are limited; people don't trust you so they will not allow you to expand your world; your own addictions will narrow your world. The idea is that your foolish choices cause you to end in a place that you do not want to be. The choices that you make right now are setting up a path that is going somewhere. You must be smart enough to think through where these choices are going. If you choose to eat too much because you like it, you will end up fat. If you choose to steal and lie, you will end up caught and not trusted. If you give in to sexual temptations, you will end up with diseases and lonely. If you give into arrogance and pride, you will end up hated and disrespected. If you give into materialism and impulse spending, you will end up poor and in debt. If you hide from your problems through alcohol, drugs, food, sex, etc., you will become addicted and consume your life in hiding.

It is amazing how many people made choices to put themselves in the exact circumstances that they are living, but they are surprised by the results of their decisions. "How did I get here?" "This wasn't supposed to happen." Project out the choices that you are making. Do not fool yourself that the typical results won't happen to you. This will happen to you, and it will be awful when you get there. Start listening to wisdom while you still can. Repent. Turn to the Lord and ask Him to direct your life. You need a new captain running the ship. You need to do things differently and God is the only one powerful enough to handle the job. You need to act differently. One decision at a time.

Please consider asking God to take over the management of your life. Tell God that you have made a lot of bad decisions and selfish choices. Admit that you need forgiveness and a new ability to make righteous decisions. He offers all of this through Jesus Christ. Submit to Jesus Christ and His leadership of your life. Submit to His way of approaching God, His way of handling marriage, His way of being a part of a family, His way of handling yourself, His way of working, His way of being involved in church, His way of handling money, His way of being in a community, His way of interacting with friends. He has a whole new life for you if you will embrace it. Do not continue to be a fool with its pressure, dread, and calamity ahead.

PROVERBS 1:28 - *Then they will call on me, but I will not answer: They will seek me diligently but they will not find me,*

This proverb is a very real but frightful conclusion that fools suffer. When they are suffering the results of their foolishness and under the crushing weight of the consequences of their selfishness, then fools will look for wisdom; but it **will** be hidden from them. They waited too long to begin the search. There is a window of opportunity that will not be open forever.

Some have suggested that this is God talking and that He will not be open to the fool's pleas for help and rescue, but that is not the case. It is wisdom that hides. The fool has been broken and there is no way to put that life back together fully. It is possible for that person to receive the forgiveness of God and receive the grace of God in their broken situation. But the fool must still live with the consequences of their actions whether that is prison, divorce, the wrong marriage partner, pregnancy, bankruptcy, being fired, being cheated, no job, no skills, no promotion, diseases, etc. What this proverb is saying is that when you spurn wisdom and act selfishly, impulsively, and rebelliously, you have a window in which you can change. If you miss that window, then you will suffer the consequences of your foolishness.

they will call on me, but I will not answer
Wisdom will be hidden from the fools for they now only want wisdom as another impulsive and selfish pursuit. They want it because it will get them out of the jam they are in. It is a level of justice that wisdom refuses to be turned into foolishness in the hands of the fool under pain. They are only interested in wisdom because it will rescue them and not because they really want to live a life of wisdom from here on out.

they will seek diligently but they will not find me

The very actions that would suggest a person has become a convert to wisdom will not work when the consequences of foolishness have already rained down on that person's life. It is too late. That is the message of this proverb. There is a time when it is too late to choose a life of wisdom. Solomon is saying to choose wisdom before you get there. Make the choices to incline your ear to listen to wisdom early. Choose to fear the Lord and realize that there is someone beyond you who wrote the rulebook to the game of life.

Unfortunately our society has a Bacchanalian point of view of the teens and twenties, believing that they can live a responsible life in their thirties. It doesn't work like this. If you live the life of the fool in your teens and twenties, you will have permanently altered the direction of your life.

PROVERBS 1:29 - *Because they hated knowledge and did not choose the fear of the Lord.*

This verse deals with the reason why wisdom will not answer people when they are in the midst of their terrible consequences. This is the answer why people feel God is being unfair when He allows bad things to happen to them. Solomon tells us that wisdom has a reason for not answering. These people refused knowledge and ignored God's boundaries and God. They are reaping what they are sowing. They are understanding at a much more fundamental level that God will not be mocked. Life is not a blank canvas where you get to paint anything you want. God has built into the universe rules, boundaries, wisdom, and laws which we would do well to pay attention to.

hated
This is the Hebrew word *sani* which means to hate or hold in aversion. In this case, those who are destroyed by their own foolishness are those who had an aversion to the learning, to skill development, and to the hard choices that were needed to build a righteous life. The rewards of life do not come at the front end but the back end.

knowledge
This is the Hebrew word *daat* which means information and skill. The idea here is of raw data and skill development which are essential to existing wisely in the world. Some kids just want to do what comes easy. They don't want to learn. They don't want to practice. They don't want to keep learning. They just want to do what they like; what is comfortable at the moment. These kinds of choices will destroy you and leave you in a place that wisdom will not answer.

Now I must say that wisdom will answer when you have repented. But if you still have your hatred of real knowledge and your contempt for the wise choice then wisdom will not help you.

choose

This is the Hebrew word *bahar* which means to choose, to decide. The idea is clearly that these people who are destroyed by their foolishness choose to ignore the warnings of the Lord, choose to run after selfishness rather than wisdom, and choose to not worship God and live in the boundaries that He has set.

Solomon saw in his day people making foolish choices that directed them toward problematic endings. He wanted those who read this book to realize that the majority of what happens to you is your choice. It is not controlled by another. It is not your destiny to live a miserable existence. You are making choices and if you make the wrong ones, there will be no answers when you are wrecked on the side of the road of life.

Make no mistake about it, you choose the fear of the Lord. You decide to listen to the Lord's voice in the Scripture and as He speaks to your spirit. It will be a choice to say no to what the world is wanting you to do and yes to the Lord's way. It will be hard to say no to the impulses of your flesh and yes to the Lord's promptings. It will take everything you have to resist the attacks of the Devil in fear, doubt, lies, accusations, etc., and stand firm in the truth of God. No one else will choose for you. You must choose each day: "Will I live for the Lord today or will I live for myself?" Wherever you are and no matter how far you may have strayed from the path of righteousness, you can choose to follow the Lord and do what He wants today.

fear of the Lord

This is the combination of the word *yare Yahweh* which means the fear of the Lord or reverence for the Lord or being afraid of the Lord. The idea of reverence is constantly brought up, but this grows out of the realization of the power, might, majesty, and knowledge of God. There is a sense that those who turn away from the reality of God because they want to do their own thing will find themselves wrecked on their own accomplishments. Life doesn't work unless it is God's way. We are constantly trying to add to God's way to invent our own way. There is no fear of God before our eyes, so as a culture we experiment with new forms of marriage, with legalizing get-rich-quick schemes, with sexualizing everything, with ignoring the power of advertising and music to tempt and seduce and destroy, with ignoring personal responsibility as the basis of a healthy society and healthy self-esteem.

PROVERBS 1:30 - *They would not accept my counsel, they spurned all my reproof.*

This proverb continues the dissecting of the reason that the person who rejects wisdom ends up with no answers and in the midst of deep trouble. Solomon here adds that those who end up in very difficult places without answers were the same ones who rejected the small little changes that wisdom suggested earlier. They didn't want to modify their lifestyle at all.

counsel

This is the Hebrew word *etsah* which means counsel or advice. The meaning of this first phrase in the proverb is that wisdom kept whispering suggestions on how to be less selfish and how to have others also win. But this was rejected.

These wise courses of action would lower the level of selfish pleasure. We see this all the time when we interview those who have had accidents and killed people or been involved in college hazing accidents or become addicted to drugs. They were just having fun and even though a little voice in the back of their mind said "don't do this" they never thought this would happen to them. The counsel came either in the form of a friend, a counselor, an internal prompting, a teacher, a book, or something. But they thought they were immune from the consequences; they just wanted to do what they wanted to do.

reproof

This is the Hebrew word *tokechah* which means rebuke, correction, punishment. The idea here is that there are consequences to foolish actions. These are called rebukes. They are meant to cause a person to stop and go in another direction. But we become addicted to our form of selfishness and push through these problems and difficulties and consequences as if they were normal. Everybody has these kinds of problems.

I am amazed at the number of times I hear that people have destroyed their marriage because of their love for a hobby or a job or friends, and yet they just continue right on doing the thing that destroyed the center of their relational life. I have listened to people tell me how they destroyed every relationship and good thing in their life to get more of a particular drug. I have listened to men and women tell me how exciting their affair is and how they are willing to give up their family and sometimes their job in order to have this illicit relationship. Then three months later have that relationship be a complete bust with more problems and more arguments, and now they have no family support and sometimes no job.

Solomon is saying that people who want to be really selfish will push through almost anything to continue being selfish. It is not as though they were not warned or rebuked or had a shot across their bow – they did. But they were not going to stop.

Now there are two lessons here. Whatever selfish thing you are right now beginning to pursue, you need to listen to counsel and heed rebuke and not let it take you too far. Second, you need to realize that people may blow your advice and wisdom off as they pursue their selfish counsel. You still have to give it and you still have to try and be there after they have destroyed their life with the solution.

The answer is always repentance. Turn away from your present ways and turn to the Lord for forgiveness and grace to live a new way. He has said that in Jesus Christ, He is willing to start again with anyone who will hear His voice and turn to Him in faith.

PROVERBS 1:31 - *So they shall eat of the fruit of their own way and be satiated with their own devices.*

Solomon wants to drive deep into the soul of his young students that you will create the world you live in. The way you treat people will be the basis of how you will be treated by the vast majority of people.

eat

This is the Hebrew word *akal* which means to eat. The idea here is you will live in and off of the kind of person that you are. If you are a mean spirited, selfish person, then you will live in and off of that kind of world where it is all dog-eat-dog and viciousness.

What many people don't realize is that how they treat people and how ethical they are is creating the world in which they live. They will find the kind of world they create for themselves.

fruit

This is the Hebrew word *peri* which means fruit, earnings, product. God's universe plays by God's rules: you reap what you sow. If you sow selfishness, then you reap selfishness. If you sow love others first, then you reap love in return.

Solomon is pointing out that those who think they are getting ahead by violence, selfishness, cheating, and predatory ways will eventually be surrounded by people who will do that to them. "According to his deeds" is a maxim in the biblical economy.

way

This is the Hebrew word *derek* which means way, road, path, journey. It is used metaphorically here for the lifestyle you lead. God says that there is an absolute correspondence between how you treat people and how selfish you are and the kind of opportunities and world you live in.

satiated

This is the Hebrew word *sabea* which means satiated or satisfied. The idea is that you will be filled up or full of. In this case you will be sick of people who are treating you exactly like you are treating others.

If it seems like everyone treats you like dirt, then it may be because you treat everyone else like dirt. If you notice the pride and ego in everyone, then it may be that you are proud and egotistical. The very schemes that you try on others will be done to you. That is why the Lord Jesus says "Do unto others as you would have done to you."

devices

This is the Hebrew word *moetsah* which means counsel, plan, principle, device. Solomon is saying how you treat people is how you will be treated. People tend to reflect back on others what they receive. Few people realize this and wonder why so many people are angry, proud, or heartless towards them. It is often because they are this way towards others.

PROVERBS 1:32 - *For the waywardness of the naive will kill them, and the complacency of fools will destroy them.*

waywardness

This is the Hebrew word *meshubah* which means turning back, apostasy, faithless, waywardness. The clear idea here is that the person is making progress in doing what is right but then turns back to a selfish way of living.

Solomon says that this is the way of the naive person. They start down the path of everybody-wins, but they turn back from it and go after the I-win solution. They can't stay with the everybody-wins lifestyle; it takes too long and it feels too complicated and indirect. At some point they just revert back to "I need to look after number one." This sometimes "I want you to win and sometimes I want me to win" is what destroys them. People don't know which orientation they will find when they interact with this person.

naive

This is the Hebrew word *pethi* which means naive, simple, open-minded. This is the person who does not understand or pursue the complex or subtle orientations of wisdom. They just want everything to be simple, easy, or straightforward.

This person understands the simpleness of "I want that, so I should go after that." They do not understand "I win when I cause the right people around me to win." That is too complex and so they turn back from pursuing the wins for others; they go back to just pursuing wins for themselves.

Once you have set out on the path of wisdom, your path to winning is much more indirect. You will win and gain what you want when the right people in your life win in the right way. It is complex but clearly true that if your spouse wins, you win; if your children win, you win; if your company wins, you win; if your church wins, you win.

Now let me just say that it does, at times, get very subtle and complex to help others win in the right way. It seems like you are losing in the short term which is what causes the naive to turn back. Don't turn back. If you want a great marriage, help your spouse win in a big way no matter how complex or subtle it becomes. If you want a great family, help your family members win. If you want a great company, help your colleagues win and the company wins in a big way. Now this does not mean that you cause yourself to lose in order for them to win; it is that you are looking for ways to benefit them that also allow you to win. Another naive game is to see winning in life as a zero-sum game. Either I win or they win but both cannot. This is wrong. Wisdom digs for the everybody-wins choice. It is there.

kill

This is the Hebrew word *harag* which means to kill, slay, murder. People who begin acting like they have the other person's best interests at heart, gains trust, and then takes the selfish tact, kills the relationship with the other person more than the person who is selfish from the beginning. The naive person who switches to a selfish tact in the middle of a relationship causes a greater feeling of betrayal than the person who just is out for themselves from the start. This is why divorce hurts so bad. This is why business partnerships that go bad are so deeply hurtful. This is why teens that rebel are so deeply painful.

complacency

This is the Hebrew word *salew* which means quiet, ease, or prosperous. The idea in this case seems to be that the fool does not want to go to extra work, so they do not take the steps necessary to change the situation to an everybody-wins scenario. They just keep existing in the status quo. "It is just too much work to change, so I will keep doing what I have always been doing and hope for a different result." They won't get it, but they will always hope.

In order to get a better result, you must enter better components. Some better things have to be added to the relationship in order to move the thing forward. This takes effort and the fool is disinclined to do that much work.

In other words, you have to love your spouse at a new level to change your marriage; you have to love your kids at a new level to change your family for the better; you have to do work at a new level or new effectiveness to change the company.

Realize that all of us see any changes as too much work. But if you do not change, then you will not get the result that you want. Be wise. Don't suffer the fate of the fool or the naive person. Strategize how to accomplish an everybody-wins philosophy in the key relationships of life.

PROVERBS 1:33 ~ *But he who listens to me shall live securely and will be at ease from the dread of evil.*

Solomon finishes his bold statements regarding the power and benefits of wisdom in this final set-piece – security and freedom from harm done by those who are wicked. These are two powerful motivators. Learn wisdom, Solomon declares, and you will gain these things you seek. You will gain them in the right way, at the right time, and without damaging others to get it.

listens

This is the Hebrew word *shama* which means to hear, to listen, to obey, to listen carefully. It means that you listen with the intent to do what wisdom says to do even if you may feel that something else should be done. When wisdom speaks, you listen in order to obey.

Realize that Solomon started this proverb with "But" or in contradistinction to what I have been saying about the consequences of foolishness. There is great benefit in learning how to act wisely, especially when you don't want to.

securely

This is the Hebrew word *betach* which means security, confidence, securely. The idea that Solomon is trying to portray is that wisdom accomplishes what you want: security. In that time period, security from enemies both foreign and domestic was a huge deal. We, in our day and age, have come to feel that security is a right and not a reward for right choices. There will come a time in the not too distant future, I am afraid, that we will again long for security like those who lived in cities in Israel.

Our insecurity does not usually deal with physical attack, although in certain parts of most major cities that is a distinct possibility. Insecurity has to do with employment, marriage, financial uncertainty, children. Learning to look for the triple-win in each of these cases will allow a whole new level of security to take place in your life. Learn to be wise and not selfish. Selfishness invites problems.

dread

This is the Hebrew word *pachad* which means dread, disaster, fear. The idea here is that when you have done wrong to better yourself, you are always fearful that someone will do that to you. There is an emotion that lies in the background of your life if you have profited at the expense of others. That emotion is dread – the feeling that something bad is coming.

Solomon is reinforcing that the blessings of wisdom are incredibly rewarding and the consequences of selfishness are repulsive. So do not choose to be a fool. Choose to be a wise man or woman and gain the benefit.

The question is: Are you listening to wisdom or to foolishness?

Do you have fear in your life?

Is it because of foolishness in your life somewhere?

Proverbs 2

PROVERBS 2:1 - *My son, if you will receive my words and treasure my commandments within you,*

Notice the word *son*. This is a young man or a person who puts himself in the position of learner.

receive my words

Notice that the writer says that even the son must put himself into an attitude to receive the words of this book. Just because you are a physical son or follower or employee, it does not mean that you will automatically be willing to receive instruction.

How tragic that sometimes the very people we would like to have receive our wisdom are not open to it. A person must be open to receive words of wisdom. If they are not open, then the wisdom of these lessons will fall like water off a duck's back.

This is a word to parents that you should make sure, in every way you can, that your children respect you enough to be willing to listen to you. You should make sure that they are not given free rein to their selfish tendencies to blow you off. You must make sure that the nature of your relationship is close and supportive so that their receiving your words is a no brainer.

This is also a warning to us. Do we have the proper attitude to receive God's wisdom even when it says things we don't want to hear or comes through a person we don't like? God is pouring out wisdom to us. If we are willing to hear it, He will make us wise. Many times we must admit that our own selfish choices caused much of the problems that we now experience. Is your heart right to receive God's wisdom – especially through this book but also as we walk through the day?

treasure my commandments within you

What do you hold dear in your life? Is it a list of do's and don'ts that will show you the path of wisdom? Are we treasuring up useless trinkets when the real treasures we treat with disregard?

Remember our world system wants to get us to attach the wrong price tags to the stuff in our lives. They want us to have a high value on

TV's, couches, cars, and homes while we put a low priority on God, family, Scripture, relationships, etc.

In this instance God is telling you to put a high value on the list of do's and don'ts that you will find in this book. It will be a healing and a life to you. There are very few things that are more valuable than a guide that will help you arrive at the right decision every time. The commandments in this book are that guide. Don't throw it away as worthless or too complicated.

The commandments in this book are over 3,000 years old and have shown their worth in every culture and every time. They are breathed with the life of God. They are inspired by God.

How many bad decisions have you made? If I could give you a list of things to think about before you made your decisions that would virtually eliminate bad decisions if you followed them, would that be worth something?

Now there is a difference between wise and foolish decisions and right and wrong decisions. Something may not be wrong, but it still may be foolish. This book will have us think about our decisions and actions at a much more fundamental level.

Three elementary guides that run through this book:

- Is this thing I want to do selfish? Am I the only one who will profit from this? Is there another decision in which God and others can also profit with me?

- Is what I want to do impulsive? Does it need to be done quickly without counsel or forethought? Impulsive decisions are almost always foolish decisions.

- Is this decision I want to do rebellious? Does it involve rebelling against proper authorities? Does it require disappointing their trust in me? Rebellious decisions are usually not wise decisions.

These three guides will help inform and educate your decisions if you will receive them. There is so much more in the book of Proverbs, but you have to have a heart to receive them and treasure them.

How tragic that many people have the greatest book on how to live life in their homes, but they do not value it enough to read it every day. Bibles on the shelf do not do any good. It is verses in the heart that build a great life.

PROVERBS 2:2 ~ *Make your ear attentive to wisdom, incline your heart to understanding;*

One of the main messages of the book of Proverbs is that wisdom is all around if we would just look for it and be sensitive to it when it shows up.

make your ear attentive to wisdom

Solomon tells us that we must make our ear attentive to wisdom.

The word *ear* is the Hebrew word *ozen* which means ear or the part of the body that interprets symbolic language or a person's responsiveness to commands or information. It is this last aspect that catches our attention. In a Hebraic mindset, one has not really heard what another has said unless there is obedience or appropriate response to it. When the Scripture says "Hear the word of the Lord," it means obey the word of the Lord, not listen for the sounds God will make or take notes on what He just says. So in this same way Solomon says you have to make yourself ready to respond positively to wisdom when you come across it. You are not really a student of wisdom if you just say, "Oh, that is interesting" or "I will save it for later." It must be imbedded in your person so that you act in accordance with it.

We have a storage-tank approach to information and wisdom, filling ourselves with information and good actions that we call wisdom to be pulled out of the storage tank and used when appropriate. This works in some cases. The Scripture has a different view when it comes to wisdom. When you are faced with a decision or course of action, you are looking for wisdom. You will not find wisdom if you do not pre-commit to doing it once you find it for it may be somewhat painful to do in the short-run. Remember that wisdom is the triple-win choice – that action or choice in which God wins, others win, and I win. This is opposed to the choice in which I win and others lose or I win and some others win but God loses. Therefore if I am facing a decision, I need to pre-commit to doing the triple-win option when I find it. If not, I will be tempted to go for the quick, selfish choice in which I am looking out for number 1.

The point Solomon is telling his young learner is that wisdom must be done or it is gone. It cannot be found if it will not be obeyed. I have counseled many people who have asked me to save their marriage or help them financially or stop their children from rebelling, but then they tell me what they are unwilling to do. Usually what they are unwilling to do is the direction that wisdom is in. They will say things like, "I have already tried that" or "Don't ask me to apologize or give more of my time or live on a budget or something like that." What they want is for everybody else to change but themselves. They want to continue to be selfish and get different results in their marriage, checkbook, and family.

Make a pre-commitment to wisdom. It may seem difficult to lessen your personal win to have others win and God get glory, but it pays rich dividends in the future just as making small investments over time in a reasonable investment option. It gets better with time.

I recommend that you tell God every day, as you are studying the Scriptures, that you want His wisdom and are ready to do it. Also, when you are facing a major decision in your work, marriage, family, church, or any aspect of your life, start by telling God you are looking for wisdom and are right now pre-committing to it.

incline your heart to understanding
This is a fascinating concept that we think we comprehend but we don't.

The word *heart* is the Hebrew word *leb* which means the actual physical organ of the heart; it means the center of the person or the place of decision, volition, and emotion. And some would connect this with the immaterial part of man called the soul.

The word *incline* is the Hebrew word *nata* which means extend, lean over, incline, bend. This word carries with it the idea of leaning to the point of falling in a certain direction; going beyond what is normal and natural and balanced. One could say that Solomon is advising us to unbalance our mind, will, and emotions to grasp this thing called understanding.

The word *understanding* is the Hebrew word *bina* which means distinguish between, between the power of judgment and perception. One of the quick ways I like to understand this word *understanding* is as the connections between things; to grasp how things are interrelated. In other words, if I do this, then that will happen. If I say this, then so and so will feel these things and probably react in these ways.

It is tragic when a person does not have any understanding of the connections between what they say and do and how other people react. They just see what they want and go after it, regularly amazed at the idea that other people may have had designs on that thing themselves or could have a reaction.

This is the place where many people in our society are today. They do not realize that all actions are interrelated with lots of other people. If a person chooses to smoke, they are doing a lot of things beyond just putting smoke in their lungs. They put smoke in the lungs of those around them; they damage their lung's ability to breathe; they increase their risk for cancer; they decrease their life expectancy; they are perceived differently; they smell different. If a person chooses to be proud, a whole host of connections and reactions are set in motion. If a person commits adultery, a massive amount of connections and reactions are set in motion. If I own a company and choose to pollute the river or air, a huge number of reactions and connections are unleashed in the society. We live in a society in which people basically want permission to do what they want to do with little regard for what will happen to all those who are impacted by their actions.

If you and I are going to be wise, then we will need to stretch out for or not rest until we see the various reactions and connections that our actions will have. If we were to just stop and think a while before we acted – What will happen if I do this? – we would be inclining our heart to understanding. It is like putting a chess piece in the place we are thinking about moving it but not taking our hand off it. We can then survey the various possibilities and countermoves that our potential move makes possible.

Too often we just grow weary of this type of hard thinking and want to do what we want before anybody can stop us. This is the fool's way. If we want a great marriage, a satisfying career, an enjoyable family, devoted friends, then we must take the time to lean over and see the various reactions and connections that our actions will have on these very important parts of our life.

If this is hard for you, then ask someone who is wise to help you. Give them hypothetical situations and say, "If I said this, what do you think my spouse would say; my children, my boss, my friends?" Keep doing this type of thing until you begin to grasp understanding for then you will be wise and most likely a lot less quick in speech and action.

At various times you will be caught completely off guard by the reaction of others. This is an indication that you have some growing to do in understanding. A person who has understanding can anticipate the reactions and interactions of others and decide beforehand whether they are worth it.

PROVERBS 2:3 - *For if you cry for discernment, lift your voice for understanding;*

discernment

This word translated in the NASB here as *discernment* is really the word *understanding* – where the person is crying out for perception into the relationship between events and knowledge. The cry is for insight into what is behind just the raw facts.

understanding

This is the only place where both words for *understanding* are used in the same passage which adjusts the meaning of these usually synonymous terms. The first reference carries the usual meaning for the word understanding – insight even discernment. The second is a cry for the object of understanding – the carrier of key information that unlocks the understanding or relationship.

This is a very interesting bit of information. One must gain the understanding through a deep and open desire for the insight about what is the relationship between events, circumstances, people, etc; but one must also be just as hungry for the object or means through which that information will come. Understanding does not just pop into one's mind; it is conveyed through someone or something and one must be ready for the teacher or the insight will be missed.

In other words, one must be very interested in understanding why things happen and the relationship between events, and one must realize that God will teach you these insights through a teacher from whom you must equally be prepared to learn.

PROVERBS 2:4 - *If you seek her as silver and search for her as for hidden treasures;*

Wisdom must be sought. It runs counter to our normal choices and is hidden from view by our own foolish tendencies. It begins to be more predictable once you have found it on a regular basis.

In this Proverb, God tells us that we are needing to conduct a search of all the available options. One or a number of them represent wisdom. We must, however, lean hard into the search so that we will discern the proper direction.

What is interesting is that you will be searching for wisdom, but your will discerns the fear of the Lord first. These are the boundaries of God's moral law. There will probably be a number of fairly obvious and easy ways to accomplish the goals you want that involve cheating, anger, lying, etc. This is where you find the fear of the Lord. Do I really fear Him and believe that He has consequences for my actions, especially when I move beyond the boundaries of the Ten Commandments and God's moral law?

The Lord will give you wisdom, verse 5 says, when you have discerned the fear of the Lord first. Where are the boundaries? Our minds will find the deviant ways to accomplish our goals. But in seeking wisdom, we must reject these. If the goal is to be happily married, our fleshly nature will come up with the new mate, the affair, the alcoholic anesthesia that will make the possibility of a happy marriage look bright. You don't get a happy marriage that way; it just seems like you would. It is just that you have to cross significant moral boundaries to do that to your spouse. This is the direction of choice for many instead of putting in the work to make their present marriage work at a whole new level.

When you are facing a business decision and do not know how to achieve your goals, there will always be some scheme with the books that will come to mind that must be rejected or you will never find stable success or wisdom.

PROVERBS 2:5 - *Then you will discern the fear of the Lord and discover the knowledge of God.*

It is absolutely crucial in the gaining of knowledge that this information not be cut off from knowledge of God – that He is a Holy God and that He keeps track of all the things that we do and that He will call a man into judgment for everything that he has ever done, said, or thought.

When information is divorced from an understanding of God and His nature and the eventual eternal evaluation, then it becomes perverted and twisted and can be used to destroy instead of to aid mankind.

Remember that what you are searching for is wisdom and understanding, not information and power. Too often we think that these concepts are synonymous. They are not. To be wise means, at times, that you give up power. At times it means that you do not gain intimate or detailed knowledge of certain things.

The fear of the Lord is a crucial concept to a righteous life. It is associated in the New Testament with the knowledge of God's review of your life when you die.

2 Corinthians 5:10 - *For we must all appear before the judgment seat of Christ, so that each one may be recompensed for his deeds in the body, according to what he has done, whether good or bad.*

1 Corinthians 5:5 - *Therefore do not go on passing judgment before the time, but wait until the Lord comes who will both bring to light the things hidden in the darkness and disclose the motives of men's hearts; and then each man's praise will come to him from God.*

There is a subtle suggestion that you do not have accurate knowledge of God until your knowledge includes fear of Him. He is a fearful being with all power and all knowledge. We are sinful and disgraced and rebellious against the Holy God who set us here.

I am deeply concerned that people have invented a conception of God that has removed all the fear. They have a tame God of their own invention. What a shock that they will see not that God is their pet willing to bend to their wishes but Holy, awesome, and bending time, space, and eternity to His own wishes. He demands my allegiance and submission just by the power of His being, and yet He asks for it as though it is not His to demand.

The ethic of both the Old and New Testament is love God and love your neighbor. Are you doing anything positive in your life to change the life of those around you or are you living a purely selfish life? Is the record of your life going to show that you were selfish to the core even when you seemed to be loving or that you are willing to be transformed by the message of God's love and forgiveness?

PROVERBS 2:6 - *For the Lord gives wisdom; from His mouth comes knowledge and understanding.*

What is interesting in this proverb is that while you search for wisdom, it is the Lord who eventually gives it to you. It would seem that in at least some cases, if not many, you cannot connect the dots to wisdom using only your rational faculty or you would not need to search so hard and the Lord would not have to give it.

Those who care about God and seek to please Him are interested in not just what direction makes sense and will bring the prosperity or goal they seek, but they are interested in what does the Lord want. It is this level of wisdom that needs to be given to you. It does not always make the most sense of all the options available to you. It is just clear what He wants you to do.

Notice that He gives it to you. It comes from Him. It will often make perfect sense in retrospect, but there is no way for us to know what He knows. He is outside the time domain and understands everything that will possibly happen down any time tangent. If something looks like the wise thing to do but He knows something that will happen in six months that we can never know, then we need His choice not just ours. If He knows that we will encounter a person who will present an irresistible temptation to us at some point down a particular path, then we need to avoid that path. We need His wisdom. If He knows that all types of support and help and encouragement will be available about three months from now going down a particular path, then while it does not make the "best" sense at the time, it is the path to go down. If He sees that we need to learn certain qualities and those will only be learned going down path Y instead of the more popular or immediately successful path Z, then we need His wisdom not just the sum total of our own.

PROVERBS 2:7 - *He stores up sound wisdom for the upright; He is a shield to those who walk in integrity,*

He stores up sound wisdom for the upright

stores up

The word *stores up* in the Hebrew is the word *saphan*. It means to treasure up or to conceal with a definite purpose. God declares that if you are willing to search for the wisdom that you need and will not settle for the easy way or the wicked way, He has concealed stores of wisdom for you – in a sense, secret knowledge that others never find and may not comprehend. This could be both in this world and in the next. What will it be like to be invited into the storeroom of God's wisdom in heaven? Are you searching for those bundles of wisdom that God has hidden along the way in your life that bring a new sense of order and understanding to life?

sound wisdom

This word for *wisdom* is a seldom used word which carries with it the idea of very practical and profitable wisdom. The idea is that living a righteous life is rewarded by God with information that will be very practically helpful. There is practical, profitable information that is stored up for those who search for wisdom with a clean heart.

for the upright

The word literally means to go straight. It means that one does not have deceptiveness about one. It means that they are following the rules of God for life.

He is a shield to those who walk in integrity

He is a shield

The word *shield* is the Hebrew word *magen* which is used for the round light shield of the infantryman, not the heavy full frontal shield. Also the words "He is" are not in the Hebrew text but have been supplied by the translators. While it is true that God is ultimately the shield, it may be a better translation to see the stored up, sound wisdom as the round shield protecting people who are in the midst of life as they seek to walk in integrity.

If one does not find the shield, then one is not protected. If one does not use it, then one is not protected. If one does not have integrity, then one cannot put on this shield.

It is often true that one of the greatest shields against destruction is to avoid temptation and sin. When one does not have to remember what they lied about or conceal unfaithfulness or hide what was stolen, then they have a protective shield keeping them from much harm.

walk in integrity

The Hebrew word is *tom* meaning completeness and wholeness. What you see is what you get. There is not a deceptive hidden part that is different from what you see.

God is declaring to those who are willing to hear that it pays to search after God's wisdom. He has a hidden stash of very practical and profitable information for those who are willing to live an upright life. It does, at times, look like those who are cheating and stealing and lying are getting ahead; but they are not. This wisdom from God acts like a shield that protects the person from many of the problems of life.

PROVERBS 2:8 - *Guarding the paths of justice, and He preserves the way of His godly ones.*

The word guarding is the Hebrew word *nasar* which is to watch, guard, keep, to keep in view. Solomon is trying to drill into the young student that there are some lifestyles that God pays special attention to with the intent of blessing. He intimately knows everyone's pathway, but the pathway of the godly, wise ruler gains His special attention for blessing and preservation. There is an element of protection and smoothing out of the way in this idea, and it shows up in Proverbs 3 when he says, "in all your ways acknowledge Him and He will make your paths straight or smooth."

Solomon is saying: Get into this lifestyle. Problems will come to everyone; but God protects, guards, and straightens the life of those who are on the right pathway. Has God been straightening your pathway? Has He protected you from some of the stuff that could have come your way? Are you in the paths of justice?

Notice the word *path* is the word *orah* which is way or path. It is used to describe a lifestyle or way of living. There are different ways of living and the one which God guards is the one of integrity and righteous leadership

The word *justice* is the word *misphat* which is judgment, justice, ordinance. It comes from the root Hebrew verb *sapat* which means to rule or govern and includes all three functions of what we call government and leadership: legislative, executive, and judicial functions. One could think of this as the right decision. God guards and protects those who lead, rule, and make the right decision. And the right decision has its own pathway. In fact, if one consistently makes the right decisions, it strings together a pathway through life that is the one that God protects.

The word *godly ones* is the Hebrew word *hasid* which means holy one or saint. It comes from the word *hesed* which is the word loving-kindness, mercy, love. The idea is that those who love God deeply are those who are called His holy ones. They keep His commandments more faithfully than others because they love Him more. Even as Jesus says in the New Testament, "If you love me, keep my commandments." We are not used to this type of thinking in terms of love. We see love as a feeling and want to respond with a feeling. To be a holy one or godly person is to live within God's Ten Commandments structure out of the desire to please God. God guards the life of those people

Remember that Solomon is trying to teach people how to begin living wisely. He is saying that there is a particular lifestyle that He has watched God protect and guard more than any other. He has watched the person who is living this lifestyle be protected from levels of trouble and difficulty that others do not experience. This lifestyle is one of godliness and justice. Therefore Solomon wants to motivate us to abandon whatever lifestyle that we have adopted that is not that one.

Throughout the Proverbs God is telling us through the teaching of Solomon, why would you want to live in a way that invites trouble and difficulty when you can have God paying special attention so that He can bless you.

Think through your life this week or this month. Are there any parts or decisions that require you to live outside of God's Ten Commandments of love? Don't do it. Stay within the pathways that God is guarding.

PROVERBS 2:9-16 - *Then you will discern righteousness and justice and equity and every good course. For wisdom will enter your heart and knowledge will be pleasant to your soul; discretion will guard you, understanding will watch over you, to deliver you from the way of evil, from the man who speaks perverse things; from those who leave the paths of uprightness... to deliver you from the strange woman, from the adulteress who flatters with her words;*

This whole section is an amazing series of promises. Almost everything that anyone could want is promised as the outcome. What is amazing is the way of activating these wonderful results. In the first four verses, we are told that only the really seeking heart will ever activate the gift of God to receive these incredible benefits. The first part of this chapter in Proverbs is often skimmed over to spend time on the incredible list of benefits, but the key to attaining the wonder of wisdom is the seeking heart. You must really want it and must cry out for it; ready to receive it from the various sources that God sends it through.

discern righteousness and justice and equity and every good course

This is a Hebraic way of talking about the key qualities in leadership. When the three ideas of righteousness, justice, and equity are combined, they form a triplet of godly leadership and authority. This is the way of saying great leadership God's way. We are tired of authoritarian leadership that has no equity or fairness. We have seen leadership that is not righteous but instead is selfish and wicked. It eventually destroys the leader and the followers. We have witnessed when leadership becomes overwhelmed with favoritism, factions, and a me-and-mine-first attitude.

God is promising to develop a new level of leadership if you will follow His plan. If you want to become a new-level leader, then you must cry out to God and listen for the subtleties of wisdom.

wisdom will enter your heart

The ability to know what is the triple-win decision: in which direction do God, others, and myself benefit the most long term. You must really seek to understand the subtleties of a process to come to wisdom. Often the really wise course is not the first one that you think of. Gold does not usually lie on the surface; it must be mined.

knowledge will be pleasant to your soul

These are skills and information that are required for a wise set of actions or decisions. Often before one can really embrace the wise course, there is a particular skill set or information that must be obtained. This proverb tells us that once it is obtained, it sits in the innermost part of your being and refreshes your soul. By the way, that makes it worth the work to obtain it.

discretion will guard you

This word *discretion* is the word for plan, plot, scheme. The course of wisdom develops a plan. Very rarely is wisdom a one-step plan. There are often many steps that must be coordinated and put in order. The plan and its various contingencies will guard you from mistakes, surprises, and temptations. Plan your work and work your plan. This takes time and desire to put the pieces of the plan together.

understanding will watch over you

Understanding is the Hebrew word *bina*. It means to understand, have insight, discern. It is the information that is more than just data collection. It is the connection between information and the interactions between groups, things, and forces. This is perceptive insight – the reading between the lines of raw information. This is a powerful ability to see what is hidden to perceive the reactions and hidden messages. This ability will truly guard you from making the obvious choice that would be disastrous. It is one of those: something is wrong and I am going to understand what it is... I can't put my finger on it... but I know it is not right.

to deliver you from the way of evil, from the man who speaks perverse things. To deliver you from the strange woman

This section of verses lists three particular villains who trip up the growing young man or woman in their pursuit to live a good life. The pathway of evil or wickedness. It is tempting and has shipwrecked many. Notice that one must be delivered from these people and pathways. One or all of them will be alluring. It does not say that you will not be tempted but rather if you follow the prescription, then you will be delivered from that which in your foolishness you would fall victim to.

Remember that the key to receiving all of these benefits is the first four verses – seeking wisdom and insight and God. In each decision you must cry out to God for the level of wisdom you need until the wise course glows like an airport runway at night. Good decisions and wise life courses will do this if enough effort and true heart cries are involved.

PROVERBS 2:10 - *For wisdom will enter your heart and knowledge will be pleasant to your soul;*

This Proverb answers one of the most important questions of life. How do we make additions to our soul or internal programming? As we live our life we will be adding to the software that runs our bodies. The place of our software is our soul. This is described as our heart in this passage. Notice that the Proverb says that if we do what has been suggested, that wisdom will enter our heart. We won't just use some wisdom or act wisely in an instance, but it will be added to the internal programming.

Remember what Moses says about our life – that it will last 70+ years and that at the end God will examine our soul to see how much wisdom we have amassed. Have we just occasionally stumbled across wisdom or have we really internalized wisdom in which it has become a part of our internal programming?

On a side note... It is clear that in the Christian worldview our bodies, brains, heart, eyes, arms, legs, etc., are the hardware of this life and our soul is the software of this life. All of our life we are adding programs to the basic software package we came equipped with. One day our soul or software will be uploaded to a different place and cleaned of its selfish tendencies and then reloaded into a new hardware in a new setting. Pretty exciting stuff! It is the stuff that we have loaded on the software that matters and not the hardware. That will wear down and become obsolete. While it is important to keep the hardware in good condition, it is not the hardware that ultimately matters – it is the software.

and knowledge will be pleasant to your soul

This is an interesting phrase because it sets up at least two directions to follow its thinking. First, that real knowledge – when accepted and embraced along with wisdom – is a very pleasant thing. Solomon is motivating us toward knowledge and wisdom by speaking of the pleasantness of possessing it.

However, the second implication of this part of the Proverb is more disturbing and that is that it is possible for knowledge to not be pleasant to your soul. That it is possible in rejecting wisdom and pursuing foolishness that real knowledge will be very disturbing and deeply painful. I think of those people who have built their life on fool's pleasure when the truth of the way life really works comes crashing down on them. I think of those who are wicked, believing that this life is all there is and that they are getting away with flaunting man's rules. What will knowledge feel like when they are still conscious on the other side of death and are moving toward judgment day? Knowledge will not be pleasant to their soul.

There are spiritual, moral, emotional, and mental realities in this world that one should pay attention to. It is only as one lives in the world that God created that knowledge will be pleasant to your soul.

PROVERBS 2:11 ~ Discretion will guard you, understanding will watch over you,

This proverb is obviously in the middle of a longer sales presentation on the virtues of going after wisdom. This whole chapter is about why you should make wisdom a life-long pursuit.

Every day you will instinctively know what you want to do selfishly but to find out that which will promote the common good – the choices that are the everybody-wins choice – will take much more searching.

In fact, the first parts of this section tell us that if you don't highly desire the wise Triple-Win choice, you will not see it when it comes by. If you miss the wise choice, then all the benefits that this chapter speak of will also not be a part of your life.

The two benefits that this verse speaks of are particularly potent benefits:

The word *discretion* is the word *mezimma* in the Hebrew which means purpose or plot. When it is used of the Lord, it is called His purposes; when it is used of wicked men, it is called schemes. We would understand this as plans, goals, designs.

What this means is that wisdom causes a person to plan a future and have goals and plans. It is these goals and plans that become major driving forces in the life of the person and keep them from many wicked involvements. This is a truth that we need to be constantly aware of. When do we get into the most trouble – when we have nothing planned and are just at the whim of our own impulses or those of others.

Young people can throw their lives away in a heartbeat if they do not have plans for the future: college, development of a skill, pursuing a dream, great marriage, good job, entrance to a military academy. Who has not seen a young person start resisting temptation because it would affect the accomplishment of the dream in their head. Having that dream is an essential part of having wisdom.

This is not just true for young people. At every point in our life we become more susceptible for temptation when we have nothing planned; when we are not reaching forward to what lies ahead, as the Apostle Paul says. When the past or the present is stronger than the future, we become more susceptible to temptation.

Let me ask you: Do you have plans for this year? For the next five? Do you have goals that will take a number of years to complete or attain? Are you still stretching to accomplish something in your life? If the answer is "no" then you need to get some. What would God want you to accomplish during the next five-year period of your life? If you were to go back to school, what would you study? What dream have you always had that you could start pursuing at this point?

Remember, it is having the goals and the plans that guard you from the pull of the temptations that are going to come.

The word *understanding* is the Hebrew word *bina* which means understand, discern, insight. It is a different word than the word for knowledge or raw facts; it means to realize the connection between two or more sets of facts. The key idea in understanding is the connection between things. In this proverb, understanding is seen as a huge angelic guarding watching over your life. Another way of seeing it is like a chess match in which you keep your hand on a piece and move it where you are thinking about moving it and see all the moves and countermoves that are possible from that point. You gain an understanding of the new possible position and can decide if you want to do it.

The person who has wisdom is able to think a number of steps ahead. They realize connections that others do not make. If I enter into a deal with this person, I will ultimately be swindled because this person is selfish. If I enter into a relationship with this person, I will be wounded because they have shown no capacity to care for anyone other than themselves. Do I want to have this size of loan following me for ten or so years? If I go to this college, I will do well because it has a student body like me; if I go to this other college, I will probably not do well as it is cutthroat and spiritually much darker.

It is understanding that allows you to realize what is going on in the world and, in many cases, to fairly accurately predict what impact things will have on your life. In this way understanding watches over you.

With this in mind, are you about to enter into a relationship which understanding is warning you about? Are you about to make a purchase that you have not really sat down and looked at all the connections? Is your insight detector going off about a group or individual in your life and you need to perceive more about this group or person?

Remember, if you are going to have these benefits as a part of your life, you have to be willing to fight to find wisdom. Do not just do what seems right to you. Look hard; investigate for the choice or action in which everybody but the wicked wins.

PROVERBS 2:12 - *To deliver you from the way of evil, from the man who speaks perverse things;*

In this section Solomon continues to speak of the wonders of wisdom and what it will do if it is allowed full entrance into your life. In this proverb he notes that it will deliver or save you from two things that are very good to be saved from – the way of evil and the person who speaks perverse things. It is important to look at the reverse of this proverb to see its import. If you are not wise and do not look for the triple-win choices and actions, then you will be most likely seduced by the way of evil with no way to break free. You will believe the person who tells you of twisted and bizarre things and move in that direction. A young person sets the course of their life, and they need to not be sucked into these problems.

What is the way of evil and the speaking of perverse things? And it is not just young people who need to be careful of these two dangers.

The word *perversity* is the Hebrew word *tahpuka* which is used only nine times in the Scriptures and eight times here in Proverbs. It is from the root *hapak* which means to turn, to overturn. It is translated *perversity* in the NASB and *forwardness* in the KJV. The idea is that of twistedness. It is the nature of festering evil to twist that which is righteous into something else; to use something in a way that was not its intended purpose. Evil is a twist of that which is good. Marriage is good; adultery is a twist – physical intimacy without the safety and emotional connectedness of commitment. Those who are evil continue twisting sexual pleasure to produce vile behaviors. Work is good; stealing is a twist – achieving gain without work. There are forms of stealing that involve elaborate schemes and deception so that the person doesn't even know they have been robbed. Relationships built on truth are good and enduring. Lying and deception is a twist – building a relationship on lies, deceit, fraud. In each of the directions of the Ten Commandments there are the ways of evil which become more twisted the further one gets from God's righteousness.

When one speaks perverse things, it means that the person is describing the twisted pleasures of those who have moved past God's moral boundaries. Usually they are speaking them to draw a person after them. A young person can be susceptible to this type of twisted speech. "Have you ever heard of..." "Oh yeah I tried it. It was cool."

It is important to note at this point that the way of evil is the way of increasing selfishness. When selfishness moves beyond the borders of God's standards, it becomes evil because it becomes destructive to the individual, those around them, and the society as a whole. The allure of the way of evil is that it makes you king of your life completely. Whatever you want to do, you can do. Go for it. It fails to realize that you live in God's universe in which you don't get to pick the consequences for your actions. God picked them a long time ago. Selfishness is a destructive force in God's universe. God never designed people to interact based upon it. It messes things up and the stronger the selfishness, the worse it gets.

If someone starts telling you about some bizarre thing that you should try, back up and realize that they are probably deep into the way of evil. Access the wisdom of the triple-win. Does this give God glory, will others win, and is there a long-term win in this for me?

PROVERBS 2:13 ~ *From those who leave the paths of uprightness to walk in the ways of darkness;*

The instruction process continues as these young people are told that there are people who choose to leave the paths of morality and instead inhabit the ways of darkness. This is shocking to many young people in the beginning of their training. Many have lived a protected, sheltered life in their youth.

Solomon is telling these naive beginners at adult living that there are "bad" people: These people, through their own choices, live under a different set of rules than you have been used to. They will do almost anything if it brings advantage to them. It is these people that you must protect yourself from. In fact, wisdom is the primary protector of those who are out dealing with people in the real world. The people who leave the paths of uprightness do not announce that they are evil. They do not have distinctive dress or distinctive features; they instead look like friends and like helpers. But they actually come to consume you and your resources for their own purposes.

Clearly in Proverbs the paths of uprightness are those actions and ways of living that are within the boundaries of the Ten Commandments. There are people who do not just occasionally break these significant moral boundary markers; they live beyond these moral lines. According to the book of Proverbs, when you choose to live beyond the Ten Commandments, you are choosing to live in the way of darkness. It is a dark way and will result in difficulties and unexpected disasters in your life. Do not go there. Now it is true that everyone at one time or another violates these laws and needs a Savior who is Jesus Christ the Lord.

Those who enter the way of darkness are more interested in themselves than the society at large or even their own loved ones. The deeper one gets into the ways of darkness, the more selfish it gets. Solomon is trying to educate and protect the naive and the simple and even the wise about those who have chosen to live by these rules of the jungle: "Get yours before someone else gets it."

Let's do a little review of the Ten Commandments so you can see who the people are who are living in the ways of darkness. Unfortunately it is always shocking to see God's standard and realize that some "good" people that you know have chosen to live on the other side of God's clear direction. Our present society is full of rebellion to God's standard and the devastation just continues to increase.

Where are God's boundary lines:
- When you place something or someone as first in your life or the organizing principle of your life.
- When you bow down to an idol or misrepresent the Almighty God in some way.
- When you speak or live in such a way as to deny that you represent God or know Him. This would include the constant use of the sacred or the perverse to strengthen your words.
- Present at least one in seven days to God for worship and physical rest. In the New Testament it became present every day to Jesus Christ as His day to work through you.
- Are you adapting to and valuing those leaders that God has righteously put in your life?
- When you become violently or murderously angry.
- When you refuse to contain sexual pleasure within the lifetime marital relationship God designed.
- When you profit by making another person lose – either by direct theft or through deception, fraud, or scheming.
- When you are not honest in your comments with a person who deserves the truth.
- When you crave, plan, or scheme to have what another already possesses.

PROVERBS 2:14 - *Who delight in doing evil and rejoice in the perversity of evil;*

As strange as it seems, there are people who delight in evil. They deeply enjoy being selfish even after they know that their deeds cause others to lose, to be in pain, to suffer. They still delight in the pleasure they enjoy doing – the evil thing.

This is the definition of *evil:* a form of selfishness that damages the individual, others, God, or the society. Everything would be permissible if there were no consequences. But because God knows how the world is wired and that there are consequences for certain levels and forms of selfishness, He has outlawed them. But we still fight against His telling us NO and want to experience those things because they seem pleasurable.

delight

This is the Hebrew word *sameah* which means joyful, merry, glad of heart. People find great joy in all kinds of things regardless of what it does to other people or the society as a whole.

One of the wake-up calls that Solomon wants young people to hear loud and clear in these early chapters of Proverbs is that there are people who don't care what happens to others as long as they get theirs. They will deceive, use, abuse, hurt, lie, damage, and impoverish you in order to get the pleasure they want. There are a lot of naive people who want to believe that everybody wants the best for them like their parents do but will not tell them NO like their parents.

Just because someone tells you YES all the time does not mean they love you. Most likely they are after what they want. Many kids only wake up after they have been severely broken or damaged.

evil

This is the Hebrew word *ra* which means that which is outside of the boundaries of the Ten Commandments. Our society has adopted the emotivistic ethic that only that which is revulsive is wrong, but that is not a biblical ethic. God has said that the boundaries of selfishness must stop at the lines of the Ten Commandments.

perversity of evil

There are actually people who enjoy the twisted nature of evil. They enjoy torture; sexual perversity; devious schemes to defraud people; bizarre demonic rituals to other gods; elaborate plans to take the property, employees, or spouses of others. There are people who find great joy in the twisted nature of evil and in making others suffer and lose. There is more and more interest in the universities of western civilizations to study the perversities of evil. This is a sick and distracting pursuit. It is usually pursued by those who enjoy the field of evil and need a cover to protect their bizarre interest. Avoid this if at all possible.

Wisdom will protect you from these kinds of people. It is best not to even be connected to these people. I constantly meet people who want to know how to rescue people who love evil. They are only savable if they want to be saved. It is best to steer a wide path around those folks unless you have been specifically called by God to minister to this group.

PROVERBS 2:15 - *Whose paths are crooked, and who are devious in their ways;*

This proverb is a continuation of the listing of the traits of people from whom wisdom will protect you.

What we do not often realize is that people do not come with labels attached to them. Evil people don't look worse than righteous people. But what we must do is discern actions. Behavior can be evaluated. It doesn't matter whether they have a likeable personality or are a relative, God's Word says that we are to look for certain actions to avoid and certain actions to embrace.

crooked

This is the Hebrew word *iqqes* which means twisted, crooked, perverse. The idea is that the behavior of certain people is twisted in a bizarre way. They act in ways beyond just being sinful. They are past basic lying. They are past sexual unfaithfulness. They are past simple theft. They embrace a twisted way of living and seek to pull other people into their crooked path.

devious

This is the Hebrew word *lazut* which means a deviation or crookedness or perversion. The translation makes it sound like they are deceptive, but the word refers to the kind of spur off the main line of normal moral behavior that they take.

God wants to spare us from this kind of person. Unfortunately, we celebrate these wacky lifestyles on daytime television. You don't want to understand the way they think or how they go to that place. You don't want to be in that world.

Wisdom will save you from ending up in these kinds of places. Unfortunately, because selfishness and moral license are being given free reign, more and more people are ending up in perverse behavior and twisted lifestyles. God, through the words of Solomon, accurately describes the result of selfishness. It gets incredibly bizarre.

Understand that wisdom will steer you clear of this kind of person. That means that their choices cannot be your choices if you are wise. It is never okay to move in the directions that those who violate the Ten Commandments take.

PROVERBS 2:16 - *To deliver you from the strange woman, from the adulteress who flatters with her words;*

deliver

This is the Hebrew word *nasal* which means to rescue, deliver, save. The idea is that if you embrace wisdom in depth you will be plucked out of the problems that come from an adulteress relationship. Now the deliverance will not necessarily take place from the midst of an affair. It will most likely take place through wisdom by never meeting the woman whose charms would be your downfall. It is not wisdom and strength to walk away from sin when you are right at the entrance point. It is wisdom and strength to keep a long way away from it. Realize that the deliverance of the Lord steers a wide path around sin and temptation. Just as in 1 Corinthians – *No temptation has over taken you but such as is common to man and He will with the temptation provide you with a way of escape* – the way of escape is often very early before you are under the full tug of temptation.

Live your life wisely and you will not feel the hurricane force of temptation, but instead you will feel the breeze and allure of temptation which is much easier to resist. Make good decisions early and it will be much easier to resist.

strange woman

This is the Hebrew word *zur* which means stranger. The Hebrew idea of marriage is that there is one person whom you are to bond with in a lifetime commitment; every other person is a stranger to you. This would apply to singles also. There is a person whom God would want you to commit to and marry. Every other person whom you could meet and marry is strange or unfitting to you. There are many people you might date or get to know, but you know immediately that "I could not marry this person". It may be because of their values, their lack of values, their faith or lack of it, their personality, etc. But it is obvious to you that this is not the person. So they are strange to you. But if you continue in a relationship with them long enough, the temptation to consider them as a potential mate grows stronger. If they are clearly not God's choice, then do not continue deepening the relationship. Be wise. I watch singles who continue in relationships with people that God is clearly not pleased with, that their families hate, and that they are not even excited about just because it is someone to be with for now. And then down the road they settle for this person the Bible would call a strange person. Then they diminish the potential of their life because they did not act with wisdom early enough and now they are married to a person who is not God's best.

adulteress

This is the Hebrew word *nokri* which means foreign, strange. It is really a synonym for the word above. It means an adulteress or a person who would have sexual relations with someone who is not their mate – their God-given spouse.

Solomon is stating a key lesson to his young students. There will be temptations to break your promises. There will be things that will promise pleasure and fun but are clearly the wrong way. If you live wisely, looking for the triple-win choices and taking them, you will not destroy your life down these dead-end roads. They seem exciting and wonderful, but they bring heartache and pain.

In our culture we are making a mockery of sexual control, abstinence, fidelity, and virginity; but following God's path of wisdom and joy – while it is counter to the culture these days – is the best life and yields a much better life than the momentary pleasures of sin.

Thankfully, also Jesus Christ offers everyone the forgiveness of their sins through His death on a cross. They need to repent, turn away from their sins, and walk into His arms agreeing with Him that what they did was wrong. He then invites them onto the path of wisdom. His grace is amazing and can empower even the worst sinner to a new life.

flatters

This is the Hebrew word *halaq* which means to divide, to share, to portion. The idea here is an interesting one in that the adulteress divides the person from his true mate through words. The translators of the NASB have chosen to use the word *flatters* to try and understand the word; but the idea is that using words, the adulteress lures you into a deep relationship with her. Having interviewed a number of folks who have been caught in the web of adultery, it is just as Solomon says here. It is the use of words – listening and conversation – that either slowly or quickly strengthens a relationship that leads to sexual unfaithfulness. Many men have said that affairs are mediocre sex but great listening.

Notice the point of what Solomon is saying. It is the words that create the wedge between you and your spouse and draw you towards someone you shouldn't be with. I weary of people who tell me that they can have a friendship with someone of the opposite sex other than their spouse and it is okay. This is playing with fire. It is through words, conversation, listening, sharing of ideas, concerns, feelings, appreciation, gratefulness, etc., that a man or woman is lured away into adultery.

Do not go there. Share these words, thoughts, feelings, and ideas with your spouse. If you and your spouse are not having these kinds of conversations, then you are weakening your marriage and increasing the power of temptation in your spouse's life.

PROVERBS 2:17 ~ *that leaves the companion of her youth and forgets the covenant of her God;*

Solomon expands our understanding of the action of the adulteress or the strange woman. He tells us that she does two things that are not seen as a big deal in our day but were huge things in that day and huge things in the eyes of God then and now. First, she forsakes the person she pledged herself to when she was young. Second, she ignores the compact and agreement that she made with God. Solomon is trying to get young men, especially, to remember that if they are with a woman who is not their wife, then she is someone else's wife and he is involved in helping or causing her to ignore the agreement she made with God and thereby increasing her guilt and shame at judgment day. There are willing men and women who do these two things, but they are not small things.

leave the companion of her youth: *Two words are key in this insight.*
The first word is the word *leave* which is the Hebrew word *azab* which means forsake, loose, leave. It has the idea of abandoning, forsaking. There is in the marriage vows a commitment to support the other person through the doing of your duties. A wife has a responsibility to fulfill her side of the marriage arrangement. A husband has the responsibility to fulfill his side of the marriage arrangement. The other person is counting on you to meet the deep emotional, mental, spiritual, and physical needs that only you can meet. If you do not meet them, then they are crippled in their ability to make it through life. Too often today people believe that "if I am not having my needs met by my spouse, then that gives me justification for leaving my spouse; they aren't meeting my needs; or I don't love them anymore." Nowhere in the Bible does it give the "I'm not getting mine" excuse for leaving. Nowhere does God give people the "I'm not in love any more; you can get out" coupon. When you got married, it came with certain privileges and with certain duties. You bonded with another young person to meet their needs so that together you could carve out a righteous and successful life.

The second word is the word *companion* which is the Hebrew word *alluph* which means tame, companion, cattle, friend, gentle, intimate friend. The idea here is clearly that this is someone that you pledged to be side-by-side with, to be gentle with, to build an intimacy and friendship with. When that is shattered by your actions, it destroys so much. Here is a picture of a pledge of gentleness and teamwork, and then one person comes at this team with a sword and spear seeking great damage to the other person and the team. All because they are selfish. All because they think they can have more if they break away from this team and chase after a different team.

The second insight into the life of the adulteress is that she made a commitment to God that she would stay by her husband. The fact that she is with someone other than her husband means that she is breaking her promise to God. This should not be taken lightly; God does not take it lightly. The word *forget* is the Hebrew word *sakah* which is forget, ignore, wither. The essential idea is that she places this commitment to God in the back of her mind and does not think about this promise.

One of Solomon's points is that wisdom will cause you to see all the consequences of your action if you engage in an adulteress affair. If you participate even with a willing woman, then you are helping her break her vow to God. This is a problem for her and for you. It also brings up the fact that she has found it easy to break a promise, so any promise that she makes to you she could also break.

People in our permissive culture have ample opportunity to commit adultery. It is available everywhere, but why would you want to slap God in the face like that? Why would you want to wound the person who was willing to die on the cross for you to save you from your sins? This is sinning with a high hand.

PROVERBS 2:18 - *For her house sinks down to death and her tracks lead to the dead;*

It is terribly hard to get young men to realize that they cannot give full vent to their sexual desires. Young men are at the height of their interest in sexuality and yet if they give into these pressures, they will destroy a great deal of their potential in life.

Solomon says if you go after wisdom, you will avoid entering into the house that sinks down to the dead. He uses this vivid imagery of a sinking house that once you enter it you will not escape as it drops deeper and deeper. This is very similar to the dark and depressing imagery that was in the song by The Animals called "The House of the Rising Sun." The young man screams from this house: *Mothers tell your sons; don't do the things that I have done.* He is trapped in this brothel by his own sexual desires to which he has given full vent.

This tempting diversion captures so many young promising men who could make a real difference in the world. They need to learn wisdom or they too will enter the house that leads to death.

I was so encouraged the other day to talk with a young man who is taking the necessary biblical precautions to guard his heart from pornography and sexual conquest. He has entered into an accountability group with another young man, and they are learning the biblical solutions to lustful temptations. We lose too many young men – especially in our day – to the sexualized culture around us.

sinks

This is an interesting Hebrew word *suah* which means bows down, submits, humble toward. Solomon chooses a very interesting word to convey the idea that this woman's activities actually submit to direction from the great alienator: death. What does death do but separates body from soul. This woman and her actions separate people from their life.

The translators use the words *sinks down* to suggest a passive result of her actions, but rather it is an active submission to destruction that is pictured here. She is an active place of death. The activities of the adulteress is the origin of much damage, destruction, and alienation within the society. A man pursues what he wants and destroys much of what he really needs in its pursuit.

tracks

This is the Hebrew word *magal* which means track. She has a well-worn track, and it doesn't go to paradise as it is often advertised. Instead it goes to the place of the departed spirits. Solomon is saying that you can see where her path leads; it goes to death. He is trying to point out the difference in the pathways of wisdom and foolishness. One is looking for and receiving life. The other is selfish and impulsive and receives the penalty of its greed and self-centeredness – separation from everyone and everything that means anything.

dead

This is an interesting Hebrew word *repaim* which means the departed spirits, the ghosts of the dead, the shades. This was a synonym for the place of the dead or the spirits of the dead. It is important to warn young men not to follow after the easy sexual conquest. It is important to tell them that while this young lady looks new and nice and pleasurable, this scenario has been played out many times before. The story of adultery, fornication, and the sexualized life always ends badly. Don't fall for this. Choose wisely. Wait to fall in love with a real woman who can satisfy you and all the aspects of your being. She will be worth waiting for. Remember, if you don't wait, you probably will never meet the woman who could have been your soul mate.

PROVERBS 2:19 - *None who go to her return again, nor do they reach the paths of life.*

It is not often clear to the person who is about to pursue a strange woman or man that this is a life-alerting decision. Solomon is standing at the edge of the cliff screaming for us not to jump off! He wants us to understand that taking action on the impulses of the flesh to pursue an adulterous situation will change you and your destiny in major ways.

Notice that he says none who go to her return again. You are not the same. To become unfaithful is huge. In our day the culture around us wants us to believe that sexual license is not a big deal. The world wants us to see this serious sin as a small thing. It is not just a little mistake. God has not changed His mind. It is a big deal. It is a life-altering decision to become unfaithful to your spouse. I remember two pastors who I knew well who had all the promise and potential in the world who threw it all away to kiss and hold women who were not their wives. They didn't even go as far as actual physical intimacy, but they had to resign their ministries. They would never be the same. A few moments were life changing. Our choices do matter is what Solomon is saying. There are some things that are not do-overs. These were separate men in separate situations, but they both were permanently altered by their indiscretion.

God, in His grace, can supply new measures of hope and comfort; but something is lost that can never be regained. Solomon gives a bleak assessment of a person's ability to recover from adultery. They do not reach the paths of life. This would seem best to take paths of life as the best life or destiny that God had marked out for you. You will not get back to that life. You will not attain to the full potential and full measure of accomplishment that was to be yours because of the detour of adultery that you took.

Men and women do not often ponder the things they give up to have a few seconds of illicit passion and pleasure. God, through Solomon, seems to be declaring that the pathway or destiny that He had for you is no longer attainable when you follow the ways of immorality. You alter your destiny just like the Israelites who blasphemed God and changed the blessings and future that God had planned for them. But God held out hope that He would be able to restore the years that the locust had eaten (in the book of Job) and that the glory of the second temple could exceed the glory of the first temple if they would humble themselves. So God's grace is able to triumph in our sin and weakness but realize that the perfect plan of God for our lives will not be attainable because of adultery. We will be shunted onto a plan B.

Solomon is trying to train young people that they should not give up the best that God has planned for a few moments of sexual pleasure. There is a someone whom God has for you. Save yourself for that person. Live out the life that God has planned for you. Fulfill the good works that God has lined out for you.

PROVERBS 2:20 - *So you will walk in the way of good men and keep to the paths of the righteous.*

It is absolutely imperative that you and I realize that there is a path of conduct that good, righteous, wholesome people live on. They keep moving forward in their lives and that path is always there to walk. There is also always the other path into the jungle of selfishness.

Notice that the path is the path of righteousness. The word *righteousness* is the word *sedaqa* in Hebrew which means conforming to an ethical standard or rule of conduct. Do you stay within God's boundaries of acceptable behavior or does your own selfishness and the seduction of others lure you beyond acceptable behavior? The edge of the path is the absolute boundary of the Ten Commandments. There will constantly be temptations to your goals by getting off the path and taking the shortcut through the jungle of selfishness. Don't do that.

- You could be tempted to blend Christianity with some other religion... don't
- You could be tempted to use religious artifacts or idols as decorations... don't
- You could be tempted to express your displeasure through cursing or swearing... don't
- You could be tempted to overwork and self-sufficiency; not daily and weekly acknowledging your need for God... don't
- You could be tempted to rebel from your God-given authorities... don't
- You could be tempted to continually expose your displeasure and anger until it becomes violent or even murderous... don't
- You could be tempted to find comfort, fulfillment, or pleasure with someone who is not your spouse... don't
- You could be tempted to take what is not yours... don't
- You could be tempted to deceive or lie to get your own way... don't
- You could be tempted to want other people's possessions instead of earning your own... don't

The path of good people is not hard to understand. It is everything that is inside of the above type of behavior.

Notice that you have a choice here. You can and should walk in the righteous path. You will need the guidance of wisdom to do it.

This whole section tries to remind us that the temptations are strong and they seem so pleasant and encouraging; but they lead to separation, loneliness, death, and destruction of all that we care about.

Stay on the good path; do not be seduced by the allure of the shortcut.

PROVERBS 2:21 - *For the upright will live in the land and the blameless will remain in it;*

upright

This is the Hebrew word *yasar* which means uprightness. Those who follow God's moral code would be the closest thinking here. They have committed themselves to His boundaries.

will live in the land

This was quite a promise when you consider that it was still in the people's mind that a foreign army could sweep through and take you to a new place. This happened all the time in the time of the judges. It also happened throughout that region.

God was promising that if the people would follow His law – not their own selfish impulses – that they would not be conquered and relocated.

How does this impact our lives? When an individual and a culture begin pushing past the boundaries of God's law – even if they do not believe in the law – it weakens the strength of that person or culture where it will be washed away at the next financial catastrophe.

PROVERBS 2:22 - *But the wicked will be cut off from the land and the treacherous will be uprooted from it.*

Solomon reminds his young trainees that there will be a day of reckoning. It just seems like the shortcuts that the wicked are taking are working. It is easy to get caught in a period where it looks like the bad guys are winning. The wicked people who cheat, lie, steal, gain by violence, are unfaithful, and even perverted seem to be getting ahead through their ways of living. Solomon is trying to remind us that over the course of a life, that form of living will be rejected. It will catch up with a person – even though for a small window or period it looks like there is no God and that there is no justice.

It is important to remind ourselves of these facts. One cannot go on being wicked with no consequences. Also there will be a judgment day when God will weigh the thoughts, actions, and speech of every person.

cut off from the land

This is the worst Hebrew punishment because the land of Israel was the holy land. It was so much a part of the economy and what God was doing for the nation. This was also a way of saying exile or death is the fate of the wicked.

What is interesting is that Solomon does not say how the wicked will be cut off from the land. He could mean that God will make sure that punishment takes place; he could mean that society will deal with this type of individual; he could mean that other individuals or groups that have been cheated or defrauded will bring about exile or death. Solomon does not say. But he wants us to know that the techniques of the wicked for getting what they want will not remain for the long haul.

We are reminded in history that even tyrants do not rule forever. They will be cut down.

wicked

This is the Hebrew word *resa* which means wrong, wicked, guilty. In the Old Testament it is equivalent to someone who regularly practices actions that are beyond the boundaries of the Ten Commandments. This person has decided what they want is more important than any boundaries that God or society might put in place.

treacherous

This is the Hebrew word *bagad* which means treacherous, deceitful, unfaithful to a deal. There is a fraud component to this idea. One is made to believe one thing while something else entirely is going on. You have been swindled. You have lost and the other person has gained at your expense. This is one of the key ideas in unethical and illegal behavior. If you do this to enough people, then you will get yours. What you think you have will be taken from you.

uprooted from it

Clearly this is intended to convey that the person does not live out the normal, natural course of life with the pleasant death at the end.

We, as a nation, are just entering into a period where the price of all the injustice is about to be enacted. The party for those who cheat, lie, and steal is over and the consequences have begun to come home. Many people who pretended that there was no God and lived like no one would hold them to account will lose everything in this whirlwind that is now upon us. This is now the time when Jesus said that the house built upon the rock (God and His principles) will weather the storm and those that are built upon the sand (the theories of the day) will be swept away.

Proverbs 3

PROVERBS 3:1 - *My son, do not forget my teaching, but let your heart keep my commandments;*

The significant aspect of this bit of wisdom is the depth of the keeping of the commandment. It must be kept by the heart – not just the outer man – to enjoy the benefits of length of days and years of life and peace. Some people seek to put a syrup-sweet coating over an unchanged heart and the power of the command is not activated. These commands deal with changing the heart or, as we would say, the attitude. The power of the internal attitude of the person is far greater than an external conformity to a rule.

The commandments that are being enjoined to be imbedded into your heart seem simple or trite, but they are incredibly profound.

- Do not let kindness and truth leave you

- Trust in the Lord with all your heart

- Do not lean on our own understanding

- In all your ways acknowledge Him

- Do not be wise in your own eyes

- Fear the Lord and turn away from evil

- Honor the Lord from your wealth

- Do not reject the discipline of the Lord

Many times in the reading of the book of Proverbs we miss the commandments in the midst of all the encouragement to embrace them. They are simple and profound and will change your life if you will bring them close and make them the way of your heart.

It is these commandments that I want you to embrace for they will ensure a successful, righteous life for you. God is so great to capsulate the righteous life in these statements. Solomon was remembering them from the teaching his father David gave to him. He decided to share them with the world. I want you to see the radical relevancy. We are too often trying to hear something new instead of spending time on the material from God that has proven itself true over the ages.

Remember that the words that are recorded in Proverbs were written down 3,000 years ago. Think about Solomon in a king's chamber writing down life lessons, little realizing that there would be people studying them 3,000 years later. They have force because they were breathed on by God. Don't miss these ancient lessons in how to have a better life.

PROVERBS 3:2 - *For length of days and years of life and peace they will add to you.*

length of days

One clearly gets the impression that God's principles in the book of Proverbs are able to lengthen your life; that God's ideas on how to live life are valuable extenders of life.

There is a corollary to the ideas of this verse: It is possible to extend one's life if the principles and ideas in this book are followed. In other words, you will live this long if you do xyz stuff; but if you live out the ideas in this book, you will 10, 20, 30 years longer. You and I get to choose whether we extend our life. And not only that, we get to decide whether it will be extended with a sense of completeness, wholeness, and peace.

Think about the opposite of what is being said. To ignore the principles in this book means that your life will be shorter, harder, and constantly incomplete. Who would want that? But many choose that road because they ignore the wisdom in this book from God.

years of life

It is consistent with the understanding that not only the actual time you have on earth will be extended but the life in those years.

Life is something to be enjoyed and used for the Lord God. We are in the midst of a training assignment here on earth getting ready for the real assignment in heaven. How well you learn to love and care and trust Christ here will determine the opportunities that you have there. It is important to extend your life, if possible, so that you can do more good works for the Lord.

But even if you have a short time on earth, let them be filled with life. Invest heavily in wisdom and righteous relationships. Life is relationships – it is not about heaping up wealth or power; it is about building and sustaining key relationships first with God then with others that God has put before you.

peace

This is the Hebrew word *shalom* which means peace. It comes from the root which means completion or fulfillment. It seems to carry with it the idea that one has stopped the harried acquisition mode and has the treasure that can be enjoyed. Too many people in our day are constantly in the acquisition mode and never have a sense of completion or rest. So they are never at peace.

It is possible to live life but never acquire those things that will actually bring a sense of completion to life. It is relationships that will bring peace. It is strong vibrant righteous relationships that will bring a sense of completion to life. If the crucial relationships of life are missing, then one is never satisfied.

Notice that in verse one of this chapter Solomon states that he has commandments to follow. In verse four he states that if you follow his commandments, it will bring favor with God and man. Therefore, the by-product of listening to and living by the wisdom of the book of Proverbs is completed and strong relationships which are peace. One can then live fulfilled without the constant acquisition mode of most.

It is tragic to constantly be in acquisition mode and then be completely unsatisfied when the acquisition is made, unable to enjoy the latest acquisition, unable to feel completed by the acquisition that one has poured so much energy into achieving.

The key acquisitions that bring peace are strong, vibrant relationships with God and man. It is these relationships with spouse, children, self, colleagues, believers, neighbors, and friends that bring peace to life. One's life is not complete until you have these. You can't have these if you violate the principles in this sacred book penned by Solomon but authored by God and breathed into by His life.

The fool constantly asks the question: What would make me happy? What do I want to do? The fool asks selfish questions. But the wise person asks: How can I enter into a deeper connection to the key people in my life? It may mean that I throw myself into a less pleasurable activity so that I can have a more intimate link with this other person. There is greater joy in deep connection with another key person while doing an uninteresting activity than the selfish pursuit of my own desires.

Selfishness, sin, and a materialistic focus rob the ability to be completed by one's gains.

The New Testament idea of peace is harmony or matching the key frequencies of the lives of those around you – primarily God but also the key relationships in your life. If you constantly are living out a melody that is out of tune and radically different from those around you, then you will never have peace. If you are unwilling to play the tune that God has laid out for you, then you will constantly be in a state of unease and lack of peace.

God wants to be the completer of your life; the one who brings you peace; the one who makes you whole. He does that differently than we would initially think. We often think that he could make us whole by giving us all the wealth that we would want and by giving us people who will do whatever we want. He does not, however, become our genie in a bottle. He becomes our God and directs us in the paths of life. He presents people, situations, and opportunities that—if embraced – will complete us and bring a sense of wholeness and therefore peace to our lives. He also presents Himself as the key completer of our lives – our guide, corrector, instructor, friend, father, judge, confidant, attorney, and object of reverence. All this is needed in a completer – one who brings peace to the restlessness in our souls.

PROVERBS 3:3 - *Do not let kindness and truth leave you; bind them around your neck, write them on the tablet of your heart.*

This is the basis of all horizontal relationships: loving-kindness and truth. The word translated *kindness* is really the word love *chesed*. It is the idea of commitment to mercy, meeting needs, kindness, compassion, etc.

This pairing of love and truth takes place throughout the Bible. Speak the truth in love in the New Testament. The message of Proverbs in terms of successful relationships is to be loving and truthful. Do not be so naive that you believe what everyone wants to tell you; but also do not be skeptical and cynical that you forget to have grace, mercy, and love for others. It is the combination that brings the best situations.

Notice the permanent attachment. These principles you will never outgrow. It is these and these alone that stand the test of time and relationships. Learn how to be in harmony with loving-kindness and truth. When you vibrate in harmony with these two pillars, then you will have found wisdom.

This is to be permanently etched on your soul. You must visualize to do that. They must go beyond simple words you memorize. You must see yourself living out these qualities in various situations until living out of these qualities is second nature.

Notice that you are doing the binding to your heart. Notice that you are doing the writing. There is not a holy zap that can do the writing for you. Now it is true that in the New Testament, God the Holy Spirit writes the New Covenant on our hearts, but you must write its application to the situation in your lives. Too often we want to learn about what these blessings are, but we do not see that we must live out the implication of these truths by yielding our bodies to these qualities.

PROVERBS 3:4 - *So you will find favor and good repute in the sight of God and man.*

The reason why one should permanently tie love and truth to one's life is that it results in favorable relationship with God and mankind.

This is the ultimate "How to win friends and influence people" verse. In fact, this is the basis of all successful People Skill Courses. You are attempting to win favor with others when you learn people skills.

We are, because of our fallen nature, internally moved in a selfish direction. We think, "What do I want first?" Many never even consider what the other person wants or needs. The basis of all good People Skill Courses is trying to overcome our basic sin nature – which keeps us/self at the focal point of our lives. If we are to find favor with God and man, we must reorient our focus toward God and man. Notice that this is what verse 3 suggests. Do not let love and truth leave you.

No matter how selfish other people get, don't go selfish and self-focus on yourself. Keep the love of God flowing through you. You will not help anything by acting just like them.

I am so pleased as I watch my daughter really catch this. She is demonstrating an amazing willingness to meet other's needs before her own. This godly quality of love is very encouraging to watch as it works its way out through her life.

If we stay self-focused, then it is not possible to be popular, well liked, respected, or enjoyed. No one wants to spend time around people who are always talking about themselves.

I have watched with a great deal of sadness as people in church have tried to make friends with people from a self-focused point of view. Trying to lure people into friendship – which is all about your stuff, your interests, your feelings, and your problems – will just not work. Learn what love really is – meeting needs, pursuing, pleasing.

If we learn to instinctively look to see what needs people have before we answer the question, "What do I want?" then there will be no end of favor and respect from others.

What are people's basic internal needs: a feeling of importance, to be heard, to be noticed, significance, security, acceptance. These and other basic internal needs are what we need to meet if we are to be experts at people skills.

Let me address another issue that comes up sometimes within Christian circles. The whole topic of whether we should, in any way, seek favor with man. Well this verse tells us how, so clearly it is not wrong to gain it. God wants us to know how to enjoy positive relationships with others. He does not want us to sin in order to gain them, but He does want us to know how to enjoy friends and relationships with all types of people. Too many Christians think it is spiritual to be a curmudgeon with an angry face and a condemning attitude. Not according to this verse.

PROVERBS 3:5 - *Trust in the Lord with all your heart and do not lean on your own understanding.*

The word *trust* is the word *batah* which is translated in the Septuagint by the word *hope* rather than the word *believe in*. The idea here seems to be that one must put one's hope completely in God's ability to resolve the issues of life. You trust in Him and do not worry or fret things that are beyond your control.

A number of years ago I was putting my daughter to sleep and she absolutely insisted that I lie down next to her. She was frightened and could not go to sleep or calm down. When I lay down next to her, she checked to see that I was there and then rolled on to her side and within a minute or two was sound asleep. She had confidence that if Dad was next to her and watching over her, then everything was okay and she was safe. Her total confidence in me and my ability to handle anything that might come was amazing. I realized as I lay there watching her that this is the type of trust that I must have in the Lord. I must rest in His ability to handle everything in my world. As long as He is near to me, I am okay. My responsibility is just to do what He says just as my daughter's responsibility was to do what I said.

When she began to doubt and lean on her own understanding, then she saw monsters under the bed and heard sounds of mice running in the closet and shadows crossing the room. These things from her own understanding were so disturbing that she was not able to sleep. But she trusted in me then, and she knew that she was safe because I would not let anything happen to her.

In the same way, when I lean on my own understanding, I invent all kinds of things that can derail a bright future – things that I can't handle. But if I just make sure that I do what God wants and submit my choices to Him, then I can have confidence in the future and know He will work it out. My job is to throw myself into the box that He has put me in and put my full confidence in His ability to change boxes and what comes into the box.

PROVERBS 3:6 - In all your ways acknowledge Him, and He will make your paths straight.

This verse is very interesting in that it tells us things we would not expect. There is truth hidden behind the plain-looking words here. The word *acknowledge* is not: let people know about... or pray a little prayer to... a little tip of the hat or cross of yourself....to acknowledge God in each aspect of your life. Instead the word is the word *to know* and suggests intimate knowledge of God and is suggested in each of the avenues of your life in order for the promise to kick in. In every arena, in every situation, in every relationship the believer is to be intimately aware of and related to God. Clearly this carries with it the idea that you are interacting and reacting in these arenas as God would.

It is this relational connection to God and understanding of His desired reaction or action that allows Him to so readily make your path straight. This is not guidance through the difficulties of life; this is road building and throwing obstacles and difficulties out of the way. God is actively at work for you, making your pathways through life less complicated. Boy, don't I need this. I gain this incredible blessing by having a deeper relationship with God.

God says that He blessed Cyrus and made his paths straight so that He would be in a situation to release the captive Israelites at the appointed time. This idea of the Lord making a person's path straight is a clear acknowledgement of the fact that the world is a much more complex place than one person can control. There are things and actions that are completely beyond the control of the individual that must come together in order for that person to live and enjoy the blessed life. One of the ideas is that it would be wise to be intimately acquainted with the road-builder of life who controls everything and can smooth the way for you. We will never know on this side of heaven – and maybe not there – how many obstacles and difficulties the Lord threw out of the way. It will be interesting to see the unedited tape of what the Lord was doing behind the scenes to give us the life we lived. Jeremiah 10:23 says it is not in a man to direct His steps. Jeremiah realized that there were forces way beyond himself that controlled how he lived his life – all kinds of forces.

PROVERBS 3:7 - *Do not be wise in your own eyes; fear the Lord and turn away from evil.*

The Septuagint has *do not be wise and sensible and prudent to yourself.* Don't be impressed with your own ability to navigate this world. The world is a far more complex place than you can figure out. Your own landmark's signals and tests will fail you. You must fear the Lord and realize that only God knows the proper boundaries and ways through various problems and situations. He knows how to live in this world He created, and He knows what not to do.

It is a sad thing when an individual – let alone a nation – thinks that it is beyond the direction, wisdom, and boundaries of the Almighty. It is headed into destruction. For the world is a far more complex place than we can possibly imagine. No mortal has it wired.

PROVERBS 3:8 - *It will be healing to your body and refreshment to your bones.*

The word *healing* in the Hebrew means remedy, healing, or health. Each of these is interesting in the context of this verse. The one who is afraid of offending the Lord – and that motivates them to turn away from what God labels evil – has the remedy for many physical ills; has a way to heal a number of physical problems; has the way to stay healthy. We don't tend to think this way in our culture. But it is a proper way to think. Much of the illness and physical ailments that destroy our body are self-inflicted through evil.

Think of all the ills that come from self-inflicted forms of murder: drugs, smoking, drunkenness, etc. Think of the diseases that come from adultery and its various deviant forms of perversion.

An actual literal translation of this verse is *health will come to your navel*. The Hebrews and this part of the world saw the navel as the center of life and the beginning of independent life; the beginning of independent strength. It was the place where the umbilical cord was attached from our mothers and when that cord was severed, we began our independent existence. It was then that we began to gain strength and move independently. Therefore healing to the navel meant growing strength at the center of our life and independent strength which was to be employed to do the right thing.

and refreshment to your bones

The word *refreshment* is the Hebrew word *shiqquwy* which has been translated as marrow or drink or refreshment. Clearly, when connected to the bones, it is the marrow that resupplies the strength to the bones. The marrow actually rebuilds and renews life to the bones.

The Proverbs are saying that there is a body-soul connection. The actions and reactions of your soul can damage your body and can determine how well your body ages and handles the stress of life. There are numerous studies which show the connection: stress and ulcers; anxiety and physical ailments; mental and emotional connection with irritable bowel syndrome. In fact, in new studies of twins, they are suggesting that lifestyle choices determine as much as 80% of the longevity of people rather than genes.

PROVERBS 3:9 - *Honor the Lord from your wealth and from the first of all your produce;*

The word *honor* is the Hebrew word *kabed* which means to be heavy or weighty. It carries the idea of a person who is weighty and impressive; worthy of respect. When a person gives *kabed* to another, they are said to make them more weighty or impressive. Therefore a working definition is to ADD VALUE. When we honor a person or God, we add value to them so that others perceive them more impressively.

In this verse Solomon is saying that no matter how much wealth or possessions a person has, he/she must demonstrate out of that wealth that God is weightier still.

This is done through tithes and offerings – giving of ten percent of your income and giving charitable gifts from the abundance of the blessings that God has given you. It is important to state that there is no percentage figure in this verse. One must give and handle wealth in a way that would clearly demonstrate that you are impressed with God and He is the most important being in your life. In many cases that would suggest that more than ten percent would be given.

Remember that this prescription is in the midst of the basic keys to life – how to get along with people and find favor with God and man. This command is at the core of what God says about playing the game of life to win. Dealing with money properly is a big deal. Money can become a god so quickly. One must make money serve a higher purpose: honoring God. If God blesses and gives you an abundance, then make sure that God is honored for blessing you.

There is a tendency in every age to suggest that things are tight and God doesn't really want me to give ten-plus percent of my income to Him. I need all of this. This would suggest that money has a hold on your heart. God has given you the ability to earn it. Bless Him with how you handle it.

I have never seen God not be faithful to those who give tithes and offerings to honor Him.

and from the first of all your produce

Don't wait until you have made or committed all the money. Give it to God right at the front end. Money continually tries to get you to love it. Money is just a means of trading goods, but it has a life of its own because it is so powerful. It wants you to believe that it can meet your needs. Money can't; God can. God blesses and provides goods and services to us. He asks that we remember that He gave it by giving tithes and offerings as a way to honor Him and as a safeguard over money getting too great a grip on our heart.

There is a warning in this last part of the verse to not delay giving to God. If we delay giving or make God the last on the list of people we pay, then we will not get around to it. In that day, right after the harvest was the time to tithe to the Lord and not at the end of the year. In our day, right after we get our paycheck is the time to tithe, not till after all the bills have been paid.

Money is the means that blessings are distributed but one must not look to the means as the bless-er but the one who ultimately allows the blessing.

I have heard people tell me over and over: "I do not have money to give to the Lord." Something is wrong with your spending if you do not have the money to tithe to the Lord. I have watched as many people who were headed to bankruptcy were brought out to solvency through putting God first in their budget through tithing. Then they can straighten out the rest of their budget.

PROVERBS 3:10 - *So your barns will be filled with plenty and your vats will overflow with new wine.*

This is a very important verse that shares a rather down-to-earth reason why wisdom is the best way to live. Solomon says that those who are wise have an abundance of the basics of life.

The barns were the place to store the grains that were the staple of the farming economy. So to have barns that are filled means that you have had a number of years of rich harvests; so much, in fact, that you have more than you can eat. Your needs are met.

The barns also were the storage place for wealth accumulation just like a savings account or an investment is for us. For them to have their barns filled meant that each of the various categories of their budget were filled and ready to be spent on the needs of life. Many of us live paycheck to paycheck and do not know the feeling of having our savings accounts filled and ready – accounts like Christmas gifts account, new tires account, back-to-school account, birthday account, vacation account, home repair and improvement account, mortgage account. These and many others are a part of life. What this proverb is telling us is if we follow the simple, yet profound, advice of God's wisdom, we will have enough to fill out these categories.

Notice what the advice is in Proverbs 3:3-9:

- Never stop being loving and truthful

- Follow the Lord's way in your actions and speech

- Pray to God and let people know that you are a Christian in every direction you take

- Don't think you have life figured out; be fearful of offending God and walk away from opportunities to sin

- Tithe a tenth of your income to God

If we do these simple rules, we will enjoy a life in which the basics of life are abundantly met.

I personally would testify to the truth of this proverb. God has done exactly these things out of His grace for me and my desire to be wise.

and your vats will overflow with new wine

Wine was the common drink of that day. It was usually diluted to be about 2-3% alcohol in that day. It was one of the safest liquids to drink because the bacteria in the wine killed or held back the germs in the water. Pure running water coming out of a spring with a known source was the best drink, but wine was safe and represented a safe and sure thirst quencher. So to have more wine than one can store meant that one would never have to go thirsty.

God is not promising that we can have enough wine to get drunk for that is not the use of wine in those days, and it would be very difficult to get drunk on the wine that was only 2-3% alcohol. The wine would have to be drunk without diluting it which was only prescribed for those whose life was especially bitter and had basically given up on life. Proverbs 31

God is promising in this proverb incredibly strong advantages to being wise. You will have your basic needs met beyond your ability to consume them.

Unfortunately in our culture this is not impressive. We want our wants met beyond our ability to conceive of them. This is not where God wants us to go. To go down this road will lead to the love of money and materialism. God is saying that there are real tangible benefits to the life of a believer who lives wisely. They will have abundance.

Our abundance will be of that which meets our basic needs. Now there is also another aspect to the having of abundance righteously that we need to talk about that is not specifically mentioned in this passage but is mentioned in the New Testament. That is that gaining wealth and abundance God's way gives a large pile of stuff; but more importantly, it does not add sorrow to it. (1 Timothy 6:5-10) It is one thing to compare the size of your pile; it is another to look and see how many sorrows and stresses have been added to gain or keep your pile.

It is better to have a smaller pile of abundance if it comes without sorrow and stress.

Abundant food and abundant drink are available and will come to the one who is wise.

One balancing statement must be pointed out that is mentioned later in the Proverbs – that the abundance that is coming to those who are wise sometimes can be wiped out by injustice and/or laziness. The Proverbs say: Abundant food is in the fallow ground of the poor but injustice sweeps it away. It will be a terrible thing to face Jesus in judgment if we have been involved in sweeping away the abundance that was supposed to come to one of God's wise children.

PROVERBS 3:11 - *My son, do not reject the discipline of the Lord, or loathe His reproof,*

It seems clear that this great proverb is written from the perspective of being disciplined by the Lord; being stretched and pushed beyond where you are.

The verses make so much more sense within that context:

- Do not let loving-kindness and truth leave you

- Trust in the Lord

- Do not lean on your own understanding

- In all your ways know Him

- Fear the Lord and turn away from evil

- Honor the Lord from the first of your wealth

- Do not reject the discipline of the Lord

All of the above things that we are tempted not to do when it seems, from the outside perspective, that God no longer loves us or has forgotten us or is against us. This is when we must redouble our trust in the Lord and our expression of love to others.

In the midst of the lean times, there must be a growing favor with God and man.

God is seeking to make you wiser; to be able to handle what is coming. Trust Him and stop only evaluating what is happening through the lens of your own wisdom and knowledge. God sees a much bigger canvas than you do.

do not reject the discipline of the Lord or loathe his reproof

The discipline of the Lord or the instruction of the Lord or the rebukes of the Lord are those places where God brings us up short; where He spanks us with problems. He is trying to get us to stop moving in the direction that we are going. Instead of getting mad when God says, "No, that is not the direction I want you to go," we should see this as a fresh evidence of His love. Also it is fresh evidence of His existence and involvement in our lives.

God wants us to be willing to see Him as supreme director and controller of our lives and to embrace that truth and allow our trust of Him and our love for Him to totally adjust our way of thinking and living.

Look at Deuteronomy 8:3 - *He humbled you and let you be hungry, and fed you with manna which you did not know, nor did your fathers know, that He might make you understand that man does not live by bread alone, but man lives by everything that proceeds out of the mouth of the Lord.*

When we follow the dictates of this proverb, we see in the problems and difficulties a message from the Lord. We examine whether our problems, difficulties, and obstacles are chastisements from God because we have violated the principles and commands that He has given us.

Now it is important to say that not every problem you have is a message from God. But God has structured the universe so that when we violate his law, there are consequences just as when we push too hard on particular natural laws, we tip over or break a bone or fall or receive a shock. These consequences in the natural world are referred to as reproofs in the relational and spiritual world.

We are not accustomed to thinking this way but think this through. When I am rude to another person, the consequence is often that the person is cold toward me. If I only talk about and constantly boast about myself, then people will not want to be around me. God is constantly sending me feedback about how I am doing in my relationships and in my life. We just regularly push back on His feedback. We only want to hear that we are doing fine, even if we aren't. Remember that God loves us and He will discipline us because He loves us. This means that He will allow us to receive negative feedback.

PROVERBS 3:12 - *For whom the Lord loves He reproves, even as a father corrects the son in whom he delights.*

This principle that has been the bedrock of parenting for four millennia has been abandoned in our day. Correcting, rebuking, chastising the child that you love. A child cannot reach its maximum potential without correction. A child cannot bring enjoyment to a family if it does not have self-control. These are axiomatic and yet our culture has become obsessed with the idea that children will do far better if they are never corrected and if they are never rebuked. This type of parenting will destroy this culture by raising a host of children who can never rise above their own selfish impulses.

It almost seems counter-intuitive, but it is a powerful truth. Children must be corrected and disciplined in order to enjoy them and take greater delight in them. Their ability to become all that God placed in them is dependent upon their ability to overcome the selfish impulses that rage within them. They must be able to say no to themselves. This ability almost always is developed with the aid of an outside agency (parent, teachers, military, police, mentors). The most brilliant children who consistently follow their selfish impulses will be diverted from the contribution that they were supposed to make to society, their families, and themselves.

In the same way this proverb tells us God cannot allow us to have everything that we want. He must rebuke us and train us so that we can overcome our foolish tendencies that our parents missed or did not train out of our lives. The fact that God would discipline us is amazing. We have often viewed God's role as only that of a loving grandfather waiting to spoil us with our every whim. This is not an accurate picture of God. We have been created to accomplish good works (Ephesians 2:10). The only way that we will be able to accomplish those good works is if we can deny our own selfish impulses at some level and work to the greater good. So God sends discipline into our lives to get us ready.

God also rebukes or corrects us when we have directly rebelled from His way. Do not do that, His Word says. Do not go there, He tells us. But we do it anyway. There are consequences and rebukes. I have seen a number of people who refuse to respond to God's rebukes, and then they get mad at God for the mess in their lives.

A crucial question at this point is how do God's rebukes come? Most of us would like it to be a verbal rebuke or a note with a severe reprimand. There have only been a few instances of this type of rebuke from God. In those cases it represents the end of God's grace and the beginning of severe judgment. Usually God's rebuke comes in the most crucial aspects of life – our relationships. He brings difficulties or allows the consequences of our actions to diminish one or more of our relationships. Why would God pick relationships as the place to land His rebuke? Because relationships are the point of life. Remember, *Thou shalt love the Lord thy God with all your heart, soul, mind, and strength. And thy neighbor as thyself.* These are the two great commandments and are the focus of life. Relationships are the focus of life. Therefore our relationships are the most crucial things in life.

Let me just refresh your thinking about our relationships. We have nine basic relationships: God, Self; Marriage; Family; Work; Church; Money; Society; Friends. God will bring rebuke to these relationships to correct our behavior. Usually it is our selfishness in that relationship that destroys or diminishes the relationship. Suffering through the diminished relationship should cause us to sit up and make correction to restore the relationship. God is not rebuking us because He wants to restrict our lives but to prepare us for a fuller life and great enjoyment in our relationships.

In our day and age we don't want to pay attention to the rebuke of God, so we have developed disposable relationships. If this marriage is not working out, I will get another one. If this family is not enjoyable, I will get another one. On and on it goes with no one ever resolving differences and learning what real relational harmony takes. I have watched people marry multiple times, never fixing the underlying selfishness and always blaming the other person for not understanding them. I have watched adult men and women lose jobs, be passed over for promotions, and be fired without ever considering that their selfishness was the problem. It was always the boss or the company but never them. This is like the child who believes that his parents are ogres because they tell him no and discipline him.

One of the most significant implications of this proverb that is repeated in the New Testament is that God loves those whom He rebukes. If He just allows you to wallow in your selfishness and you are given free rein to pursue your selfish desires; this is evidence that He does not love you, not that He does love you. When God tells you NO. When He disciplines you for acting in a selfish way with Him or in your marriage or at work or with your family, take this as a good sign. When you feel the conviction of God over your actions, become excited. God loves you. Respond to His love with humility and submission. Change your behavior and move to the center of His love. Bring delight to His heart.

PROVERBS 3:13 - *How blessed is the man who finds wisdom and the man who gains understanding.*

Wisdom is not something that you stumble across. You must be looking for it. You must find it. Solomon is saying that the truly right choice is not always easy to find. It often takes investigation and thought. It may require a process that is much longer than the easy and selfish choices that quickly present themselves.

blessed

This is the Hebrew word *esher* which means happiness or blessed. This word has the meaning of being in an enviable position. You have attained or have something that others would clearly want.

It is interesting that in this case it is attached to the possession of wisdom. When you have wisdom you will be in an enviable position. People will see the choices that you make and the type of life that you lead, and they will be hoping that they can also have what you have.

There is another way of looking at this word *blessed* and that is to see it as fulfilled or satisfied or filled up. You are satiated with what your life is bringing to you. This is the idea that when you do the work of making the triple-win choices, those choices will fill up your life to a level that others don't have. Enjoy the blessing of that fullness.

wisdom

This is the Hebrew word *hokma* which is the typical word for wisdom. Wisdom, in shorthand, means making the right choice of all the choices that you have in front of you. It means that you have ferreted out the choice that satisfies the three prongs of wisdom: it honors or glorifies God, it is a win for the other person, and it is a win for you. If any one of these outcomes is not obviously involved in what you are about to chose, then it is not wisdom and you should back up. Remember that there is a wise choice in every situation. Sometimes it takes awhile to see it. Sometimes it takes awhile to embrace the wisdom in a choice.

understanding

This is the Hebrew word *bina* which means understanding. It carries the idea of being able to discern between choices and to see the connections between items. This is often thought of as the ability to know what will happen if you do this or if you do that or this happened because someone did this or someone did that. Understanding is a powerful tool because it so strongly informs wise choices. If you know what the outcome will be of your choices, then they will be easier to make.

I have watched so many people do what seemed right to them only to see disastrous consequences flow from that decision because they did not have understanding. I have also watched as people kept making the selfish or impulsive decision in their life and knowing that they always get destruction in their family or their business but hoping this time that the outcome will be different. It is like playing chess – you put your hand on the piece and hope to predict all the things that will happen if you make that move. So understanding means that you must look at all the ramifications if you take various actions. You must have a clear-eyed view and not be colored by the choice you want to make. If the choice you want to make will be destructive to you, your family, or God's honor, then true understanding will lead you away from that choice no matter how tempting it appears.

Every week and every day we face these kinds of choices. Be prepared and gain understanding so that you can truly have wisdom and be blessed.

PROVERBS 3:14 - *For her profit is better than the profit of silver and her gain better than fine gold.*

Solomon must shake us out of automatically internalizing a destructive goal for life: being rich. Without wisdom it is not all it's cracked up to be. There is nothing wrong with being rich if God gives you the ability, but one needs wisdom more than riches. From ancient times to modern times people tend to automatically embrace the idea that lots of money is the right goal for life and that money, wealth, and resources are the answer. It is not.

profit
This is the Hebrew word *sahar* which means to gain from trade or merchandise; to turn around as in buying at one price and selling at another. The difference between those two prices is your profit. This is how businessmen have made their money for thousands of years. It is this profit that is the aim of most. They have internalized a goal of a pile of resources next to them that they can spend any way they want.

Solomon says that the pile of resources available to a person who has heaped up wisdom is so much greater than the one who has heaped up financial resources. Solomon sees this huge pile of wise choices as wise actions, connected relationships, goals, protection from temptations, restful nights, insights, information, skills, people skills, freedom from diseases, etc. This forms this huge mountain of wisdom that the person can draw on as they face the future. This means that there is nothing that comes their way that is overwhelming or inscrutable.

On the other hand, if a person just has a pile of money but no ability to see the triple-win choices and actions and all the other good things that come from wisdom, they will throw money at problems and follow their own impulsive path usually to some form of destruction.

profit of silver

What is the profit of silver? It is highly valuable. It appreciates. It has long-lasting value. It is transportable. It produces power for its possessors.

Solomon is trying to get us to realize that wisdom is so much more valuable than the value of money. It is amazing that 3,000 years ago money was considered the most valuable thing; and Solomon is trying to wake us up to the fact that even if you have money but you don't have wisdom, your life is not enjoyable.

Solomon is trying to get us to grasp that you get one with the other but not the other way around, and that we are all most tempted to go after the wrong one. If you aim at wisdom, you will most likely gain monetary wealth, so financial resources usually come with wisdom. But wealth does not guarantee wisdom. There are lots of wealthy fools who never really understand what is happening to them.

There are times when you must pass up the most profitable opportunities monetarily in order to pursue wisdom. Solomon is saying: Go after wisdom; you won't be sorry. Don't run after the quick profit or the higher profit necessarily. Set your sights on something higher – something that will allow fuller enjoyment of the wealth: wisdom. Make it your goal to be able to discern the win-win-win choice or action. If you can hone this skill, then you will truly be rich.

PROVERBS 3:15 - *She is more precious than jewels; and nothing you desire compares with her.*

This striking description of the value of wisdom is meant to cause you to stop and focus on what you gain when you know the wise thing to do in a given situation. It is amazing that even 3,000 years ago people undervalued the importance of wisdom and overvalued the significance of jewels. Whatever material delight you would like to have cannot be fully enjoyed unless you have wisdom along with it. To achieve your desires but to remain selfish, impulsive, and rebellious is to rob those desires of a level of their satisfaction.

The book of Proverbs is about the pursuit of wisdom. Wisdom is, in each situation, digging for that which is the triple-win (where God wins, others win, and you win). Collecting what to do in a number of situations; making the right choice when various options present themselves; knowing how to deal with various types of people; knowing how to live a fully enjoyable life; being on a path that will bring honor, riches, and joy; avoiding the traps of pride, cynicism, sloth, greed, lust, gossip, violence, anger, lying, etc. – all of this and much more are waiting for the persons who commit themselves to a lifelong search for wisdom.

Right now you are being tempted to go after something other than wisdom. Right now you have choices to make about whether you should do one thing or the other. One of your choices is a shortcut: a small hedging of what is right or a purely selfish pursuit. The other choice is clearly the right way of acting. It is harder and often longer and more people benefit from this way. You personally don't gain as much from this way until much later. These are these choices that are between foolishness and wisdom. They are these choices that will define your life.

If you consistently choose the selfish me-first way, then you will reap the short-term gains of that way and the long-term rebukes – difficulties and pain of that way along with the change in your destiny.

If you begin to consistently choose to do the wise thing – the thing where God wins, others win, and you win – then your rewards are much deeper, richer, and fuller than you thought they would be.

PROVERBS 3:16 - *Long life is in her right hand; in her left hand are riches and honor.*

long life

This is really the phrase *length of days* which would be the Hebrew way of saying long life; the amount of days that you are on this planet is lengthened. Following the path of wisdom will cause your destiny to change. You will select that destiny in which you live longer. God knows all the possibilities of the all the possibilities, and He knows what your life will look like if you begin making wise choices. You can change your destiny. You can select one of the good and beneficial destinies that God has chosen for you. It is not possible to get off the map of God, but God has marked out several possible pathways that you can take. Those who follow Him and embrace wisdom, forgiveness, and righteousness live a completely different life than those who just go with selfishness, bitterness, greed, materialism, and arrogance. It is important to realize that God is holding out hope. You can live a different destiny than the foolish broken one that will be your lot unless you change. If you choose wisdom as your guiding principle, then your destiny will change to include longer life; higher monetary levels; more respect; higher comfort; and less strife, fighting, and contention with others. It does not matter when you decide to get on the wisdom road; your future will be different. It is best when you are a teen; but if you are in your 20's or 40's or 60's, the wisdom road will still pay out a better result than any other plan you might come up with.

Notice that these results are the consequences of choosing wisely during your life. It is not magic or some special power. It is that the choices that wisdom would direct you to make accumulate completely different results than foolishness does.

right hand and left hand

In Hebrew thinking, the right hand was the place of prominence and significance. Even in our own thinking, we call a person my right-hand guy when we want to say that they are indispensable and the key player. Solomon is saying that the path of wisdom builds long life and long life is the key player in establishing the path of wisdom. Its benefits accumulate over time. The path of wisdom is not a get-rich-quick scheme. It is a gain-blessings-slowly scheme.

In other words, you must have a longer time for wisdom to show its benefits. Over a short time it may appear as though the fool's path pays out as well as the wise path. This is what happens over the course of the short four years of high school or college. It looks like the fool who gets drunk and parties and takes all the selfish risks is winning. After all, they don't seem to be paying for their embrace of selfishness and instead they get the girls/boys, the popularity, the "fun," etc. But what is not seen is the virus of selfishness that is infecting their soul and its cancerous effect. What is also not seen is the rich advantage that the person on the path of wisdom is gaining.

Jesus' comments here are very important. "What does it profit a man if he gains the whole world but loses his soul?" There are people who pursue the world's goods and, in the pursuit, infect their soul with a bacteria that destroys it so that they are rich in this world's goods but have no soul and no relationship with God or others. Instead, Jesus would suggest – as Solomon did 1,000 years before – that one seek first the kingdom of God and all these other things will be added to you. Seek a rich, deep soul knowing God and enjoying deep relationships with others. What good is having a beautiful piano if getting it made you deaf?

riches

This is the Hebrew word *oser* which means wealth, riches. The idea is that one has riches when one has an abundance beyond what is needed to sustain one for the next day or week. Riches are treasures that have been built up so that one can sustain oneself into the foreseeable future and so that one can be generous with others who are truly in need.

In our day the majority are not encouraged to be disciplined with their money so they can accumulate wealth for their later years. Our culture is all about spending and consuming now. Therefore we have no savings and little retirement investments. We do not see that our cultural value of "enjoy it all right now" is foolishness and a form of selfishness. All financial advisors tell us that if we would be willing to send a little bit away each month automatically deducted from what we make, we will end up wealthy when we can no longer earn a living. All it takes is ten percent of our income sent away to some reasonable investment savings. But we are too often pursuing a fool's lifestyle in the here and now.

Choose your destiny today. Talk to people at your work and set up a retirement account in which the ten percent or the maximum contribution you can make will be automatically taken out of your paycheck. Then figure out what standard of living you can maintain. Or tell the person in payroll that when the next raise comes, you want it to be completely given to retirement. Do that twice or three times and then you can get all the raises.

Remember, wisdom is small choices now that are righteous and glorify God, benefit others, and yourself. They usually are long-term decisions. Don't wait; start doing this now.

honor

This is the Hebrew word *kobed* which means great. It means significant, valuable, worthy of honor for their contribution. When one chooses wisdom over folly, they are choosing contribution over consumption. Wisdom chooses to make small important contributions to society, to family, to church, to themselves, to friends. It is those seemingly small but important contributions that build up and cause those around you to realize how valuable you are to them.

It is important to realize that one must continue to make these contributions until they become second nature. When it is your habit to make choices and pursue actions that do not just benefit you but also benefit the people in your life, it builds up bonds and joy in your life and in theirs. Do not underestimate the value of the people in your life; their opinion of you will make you or break you. It is their opinion of how valuable you are that changes everything. Choosing the path of wisdom is making the decision to make a contribution to their success.

You will all succeed together; wisdom is not a doormat philosophy in which you destroy yourself for their success. No, wisdom is finding the choice and the action in which they are benefited and you also are benefited. It is the triple-win that you are after.

PROVERBS 3:17 - *Her ways are pleasant ways and all her paths are peace.*

Solomon continues his selling of the advantages of the path of wisdom by describing what being on the road of wisdom is like. In this case he points out two aspects of the path of wisdom that many do not realize. They think that these two important joy-producers are available everywhere.

pleasant

This is the Hebrew word *noam* which means pleasantness, beauty, kindness, favor. Solomon is pointing out that when you dig hard to find the triple-win choices and actions, you will be introduced to a lifestyle of pleasant interactions between people or symmetry and teamwork. On the other hand, if you take the fool's road, then it is "every man for himself and dog eat dog." When you – through your choices – look for the choice that glorifies God and gives a win to others and a win for yourself, it creates a much more pleasant world than if you just push for the maximum win for yourself.

peace

This is the Hebrew word *shalom* which means peace. It means to not be at war with others. It means to vibrate in harmony with others and create beautiful melodies and music together with others. Solomon is pointing out that when you look for the triple-win choices, your world is filled with connection and harmony between you and the other people in your life. If you choose the selfish road, then your life is filled with war and strife and contention.

This is something to think through. If when you make a decision the people closest to you are upset and angry with you, it may not be the wise decision. Other people must see the win in this decision for them. I am amazed at the number of people who choose to ride the picket fence of selfishness and then wonder why everybody is against them. When you make decisions that only allow you to win, then it is to be expected that others would be upset. Every person is surrounded by a web of relationships and those people are important to you. When you dig for wisdom, you consider all the ramifications of your decisions into those relationships.

PROVERBS 3:18 - *She is a tree of life to those who take hold of her, and happy are all who hold her fast.*

Wisdom is an orientation to life. Looking for that which honors God brings a win for others as well as a win for yourself. It is this triple-win embrace that reorients life as God intended it to be. It is hard in our increasing selfish and broken world to think and live this way. It seem off and needlessly delaying your own gratification. But this verse tells us that it will bring a level of fulfillment and happiness to those who evaluate all their decisions by this measure.

Wisdom was normal thinking before the fall of Adam. Adam and Eve sought God's glory and pleasure first and the other's benefit, assuming that they would be profited personally with those other two.

tree of life
It is mentioned in a number of places throughout the Scripture. In Genesis 3 it is the life-giving substance that Adam and Eve must be kept from in their sinful state lest they eat and permanently confirm their state of rebellion. Throughout the book of Proverbs it is a symbol of that which brings joy, meaning, and fullness to life. There are times when it initially seems like one is moving away from life when you take the path that wisdom marks out, but this is not the case. Wisdom results in the better life, but sin has a better advertising budget. Sin looks more satisfying and more alluring and as though it will be more fulfilling, but it won't. It leaves people empty and alienated from each other and many times from yourself.

Solomon is saying that if you want to plant a tree of fulfillment and satisfaction in your life, then go after wisdom and a full crop of blessing, meaning, joy, life, and significance will continually be available to you.

On the other hand, if you choose the fool's road, then a tree of death will be planted in your life – a life filled with broken relationships, a life filled with missed opportunities, a life of unfulfilled potential, a life filled with regret. The road of selfishness is a highly promoted fun house that turns into a house of horrors.

happy

This is the Hebrew word *eser* which means happiness or bliss. It is also a synonym of the word *blessed* with a slight difference. God is never said to *eser* a person but He does bless people *barak*. When a person is blessed in the *eser* or happy form, he has had to do something. When Jesus issues the beatitudes, he uses the word *makarios* which is the Septuagint version of *eser* as he begins each beatitude. In other words, if you want to know how to lead a fulfilled life and how to be a blessed life, then strive after these qualities. Happiness is the result of living a life of wisdom.

Selfishness and sin – while it looks like it will produce the happier life – ends up producing a life filled with brokenness and sadness. Remember, this when you make your choices. You will not want to give up what you want to pursue, what God wants, or what will cause others to win; but if you look down those paths for your choices and personal victories, you will end up with a much better life than if you go after only what you want.

PROVERBS 3:19 - *The LORD by wisdom founded the earth, by understanding He established the heavens.*

This is an important statement doctrinally, practically, and foundationally. It states that God, who is personal, applied knowledge in a specific way as to bring about the greatest good for all those concerned and realized the connections and possible interactions between all the astronomical factors.

This statement in the proverb is used for illustrative purposes to demonstrate the effect of wisdom. It also shows that God is not asking us to do something that He Himself did not also use. It is not very often that God's actions are a practical illustration of what we should do. Usually it is because God did this or will do that you should do this other thing.

LORD

This is the Hebrew word *Yahweh* or the Tetragrammatons'; the unutterable name for God. This title for God appears 5321 times in the Old Testament for God. It is His revealed name to the people of Israel. He gives it to Moses as His personal name, intimately associated with Himself and revealing of His nature. It is a form of the verb to be. It is what Jesus was referring to when He said, "Before Abraham was born, I AM" – a direct claim to deity. This word has been transliterated in German to be Jehovah, but the Hebrew letters are YHWH.

In these statements we are being given an inside look at the planning and birth into being of our universe; peering behind the curtain of time and into the divine interaction. This proverb states that God had a number of options that were available to Him in the creation of the earth and the universe as a whole. This is the possible world's idea that floats around in philosophical thought. God did have any number of possible worlds, but what this proverb says is that He chose by an act of His will to make this one that we are dwelling in become the actualized one because it was the wisest course. This universe and this earth met the criteria of the best application of knowledge and the highest glory for His name, as well as the greatest good for the creatures inhabiting the worlds He was creating.

This verse is fascinating that it suggests that God had options. He could have created some other world in which things would have been different. It does not tell us as much as we might like to know about these possible worlds except that God, in His infinite wisdom, did not pick any of them. He picked this one to actualize. It is significant that He had choices and that He used this new thing called wisdom to make the final decision about which world He would create. Proverbs 8:22-25 suggests that wisdom was one of the first of the newly created things. God created or brought forth this thing called applied knowledge for the greatest good for the development of a universe that was going to be actualized within a small number of dimensions. The decision to create or develop applied knowledge or wisdom necessarily preceded the actual creation of an actualized place, even though this creation occupied some small number of physical dimensions.

Wisdom was and is one of the building blocks of this world in which we live. It was a part of its planning, creation, and development; and it is a part of effective living within the perimeters of its boundaries. Solomon is trying to get us to understand that wisdom is essential to living here effectively. This is not just a technique that you should use occasionally; it is a way of living that is foundational to how the world was put together.

Think about today. Will you live at odds with wisdom and follow your own impulses and temptations, or will you live in harmony with how God made the world? Will you ask the right questions today? "Will this thing bring God glory, others' benefit, and myself success?" or "What would make me happy?"

Now this embrace of wisdom is not just important for Christians; it is important for businessmen, politicians, students, parents, friends, husbands and wives, church officials, etc. A lack of wisdom and, therefore, a grasping at selfishness will bring a measure of destruction to these endeavors. Each of the problems in each of these arenas can be traced to a lack of wisdom. That is why God, through Solomon, screams at us: SEEK WISDOM!

PROVERBS 3:20 - *By His knowledge the deeps were broken up and the skies drip with dew.*

This proverb continues the amazing glimpse back at God's wisdom in creation that began in verse 19 and will occupy huge sections of chapter 8 of the Proverbs. Solomon realizes that God had an infinite number of choices present before His infinite mind in the planning of the creation of the universe and yet wisdom dictated that He create this universe with these parameters and these qualities and these interconnections.

The universe did not just happen. There are too many different variables and constants that have to be fine-tuned for this particular universe to exist. And scientists are finding more and more ways that this universe has been fine-tuned for life.

When planning the creation of the universe, He chose the potential universe that would bring Him the most glory; His creatures the most joy and fulfillment. It was wisdom that dictated that choice. In the same way the potential lives we have available to us should be dictated by wisdom and not selfish impulse.

The exact reference that Solomon is referring to in planetary history would seem to be the creation of land and the wonder of rain and the water cycle. These things that we take for granted are actually amazing things which make the world we call home possible. Without land we would not exist. If the world had remained only water, human life would not exist. Without rain we would not be able to survive. These are just two of the choices that God made that display His wisdom in this universe. Solomon is amazed at them. Solomon's keen mind penetrates through the hidden to see the choice of God. He uses them to show the power of wisdom to keep giving over long time spans. Our wise choices also will make lasting differences in our lives as well as our families.

Stop and contemplate the wonders of creation and the various choices that God could have made. He used wisdom with the clear goal of glorifying Himself and making a world that was a huge win for us.

PROVERBS 3:21 - *My son, let them not vanish from your sight; keep sound wisdom and discretion,*

vanish

This is the Hebrew word *"luz"* which means to turn aside; to depart. It is translated vanish to convey the idea that wisdom and discretion must always be on our radar system.

sound wisdom

This is the Hebrew word *tushiyyah* which is a rare word which means sound wisdom or efficient wisdom. There is a large part of this word which means the application of knowledge that has proven to be effective. It is not potential wisdom; it is known ways to allow a triple-win to take place.

Solomon is saying that young people need to be surrounded by what has worked in the past so that they can embrace proven ideas and add the new twists and applications to the unique situation they find themselves in.

discretion

This is the Hebrew word *mezimmah* which means discretion, purpose, device, schemes. The idea here is clearly a goal and the plan to get there.

Solomon wants young people to realize that they must always know where they want to go; what they are after; what their goal(s) in life are; and have a satchel of proven strategies and methods that produce win/win outcomes for people.

We all have a tendency to believe the world is all new to us and that we can shoot from the hip or do not need to do things the same way that they have been done in the past. Solomon is saying that this orientation is a mistake. He is screaming at us to realize that proven methods are proven for a reason and that your goals keep you from being seduced away from accomplishing your purpose in life.

Keep goals and proven methods in your satchel at all times. What are you trying to accomplish with your life? What is your goal in life? What is your dream? It is amazing the number of people that get turned aside from their dream by lust, by a relationship, by a mistake, by greed, or by laziness at a critical juncture. You have to stay focused to accomplish your dream.

Solomon is giving us critical insight into how to live the life we know we were meant to live. Don't throw it away by ignoring this ancient wisdom.

PROVERBS 3:22 - *So they will be life to your soul and adornment to your neck.*

Solomon continues his persuasive discussion of the power of sound wisdom and discretion. It makes a significant difference in your life – both internally and externally – if you do not go down the path of foolishness but instead cling to sound wisdom and discretion. It is interesting that this is not so much about avoiding foolishness but instead the positive benefits of wisdom and discretion.

life

This is the Hebrew word *haya* which means live, live prosperously, be alive, sustain life. It is about the animating principle of life. Notice that in this instance it is spoken about the soul. Solomon is saying that it is possible to inject more life into your soul; to have a soul that is truly alive, living prosperously. This means, on the other hand, that if you focus on selfish behavior, impulsive actions, and rebellious actions, then you will inject death and damage into your soul.

How does this work? Well LIFE IS RELATIONSHIPS and your ability to manage, develop, and strengthen those relationships is what the inner man feeds off of. If you are stupid, selfish, impulsive, proud, sarcastic, rebellious, you destroy relationships and therefore your soul has less to live on. It then deals with the relationships that your actions and words have crushed. When are you the most down and depressed? When a relationship that is really important to you has been lost or severely damaged. It is the relational energy of life that allows your soul to dance. When you – through willful actions – destroy the very things that you need to enjoy life, you lose even while you are doing what you want.

I watch husbands and wives destroy their marriage through selfishness, sarcasm, and denial and then they wonder why they have such a bad marriage. I watch people work slowly, bad mouth their boss, do personal work at the job, and then wonder why they don't get the raise or the promotion. I watch people focus on themselves, put others down, gossip about their friends, and then wonder why they don't have as many friends as they would like. Solomon is screaming at us: *Wisdom: looking for the triple-win will preserve the relationships in life and feed your soul what it needs to live off of.*

adornment

This is the Hebrew word *hen* which means favor or grace but also refers to a charm or adornment in a few cases. Solomon is saying that if you feed your soul with wisdom and discretion, it will show on your face and body. You will be a different person to those who look at you. Physically these inner righteous ways will change your look. It is a good change.

PROVERBS 3:23 ~ *Then you will walk in your way securely and your foot will not stumble.*

The key word in this proverb is <u>then</u>. After you find wisdom, all these wonderful things will happen to you. Solomon is selling the benefits of wisdom.

In this proverb he points out that when you act with wisdom in which God is glorified, others win and you win and you do not have to worry about as many dangers and problems. You have eliminated them by your wise actions and choices.

Think this through: Every time you choose the wise action instead of the selfish one, you gain the opportunities that come after the wise action – you get the benefits of the wise action. You miss the problems of the selfish action, and you miss the new selfish opportunities that would be available after the selfish action. You are in a four times better place than you would have been if you did the foolish action.

securely

This is the Hebrew word *betach* which means security, confidence, safely. What the wise person is stepping on is secure and not shaky or suspect. He has checked it out and has received confirmation. There is no impulsiveness and shady dealings as there are when you are pursuing what is selfish or foolish.

The foolish path is the quick, hidden – maybe illegal – deal that is too good to be true. The wise path is full of checks and balances and confirmation.

When you go down the wise path, you don't have to wonder if the police will be knocking at your door soon. You don't have to wonder if the IRS will be taking all you have. You don't have to worry about the boss finding out about what you have been doing. You don't have to hope that your wife never finds out. Instead you are secure. What you are doing is good, right, open, and aboveboard.

stumble

This is the Hebrew word *nagaph* which means to strike, smite. In this case, when connected with foot or walking, it means tripping over something that your foot hits.

One of the dangers of walking on dirt paths is that there is a rock sticking up that you don't see. Your foot hits it, and you fall flat on your face. This is the picture that is brought to mind in this part of the proverb. If you are following the path of wisdom, this hidden rock that makes you fall headlong on the path is not there. You do not have the fall that destroys everything. You may trip, but you can recover. Wisdom makes you cautious and aware of what is around you.

PROVERBS 3:24 - *When you lie down, you will not be afraid; when you lie down, your sleep will be sweet.*

People don't tend to realize all the connections between things. We don't realize that the positive, righteous things that we do for others impact the direction of our life. We don't often see the connection between choosing to glorify God with our speech and actions and a lessening of stress and anxiety. Wisdom is that course of action that looks for the triple-win: the action, the choice, the words that cause God to be glorified, loved ones to win, and us personally to win.

Solomon points out in this proverb that how wisely you win has an impact in how sweetly you sleep. Wisdom is not the only contributor to how you sleep, but it is much bigger than you think.

afraid

This is the Hebrew word *pachad* which means to dread, to be in awe. The idea here is fear that grips your life: fear of what you have done coming back on you; fear of what others will do to you; the spirit of fear surrounding you and creating scenarios that you embrace.

When a person is foolish, they expose themselves, their children, and others to circumstances that are unstable, dangerous, and fearful. Impulsive, selfish, rebellious, and proud actions move you in a direction where there are more dangerous and threatening things. It is best to just miss those experiences all together by not being anywhere near where they happen or with people who live like that.

It is a shame when the foolish choices of parents subject their children to fear every night. Don't do this. Start making wise choices and remove the cloud of fear from your own life and your loved ones' lives. Yes, wisdom is less exciting on the front end, but it becomes far more fulfilling on the back end.

sweet

This is the Hebrew word *arab* which means to be sweet or pleasing. Your mind won't be racing to all the bad things that could happen but will be able to slow down and rest in God's goodness and the environment your choices have created.

A good sleep requires trust. You are turning off the mechanism of your body and going offline for a while so your internal processes can do system checks and repairs. You must trust God, the environment, the people around you, etc., to have a deep, restful sleep. That is why it comes from wisdom.

A good night's sleep is wonderful and it happens far more often in the path of wisdom. Choose to live wisely, not selfishly.

PROVERBS 3:25 - *Do not be afraid of sudden fear nor of the onslaught of the wicked when it comes;*

afraid

This is the Hebrew word *yare* which means fear, afraid, even reverence. Do not build your life around the possibility of something bad happening to you. Don't rehearse all the bad things that could happen to you.

You have a choice whether you will let your soul be gripped by the emotion of fear. You don't have to let this happen.

sudden

This is the Hebrew word *peta* which means suddenness. It has the idea of quickly, unexpectedly, impulsive. Solomon is saying that if you follow the path of wisdom, then you do not have to be afraid of sudden fears. You will be ready for these. You will have seen the signs coming.

He is saying that you should not give into a paranoid point of view. Some Christians have developed such a negative evil-is-everywhere mindset that they are skittish and pessimistic. Don't let this kind of thinking grip you. If you are following wisdom, God will protect you.

fear

This is the Hebrew word *pahad* which means dread, fear, terror. The idea is that some thought rises up in your mind and begins to consume your thinking – some terrible thing that could happen to you. Don't give into this intruder in your mind. Don't give over your thought processes to an emotion. Push back on the emotion and express confidence in the Lord.

For some this sudden fear is rooted in reality; for others it is bizarre. It could be an IRS audit; it could be a past sin coming out; it could be an unlikely attack; it could be a series of improbable events. The point is that these are not events that are happening but are, instead, things that "could" happen that are invented by your mind that seek to pull you into a pool of fear.

When one of my daughters was little, she saw a TV show about a fire in a house. We had to spend a lot of time praying and reassuring her that our house would not burn down. She had allowed herself to be completely gripped by a fear that was not going to take place.

I watch as grown-ups do the same things and change their whole lives to try and avoid an imaginary fear. Don't do this; don't let fear dictate what you do or how your live your life.

Notice that this verse is in the midst of a section about what following wisdom will do for you. But Solomon still needs to tell us not to let these imaginary fears take over our thinking.

nor of the onslaught of the wicked when it comes

onslaught

This is the Hebrew word *shoah* which means devastation, ruin, storm, waste. The idea is clearly that the wicked will try and bring their destruction upon the society and the righteous, but those who are following wisdom do not have to give into the fear that this will destroy them. It may destroy your worldly possessions, but you don't have to give into fear over the thought of the wicked succeeding.

Solomon is talking, in this proverb, about two kinds of fearful things: one, a sudden fear that pops into your head; and two, the agenda of the wicked to get what they want. Solomon's advice is that you should not allow either of these kinds of fears to grip your mind.

PROVERBS 3:26 - *For the Lord will be your confidence and will keep your foot from being caught.*

I am amazed at how often non-believers want to see everything good that happens to them or others as a coincidence or directly related to what they have done. There is so little understanding of God's providence that we don't even look for it anymore. There was a time in this country when we understood that God is in charge and if He wants to block you, then you will be blocked. If He wants you to make progress in a certain direction, then against all odds, progress in that direction is possible. This does not mean that just because an action is allowed it is therefore good. God allows us to make foolish and even wicked choices.

This proverb says that God plays favorites for those who follow His laws, His precepts, and His direction. Those who ignore what He has said and what He is saying bear the consequences for their pride.

confidence

This is the Hebrew word *kesel* which means – surprisingly enough – foolishness, stupidity, or confidence. The idea here is that sometimes when you do what wisdom dictates, it has very little support from the people around you. Why would you want to sacrifice your own accomplishments to help others win? It just doesn't make sense to people. Why would you refuse to do something that would be pleasurable and legal just because it would not honor God as much as another option? This is beyond comprehension to some. But this is what wisdom does. Wisdom looks to the long-distant future and looks for that choice that allows God to receive great glory, others to win, and you to win. This choice will not make sense to some and, therefore, you will look like a fool. In those cases Solomon is saying that the Lord will be your foolishness. You will appear to be foolish because you actually believed in what He said to do.

I was reading recently an account of the landing of the Puritans in America at Plymouth. The book was written from the point of view that the Puritans were all bad and the Indians were the oppressed victims of the story. Even in this type of biased history the providence of God could not be buried. There were any number of unexplainable events that should not have happened the way they happened. There were miracles supporting the Puritans.

God says, through the mouth of his servant Solomon in this case, that He will strongly support those who strive to conduct themselves with righteous wisdom. Even if they are fooled into a trap, He will fight for them so that they will not get caught. He will gladly be their foolishness when they put His honor ahead of their own prosperity, comfort, and pleasure.

Realize that the Lord will not be the confidence or defender of those who just say that they are believers or Christians or religious but who demonstrate no wisdom. If a person embraces selfishness, rebellion, pride, mocking, and/or impulsiveness, they will reap what they sow – no matter how much they say they believe in God. *Do not be deceived, God will not be mocked, whatsoever a man sows that shall he also reap,* Galatians 6:7 tells us.

It is a great thing to watch the Lord go to bat for you. It is a great thing to watch Him discipline you with a loving hand. It is a great thing to have Him calm your heart with contentment while others are running after the trinkets of the world which in a few years they will have to surrender.

Yes, there will be times when you must be the Lord's fool. The things that He asks you to do will not make sense to average folks. And you will have a choice. Will I emphasize relationships with my talent, time, and treasures or will I emphasize selfishness? There will be times when He will demand that you not do things that everyone else is doing. It will be worth it. Yes, you may have to surrender a little of your cool factor, but you gain so much more.

PROVERBS 3:27 - *Do not withhold good from those to whom it is due, when it is in your power to do it.*

withhold

This is the Hebrew word *mana* which means to withhold, keep back, refrain, deny. Clearly Solomon is trying to help us understand that when we have the chance to benefit someone else, we should take that opportunity.

Unfortunately we are often too eager to only look for our own benefit. The wise person is the one who spreads benefit and blessing whenever they can. One of the basics principles of wisdom is looking to do good to others. This may mean a kind word, a note, an opened door, a listening ear, a helping hand. But when there is an opportunity to actually do something good for others, it is not missed.

good

This is the word *tob* which means good; the quick overarching idea is something that is of benefit to another person.

Solomon suggests that opportunities for benefitting others should not be missed. While this seems trivial, it makes all the difference in the world. People will see you as either a selfish person always thinking about yourself or a good person looking to benefit others and not just yourself. Living a wise life, which is Solomon's goal, requires that you develop the good-for-others focus.

What is interesting here is that one of the basic principles of wisdom is dealing with sins of omission. There is the constant danger of being solely focused on yourself and missing opportunities to really bless, help, and benefit others. This self-focused mentality is being trumpeted in our day as the way to get ahead, but Solomon warns that missing opportunities to bless and benefit others will come back to bite you.

We are also often protective of being taken advantage of that we miss many of these opportunities. In this idea you will freely allow yourself to be taken advantage of to help the other person. They will get the better end of the deal, but you will gain the emotional satisfaction of doing good and you will be pleasing to God.

I get concerned about the culture of schools, business, and government where it is seen as cool to put people down and gossip rather than do good to people. I am troubled by the fact that many kid's cool factor goes up if they can put other kids down. It is not helpful when the office gossip is designed to find the flaws of the people in the office and broadcast them.

due

This is the Hebrew word *baal* which means owner, lord, ruler. In this case the translators used the words *to whom it is due* to make it clearer but unfortunately clouded the idea in the original that one should do good to one's authorities. This is the last person who you want to benefit.

This proverb, properly understood, talks about a forgotten secret in our culture: the secret of honor, submission, and gratefulness above what is required. Our culture so values independence that we have made the rebel that hero. The rebel does not get ahead; the rebel takes the obstacle-filled path.

Solomon was trying to hold the faces of his young charges and let them know that when they have the chance to benefit their superiors, they should take that opportunity. It is the wise thing to do.

power

This is the Hebrew word *hand* which means hand. The idea is that if you have the ability to bless others, then take it – especially if it is your superior.

Too often we push our hand down back into our pockets rather than reach out with the help that is needed. We turn away the words that others need. We are so afraid of puffing them up that we hold back needed gratefulness and praise. Don't be like this. This week when you have the chance to say something nice to the people around you – especially your boss – then do it. When you have the chance to do something that would really benefit them, then take that chance.

PROVERBS 3:28 - *Do not say to your neighbor, "Go, and come back, and tomorrow I will give it." When you now have it with you.*

One of the principles of wisdom is that you do good to people when it is available to do.

Too many of us put off good things for silly reasons. We don't tell our spouse that we love them because it seems silly. We don't compliment our children on a job well done because they should just do it that way all the time. We don't encourage the person who is down because they might take it the wrong way. We don't put on a positive attitude because we just want to be grumpy and negative.

This proverb deals with the issue of someone in need coming to you to borrow something you have. But you make them come back again because it is more convenient for you at that time, or it could be that you have the person come back to suggest your superiority over the person in need.

This proverb also deals with the issue of a person who works for you and has come to be paid. It is not right to withhold payment to that person when you actually have the funds to pay them.

Wisdom does the positive, right thing every chance it can. It doesn't wait to give compliments. It doesn't wait to express love and care to loved ones. It doesn't procrastinate in helping or doing something for another. It doesn't have the mindset that "I will help if it suits my schedule or it's convenient for me." It helps.

PROVERBS 3:29 - *Do not devise harm against your neighbor, while he lives securely beside you.*

This is one of a series of basic prohibitions that Solomon includes at the beginning of our training in wisdom. There are five major "do not's" from verse 27 through verse 31. Solomon seems to be saying: Here are basic and fundamental issues that need to be stated as we are getting started in wisdom training. Don't do these things. What is interesting about these things is that they don't seem earth shattering, but they are crucial in the development of a positive orientation to the world. There is a much longer three chapter list of prohibitions near the end of Solomon's instruction on wisdom. But these five catch our eye because they are of such a fundamental nature. Will you be a positive actor in the drama called life or will you take a negative part? It is your choice: the positive one is wise; the negative one is foolish.

devise

This is the Hebrew word *charash* which means to engrave, to devise, plot, plow. It involves a planned process. In this case it is some planned action or process that involves or will impact your neighbor in some negative way. This could be your neighbor where you live, where you work, where you worship, in your family. There are people all around you who are impacted by your actions and plans.

In a roundabout way Solomon is saying that you have to think through what you are planning on doing; what you want and your goals. Do any of them negatively impact the people around you? Unfortunately this type of thinking is almost unheard of in our day and age. People have been told that they should just pursue what they think they want with no thought about how it will impact their family, their friends, their neighborhood, their colleagues, etc.

In reality this is a basic ethical principle of which there are only two at the most basic level. Does your goal or action harm anyone? Who does your goal or action benefit? If you are the only one who benefits and others will be harmed, then your proposed action is unethical. This is basic training in ethics and morality.

I have watched, however, people pursue their desires or goals with little or no thought to the wider ramifications of what they are doing. Let me give you some examples:

- Men, and now even women, who take promotions or jobs that require significant amounts of travel right at the critical stages of their children's development with the result that their children are significantly psychologically harmed by their absence.

- Neighbors who want to make alterations to their home which are completely at odds with their neighbors' homes and may reduce property values or enjoyment of the area. These folks just do what they want because "it is my property" without regard to the harm that will come to their neighbors.

- Men and women who want a particular promotion at work, so they either purposely or even unintentionally put their competitor in a bad light so they will get the promotion.

- People who pursue a sport or activity that will put one of their friends in danger or the position of major embarrassment. They do not think that Bill cannot handle this; they only think that they want to do that and if Bill is dumb enough to try, then that is his problem.

harm

This is the Hebrew word *raah* which means evil, misery, distress, injury. This is either the intended or unintended result of a particular action. Most of the time it seems that harm is the unintended result of their desired action.

Although there are times when people actually devise harm against those they know. This may be because you think they have slighted or wounded you in some way or because it will allow you to have more of what you want.

This happens at all ages, but it is especially tempting early in life – the teens and the twenties. It doesn't seem that big a deal to shame, embarrass, put down, slight, and disrespect people that are all around you when you are young. Solomon is screaming: Don't start down this negative path! Make a positive contribution to everyone you can. It may cost you a few cool points in the short run, but you will have a much better life in the long run.

neighbor

This is the Hebrew word *rea* which means friend, companion, neighbor, mate, etc. – those who are connected to you by location, activity, relation, goal, etc. These are the people in your life. Don't use them or harm them to advance your goals in life.

securely

This is the Hebrew word *betach* which means securely, unsuspecting. These are the people who do not expect you to gossip about them; who do not expect that you would take advantage of them; who do not think that you would purposely harm them to advance yourself. These are the people who trust you. Solomon is saying that you should make sure that people who do trust you keep on trusting you because you reject possible actions that could harm them.

PROVERBS 3:30 ~ *Do not contend with a man without cause, if he has done you no harm.*

contend

This is the Hebrew word *rib* which means to strive, to contend. There is an interesting tendency among people to push back against what others want to do just because it is not their own idea. Solomon is talking about this issue. We just naturally want to present the other side of an issue. We bring out the exception to the case. We take the devil's-advocate position and oppose the new idea or plan rather than discussing and exploring it.

I see this tendency damaging marriages, disrupting businesses, stirring up churches. Solomon says: don't oppose or contend with someone's ideas for no reason. Solomon doesn't say this but doing the opposite is implied. Allow the other person to put out their ideas fully. Explore with the other person what they are thinking. Many times the idea has to be shelved because it has serious flaws, but the supportive environment goes a long way to helping the next project or idea.

Don't be so quick to oppose new ideas and suggestions. Don't become known as the person who is against everything. It is appropriate to oppose some things even as Solomon says, "with a cause." But do not just oppose something before you have heard it.

cause

This is the word *chinnam* which means without a cause, for nothing, uselessly. If you ask yourself why are you involved in an argument with a particular person or over a particular issue and the answer is, "Oh, no reason in particular," then you are violating this bit of wisdom.

harm

This is the Hebrew word *raah* which means evil, misery, distress, injury. Solomon is pointing out that we can get all worked up against something that has not affected us in any way.

There is another possible issue involved in this proverb: taking up an offense for someone else. This is where someone you know was harmed by an individual and you begin to carry that person's hurt. If you begin contending with that person based upon someone else's hurt, then you will draw a truckload of troubles to your life needlessly.

PROVERBS 3:31 - *Do not envy a man of violence and do not choose any of his ways.*

Solomon specifically says not to envy the man who gains through his aggressiveness and harm to others. Don't envy what he gains and do not envy that he is always able to assert his rights and his point of view.

envy

This is the Hebrew word *qanah* which means to be jealous or envious. To want what someone else has is the basic idea in this context. We may want this person's ability in order to bend others to our point of view. But Solomon says they pay a very steep price for their ability to gain what they want.

When we gain by others, loss it is only a short-term gain at best. That seems to be a project with the Lord.

violence

This is the Hebrew word *chamas* which means violence, wrong, malicious. The idea is that harm is being or will be done. It is the sure sign that ethical misconduct or wrong has taken place. Someone has been harmed or their profit has been diminished in order to accomplish your personal profit. We do not think in these terms; but we should become increasingly aware of how our actions, words, attitudes, and motives impact others.

The violent person does not necessarily want to be violent. They just have to have their own way, and they are willing to threaten violence or do violence to get it.

choose

This is the Hebrew word *bachar* which means to choose, to make a choice. You do have a choice what kind of lifestyle you will embrace. Once you have embraced a lifestyle, then your choices may become inevitable as certain behaviors come with a certain lifestyle choice.

Think this through: The life of person who makes a living selling drugs is different from the person who sells clothes at a department store. The person who keeps out of trouble by lying has a completely different set of friends than the person who tries to keep out of trouble by not needing to lie in the first place.

ways

This is the Hebrew word *derek* which means path, way, direction. The Hebrew mindset was that a person's life was on a path and certain predictable things are a part of each lifestyle path. The things that are a part of a person who gets their way through violence, intimidation, or over aggressiveness is not a way of life to embrace. It entails far more than just getting your own way. It is clear from the fact that this is a plural word and that there are a number of different ways that this person uses harm, violence, threat, and/or intimidation to assert his perspective. Don't make the choice to have your claims met through this volatile, aggressive behavior. You may think that you are accomplishing lots of stuff, but you are not.

PROVERBS 3:32 ~ *For the devious are an abomination to the Lord; but He is intimate with the upright.*

devious

This is the Hebrew word *luz* which means to turn aside, to depart. It is translated as depart, devious, guile, vanish. This is the person who trusts more in their own schemes than in a straightforward approach to things. They operate through backroom deals and complicated deceptions in order to get what they want. When everything has to be hidden, there are elements of unrighteousness. Why can't everyone see what you are up to?

Solomon is trying to help the young person studying wisdom under his care. Don't get too enamored with schemes and deception. It looks like it produces winners, but usually it has to be hidden because there is a major loser hidden in there somewhere. Wisdom looks for the triple win. It digs for the way to have everyone but the wicked win.

intimate

This is the Hebrew word *sod* which means counsel, fellowship, consultation, secrets. Solomon is clearly setting up a direct contrast between the secret schemes of the devious person and the straightforward person who gets let in on the secrets of the Lord. Which do you want to have – your own schemes or the Lord's secrets?

upright

This is the Hebrew word *yashar* which means straight, right. This word conveys the idea of the person who takes the straight path. This is the one who does not have a lot of schemes and trickery to their life. It is a direct contrast to the person who is devious. The upright person stays within the boundaries of the Ten Commandments. This person looks to glorify God – to bring about a win for those around them, for themselves, and for God.

PROVERBS 3:33 - *The curse of the Lord is on the house of the wicked, but He blesses the dwelling of the righteous.*

curse

This is the Hebrew word *meerah* which means curse. These can generally be seen as the punishments or natural consequences of actions outside of God's moral boundaries. It has been Solomon's observation that those who live outside the Ten Commandments have a lot of bad stuff happen to them. They may think that they are getting ahead in one area, but other areas keep falling apart. They have sacrificed their life for prosperity in one area.

What is interesting about our day is that we have failed to recognize the curse of the Lord for what it is; we accept it as normal parts of living. We don't know why children rebel; they just do. We don't know why marriages break up; some just do. We don't know why some people constantly have financial troubles; they just do. We don't know why some people have a hard time getting or keeping a job; they just do. These are the kinds of reasoning's that go on in our day. But each of these is completely understandable by the actions the individual takes. They were off doing something else when they should have been focused on those positive relationships.

The wicked are selfish and no longer respect any moral boundaries on their behavior. They want what they want, and they will do whatever they have to do to get what they want. If it requires stealing, then they will steal. If it requires adultery, then they will commit adultery. If it requires lying, then they will lie. If it requires worshipping another god or practicing another religion, then they will do that. If it requires that they intimidate or hurt another person, then they will do that. There is little or no remorse and even if there is guilt or remorse, there is no change in behavior.

It is for these reasons that God says He has designed the universe to curse those who live this way. You may get what you want but lose your soul. Many of us have watched too many Mafia movies where the killer kills during the day and then enjoys a loving family life in the evening like everybody else. This does not happen. The curse of the Lord resides on that house. It is not normal.

house of the wicked
Notice that the curse resides on the whole of the family or house of the wicked. It is not just the wicked person, and it does affect the other people in the house.

blesses
This is the Hebrew word *barak* which means to bless. To profit in some manner is the idea. The Lord has promised to profit those who follow Him and live a righteous life.

The righteous life is the life of blessing God and blessing others while you stay inside the boundaries of the Ten Commandments. It is not just staying inside the Ten Commandments. One must glorify God and meet the needs of those around you in order to be a righteous person. Jesus states this clearly when He says that the two greatest commandments are *Thou shalt love the Lord your God with all your heart, soul, mind and strength and your neighbor as yourself.* Each of these is positive. It requires that we seek to please God with our life, words, thoughts, and attitudes and to be open to the needs of the people that we are in a relationship with.

God says that He will add blessings and good things to the whole family of those who follow the righteous path instead of the selfish path. The children, spouse, and grandchildren of those who are righteous benefit from the righteousness that this one individual exhibits. Many times we are being blessed because of the righteousness of another person in our family.

I have watched sometimes as the righteous family is blessed and yet raised up within that family enjoying the blessings is a child that keeps choosing selfish and then eventually wicked choices. They are surrounded by the blessings of their parents and are not feeling the full impact of their selfishness. They do not see the direct correlation between foolishness, wickedness, and harmful effects. They are protected by the blessing of God as they lead the foolish life. Then they are forced out or grow up or even rebel and leave and then the full force of their foolish and wicked ways slams them in the face. They did not realize that the good life that they enjoyed is not normal; it is the blessing of God.

This prodigal then establishes a foolish or even a wicked house and begins a different experience in their relationships.

PROVERBS 3:34 - *Though He scoffs at the scoffers, yet He gives grace to the afflicted.*

Biblical wisdom means that one reaps what one sows. One is recompensed for his deeds. You acted and behaved in a certain way; that is how you will be treated. People and the world – and even God – reflect back to you what you give off.

This verse is a slight variation of the verse that is repeated in various parts of the Old and New Testament. God is opposed to the proud but gives grace to the humble. Proverbs 3:34; James 4:6; 1 Peter 5:5.

So many times people are upset at what other people are doing to them when they are often just getting a taste of what they do to people.

This proverb is a continuation of this basic biblical truth: If you are a scoffer then God will scoff at you. If you afflict yourself for God's sake, then He will give you grace.

scoffs

This is the Hebrew word *lits* which means to scorn, scoff, deride, mock. The word means to express negativity or contempt about something through speech. To be a cynic. To always take the negative side and criticize.

If your life is full of finding fault and pointing out the mess-ups and negative in others – with little regard to constructive criticism – then you are a scoffer. Don't tell me it's because people around you are such screw-ups or that you just see what is wrong with things. It is a perspective on the world, looking for the negative, looking for what is wrong.

This is a form of foolishness and pride. It puts you in the superior position. It puts you in the judging role, which is where the cynic thinks that he belongs.

We have to be very careful about this tendency in ourselves to judge how people dress or how they speak or how they work or how they eat or how they act and then put them down for these things. This is scorning, scoffing, or mocking.

What God says in this proverb is that if you act this way with others, God will act this way with you. This is His curse on you. You will be treated by Him the way you treat others. Think through this: He will point out all your flaws and all your shortcomings and all your mistakes. He will never let any of these things go without pointing them out.

If you want God to be gracious and overlook your mistakes and not point out your flaws then stop doing it with others. Suffer through others' mistakes and inadequacies. Meet their needs anyway; don't take the superior position, the "I am better than you and have the right to judge you." But instead see if there are needs they have that you can meet. Love them by meeting their needs.

The fruit of the spirit can flow through you to others -- love, joy, peace, patience, kindness, meekness, goodness, faithfulness, and self-control -- and these will be welcome gifts to others.

grace:

This is the Hebrew word *chen* which means favor, grace. The idea is clearly that God is favorably disposed towards this kind of person who afflicts themselves for others.

The wonder of God's nature is that He is gracious at all to sinful beings. We have broken his commands and turned away from His direction. But He continues to offer His favor and mercy and place of privilege to us if we will just humble ourselves. It is crucial that we get out of this superiority and pride. We must come to Him and admit that He is God and we are not. We need to admit that we have broken His laws and pushed away His direction. We seek His forgiveness through His Son Jesus Christ, and He is merciful and gracious and gives it to us.

afflicted:

This is the Hebrew word *anav* which means poor, afflicted, humble, meek. I believe that this word should probably have been translated humble in this passage because it is this quality that is the opposite of scoffing with its superiority issues.

To humble yourself and not push out your judgmental attitude or superior knowledge or information is to invite the grace of God. Of course people do things wrong. Of course they don't do things perfectly. Of course you can point out the mistakes and problems with things; but if you take that scoffer's position, God will not be gracious to you.

To be a scoffer is to act and speak like you are God and can correctly and accurately see the faults and mistakes in others and should be given the right to correct them.

Haven't all of us been caught acting like we know it all and are the corrector for everyone and everything? There are times when a little correction is needed, but it should be done positively and by the appropriate person.

As you go through the day today, let other people be corrected by God and their appropriate authority. Mind your own business and do the best you can. Humble yourself under God's direction for you and watch as His grace and blessing flow towards you.

Do you want God's grace and blessing in your life? Stop criticizing everything and everyone. Stop acting like you know everything and can correct everyone. Look for places to serve and help.

PROVERBS 3:35 - *The wise will inherit honor, but fools display dishonor.*

the wise will inherit honor

The person who seeks out the best and godly choice consistently is given greater value. People trust them and are encouraged to give them greater responsibility. We should not seek to gain advantage on the backs of the honor of others.

If you want people to give you honor – to see your value and give you more value – then you must push for the triple-win choice constantly and not pull another down to make yourself look smart.

but fools display dishonor

The key here is that the morally foolish are constantly devaluing themselves and others. If doing what you have to do causes others to be devalued, then it is foolishness. God would have us dig for that which is valuable in others. He would not want us to be involved in promoting that which devalues others or ourselves.

When you have to take someone else down a few pegs to accomplish your mission, then it cannot be the correct idea. It is not reflective of wisdom. Not too long ago I was seeking to explain a situation which had happened to me, and I realized that the easiest way to explain it to others was as someone else's fault – which I could prove. But then I would be a fool in my explanation. I needed to dig for a wise way to explain the circumstances and my decision that did not require me to expose another person to shame, ridicule, and mistrust.

Many times our stories, jokes, or even manner puts others down and destroys the other person's reputation. This course should not be pursued unless absolutely necessary to protect others from harm. It must not be pursued to bolster our reputation or position.

Proverbs 4

PROVERBS 4:1 - *Hear, O sons, the instruction of a father, and give attention that you may gain understanding,*

Hear, O sons

The word *hear* is the word *shamah* which means to hear but also carries with it the idea of hearing to obey. This is not just listening to sounds but hearing so that you may do. You have not heard if you do not do.

The word *sons* is the typical word for son or grandson. Notice in verse 3 of this chapter that Solomon's father, David, sat him down and taught him this information. This is Solomon doing for the whole world what David, his father, did for him – sitting him down and trying to give him life lessons that will allow him to avoid many of the difficulties that will come at him. It is so hard for teens to listen because they think they know all about everything. It is the information in this book of Proverbs that they often know the least about. In fact, most people are not wise and understanding and walk right into problems, difficulties, and sorrows because they do not understand.

However you do it, you – who are wise are responsible – sit down with your children and grandchildren and pass on the wisdom and understanding that you have. There is a shrinking amount of God's true wisdom in the world. It is covered over with nonsense and foolishness. I know one man who every year bought a different Bible and made notes in it all year for one of his grandchildren. Then he presented that Bible to that grandchild at the end of the year. These notes that you are reading are really my attempt to record insights on life for my grandchildren and great-grandchildren. I hope that my daughters will keep them and present them to their kids and their kids' kids if I am not around to do it.

the instruction of a father

The word *instruction* is the word *masar* which means instruction, training, even chastisement. This is not just lessons that Solomon is sharing; it is a training manual. This is training for life.

I am concerned that fathers are shirking their responsibilities as moral teachers and guides of their children. There is no one that your children would rather hear from about life than their dad. They need to hear from dad on these matters. Do not let mom be the only voice that children hear about morality and life. Don't think that the schools will teach this stuff; they won't.

Every time you read an article in the paper about something that your kids should know, clip it out. Every time you come across a verse in Scripture that would help them, write it down and bring it up. Every time you interact with a person and have an interesting interaction – whether it is good or bad – tell them about it. They need dad's perspective on life.

Too many fathers are being sucked into the world system way of thinking that we will make our biggest contribution at work, so put in your highest levels of energy and effort there. No, you will make your deepest impact and most long-lasting effect in your children. It will be a good impact or a lasting legacy of neglect and alienation. Your children are wanting to spend time with you; don't put them off until they are interesting to you. It will be too late. Enjoy them at every stage of life; but most importantly, constantly point out the insights that you have gained about life. These will echo in their lives forever. Be a dad.

and give attention that you may gain understanding

The words *gain understanding* are interesting because they are the words *know understanding*. God wants His children to really intellectually grasp and experientially realize the connection between behaviors, people, events, actions, etc. The key word in this phrase is the word *understanding*. It is the word *binah* and means distinguishment, power of judgment, perceptive insight. It is the ability to see connections between things – cause and effect – and to use that insight to make accurate decisions.

There are all kinds of connections between things that people miss. In the rest of the book of Proverbs, there are over sixty different types of fools mentioned along with their corresponding tendencies.

Solomon also catalogues almost ten different types of positive characteristics that group around real wisdom. In other words, find the one and you find the others.

Why is this so important? Because young people do not always pick up on the subtle clues that tell them whether the person they are dealing with is lying or a cheat or using them. So they wander into relationships, enter into business connections, and get burned. God is trying to save us from this. He is saying that there is a connection between how a person carries themselves and what they are like. God is trying to get young people to make the connection between hard work and profit; between slothfulness and poverty; between borrowing and slavery; between planning and accomplishment; between teach ability and success; between independence and failure and interdependence and success. Hundreds of these types of comparisons are in this God-breathed book. God had the wisest man who ever lived, other than Jesus, record insights on life in a book so we would enjoy Solomon's success and not repeat his mistakes.

PROVERBS 4:2 - *For I give you sound teaching, do not abandon my instruction.*

This proverb speaks of a deep fear that many parents have – that their child will listen to them and agree with them when they are at home; but at some time later when they are in college or sometimes even earlier, they will abandon all the rules, ideas, and values that their parents have taught them.

Solomon is acting as a spiritual father here and wants to anticipate this dynamic. Don't get rid of this stuff later. What I am teaching you is sound teaching; it is the stuff that will last. Don't think that it was okay when you were a little kid but now you need to follow the "modern" ways of looking at things. In whatever century or period of time all the way back to Solomon's time, the "modern" way has been another name for the selfish way. Now there are advances in knowledge, but these advances do not abrogate moral knowledge especially that given by revelation of God.

sound teaching

This phrase *sound teaching* comes from two Hebrew words *tob* and *leqah*. They literally mean good and learning. The idea is that what Solomon is teaching is beneficial and it is new information. Solomon is saying that I am giving you information that you have not had before, and it will significantly benefit you. You will rejoice if you follow it, but do not make the mistake that many people make in later moving on to some other new information that happens to tickle your intellectual or moral antenna. This is the stuff you should stay with because it is good, beneficial, and righteous.

abandon

This is the Hebrew word *azab* which means leave, forsake, loose. The idea is clearly this tendency for young people to forsake the teaching that gave their life meaning when they learned it at home and in the community that shaped them. They grow up a little and they need to update their learning about God and begin to trust Him and find Him

218

reliable at this new age, but they do not need to scrap all they learned to embrace some new philosophy that seems more adult and able to handle the dog-eat-dog world. I am tired of seeing young men and young ladies destroy the innocence and joy in their lives for some selfish, secularized values. Often these same youth come back to God and church and their parents when they have a family of their own, always ashamed of what took place during their period of rebellion. Some never make it back from their rebellious years. It may be average to rebel, but it is not normal. Normal is what God says ought to happen. Too many kids stop using their faith and the values that God injected into their life and then they say that Christianity didn't work for them. Christianity was not tried and found wanting; it was not tried.

The power of God's wisdom is sufficient for every age and stage in your life. Your understanding of God's wisdom and what to do in particular situations may need to be expanded and understood in new contexts, but it is still worthy of your trust. DO NOT BELIEVE THAT YOU HAVE GROWN PAST YOUR FAITH. No, you have only wanted to become more selfish and your faith will not allow you to do that.

instruction

This is the Hebrew word *torah* which means law and is where we get the title for the first five books of Moses. Now it is important to talk about the nature of law more than a minute. Laws are boundaries in which individuals in authority and society say that behaviors beyond this line are not allowed. Laws are by nature negative. They are trying to boundarize the selfish impulse inside of each person. God has said in the Ten Commandments that individual behavior becomes a threat to the individual, others, and the society as a whole when it goes beyond these ten places. It is not because God is an ogre and He wants to limit our fun and enjoyment of the world. He just knows how He set up the world and the tolerances of the moral order for selfishness. It will not sustain order when selfishness is pushed past these limits. We see the consequences happening all around us as people believe they have the right to be as selfish as they can get away with: children permanently scarred by the divorce, abuse, adultery, and anger of their parents; women and children permanently scarred by the selfishness of men; men permanently scarred by the selfishness of the men and women around them. When selfishness is allowed to reign, love grows cold, the innocent suffer, and the society becomes morally polluted and begins to break down.

In this case Solomon is stating the fact that he is going to give moral boundaries that his pupils should follow. They may seem restrictive, but they will benefit you in the long run. These are his laws or boundary markers.

On this note, every family has boundary lines which they say people should not do this or not do that. Sometimes it is these restrictive boundary lines that the children rebel over when they leave the home. This is often the attempt to differentiate themselves from their parents. This is fairly typical and does not have to constitute rebellion. Each child needs to be able to establish the personal boundaries they will adopt that will keep them from violating God's law. Some children will adopt a different personal boundary than their parents had. This is okay as long as it is still inside of God's clear moral boundary.

Coming back to the point of this proverb – have you needlessly abandoned a Godly philosophy of life only to find the new selfish out-for-#1 philosophy is not working out like you thought? Abandon it and come back to God and accept the forgiveness that is in the person and work of Jesus Christ.

If you are a youth, drink deeply of the wisdom in this book called Proverbs. There is no need to learn a different or better philosophy of life later. This is the only one you will need.

PROVERBS 4:3 - *When I was a son to my father, tender and the only son in the sight of my mother,*

then he taught me and said to me

This is one of Solomon's tenderest memories – when his father, King David, took time to instruct him in the ways of God's wisdom. It was those lessons that were imprinted on his soul. There is not enough emphasis on the instruction responsibility of fathers to take time and direct their children in the way of wisdom.

Notice that David did not try and instruct when Solomon was older and could interact with him. No, David taught Solomon when he was tender and the lessons would make the greatest impact.

It is too often that we wait to teach valuable lessons, thinking they won't understand. But if you teach when they are still in the elementary years, they internalize the lessons much deeper. Later the lessons may be met with more cynicism and resistance.

If you are a father, schedule time every week – even every day – to teach your young children the lessons of life that they will need. Impress on them the need to acquire wisdom. Become a person who discerns between possible decisions and chooses the one that causes many to win.

Notice that this teaching took place between David and Solomon before Bathsheba had any other sons.

PROVERBS 4:4 - *Then he taught me and said to me, "Let your heart hold fast my words; keep my commandments and live,"*

Solomon is remembering back when he was just a boy and how David, his father, would take him aside and talk with him about how to live and what to do in various situations. This makes a radically important impression in Solomon's life, and it is an important rite of passage for parents and children to participate in. It is the work of parenting.

To be a parent means to try and shepherd your children through the various choices that are out there so that they will have a great life. If they can avoid some of the mistakes that you made, they will be better off. If they can make the right choices that you made and that you would now make, they will have a much better life. Your children, however, are seeking to be independent and establish their own identity separate from you.

Notice Solomon's admonitions here in this proverb through his father's mouth: Let your heart hold fast my words; keep my commandments and live. You must begin to make decisions like I would make them or you will be embracing a life of death, needless pain, separation, and loneliness. Don't go down that road.

David's commandments, which were passed on to Solomon in these intimate encounters, were based on the Ten Commandments and the two great Commandments. This is why God could inspire and include Solomon's admonitions to us. It is absolutely imperative that you pass on to your children that fact that there is a way of life and a way of death in this life. One way pulsates with life through choosing to honor, respect, and cultivate other's ideas, needs, and interests. One is purely selfish, constantly asking the question, "What do I want?"

It is important that children realize that many times the right choice is counterintuitive. The way to really live is to get a little less of what you want and more of what everyone would want.

When David taught his son Solomon, he was carrying on an important function of fatherhood – teaching his children about life.

Our culture has reduced fatherhood to a paycheck and a distant enforcer. God's role for fathers involves active relationships with their children and teaching life's lessons to them when they are ready to listen.

I recommend to parents and, especially, fathers that they set up a regular time to get together individually with their children. It should be the same time each week so that it is remembered. It should be with each child individually. Notice how Solomon says that David taught ME. He took time out of his busy schedule to spend time with ME and teach ME important things I need to know. Notice that there is a focus on interaction on important issues. As a child gets older, it is important that there is more listening and questions. A teenager needs to know that they have been listened to before they are willing to interact or hear what you have to say.

I recommend that you memorize the nine major relationships of life and be prepared to ask questions about how each of these is going in their life. If there are problems, questions, or difficulties, they will come out as you show specific interest in their life. Each week they may want to talk about a different relationship or the same relationship. Stay with the topic that they want to talk about. Be careful that you do not do all the talking and telling: How do you think you should handle it? or What do you think you could do?

As for those teens who are reading this, you have probably already made choices that have destroyed friendships or damaged grades or peace with your parents. It is important that you realize that your choices will largely determine the amount of peace you have in your life. That is why David drilled into Solomon, "Keep my commandments and live." If you do not keep God's commandments, then you will not have much life or peace. This is not a game where you can always proclaim that it is time to start over. This is life and the choices that you are making will create a life worth living or a hell on earth.

Ask yourself the question, "If I were to really do what my parents wanted me to do, what would it look like?"

PROVERBS 4:5 - *Acquire wisdom! Acquire understanding! Do not forget nor turn away from the words of my mouth.*

This is the first commandment that David gave to Solomon. After a lengthy build-up in the beginning of Proverbs 4 about the wonder of being taught by the father and the importance of remembering what dad taught, this is actually what dad taught.

How to make the triple-win choice within the boundaries of God's morality and how things are related to one another – especially those things that seem unrelated.

acquire

This is the word purchase, buy, or gain in some way. Since this is a command, it means that the idea must be to procure wisdom that you don't have. You must be willing to listen to the advice of others. More than that, you must be willing to pay for wise counsel to help you avoid the pitfalls of others. Since the opposite of wisdom is foolishness which leads to wickedness, we can assume that Solomon is being taught about how to live a righteous life and how to make decisions in which every righteous person and God wins through the things you decide. It is easy to do the impulsive thing and to be tempted to do the wicked thing. But we must realize that it is wisdom that truly wins the day, and you do not always have it in yourself. Trusting yourself alone for your decisions is a good recipe for disaster. There is a need to purchase or gain by sacrifice, if necessary, the best course of action.

wisdom

Wisdom is the ability to discern the best course of action in any given situation which will result in a win for God's glory, a win for others, and a win for yourself. The wisdom of the ancients was regularly capsulated in pithy sayings called proverbs or riddles so that they could be more easily remembered. These sayings were meant to inform you of directions to go when these directions were counterintuitive. The instructions of the wisdom literature was the collected wisdom of the ages by those who had lived both good and bad and in the case of the biblical wisdom literature, it was inspired by God. Thus this God-breathed set of counterintuitive guides were to keep you from making the same mistakes that 90% of the population makes because it seems right to them.

David was saying to Solomon, his son, that you must always be on the lookout for practical knowledge that truly works. We would almost call these the slogans of life and the bits of truth that make life work. I believe David is saying that these practical bits of knowledge that make life work are everywhere, and we must collect these so that we will know what to do when the time comes. They must fit the triple-win parameters, but they themselves are lessons that we need to make life work. Let me give you some examples:

- Always put God first
- Never have the first argument with your wife
- Put your wife on a pedestal
- A penny saved is a penny earned
- A team can accomplish more than a talented individual
- God can do more with your 90% than we can with a 100%
- Set goals and go after them
- Cease striving after wealth

Some of these sayings are Scripture and some are things we pick up from parents, mentors, teachers, and others. We must make sure that they are true, and we must hang on to them so that they will guide us when we don't know what decision to make. We can then pull out these bits of wisdom from our memory bank and apply them to the triple-win grid and the current situation and see if they fit.

Jesus gives us a helpful corrective about these bits of wisdom. Not all of the slogans of wisdom that we have rattling around in our brains are actually wisdom. They may, in fact, be the opposite of wisdom. Jesus says, "If the light that is in you is darkness, how great is the darkness." In other words, if every time you dip inside yourself for a bit of wisdom to help you in a certain situation and the wisdom that you pull up is actually wrong, then you are going further afield when you do what you think is wise. Let me give you some examples.

- Let's say that you are playing a game and you wonder which move to make. Up pops the slogan "Winning isn't everything; it's the only thing." You let that idea guide you to be ruthless in some game so that you can win, but you lose the respect of the people you are playing with.

- Let's say that you are in your 20's and you are at a party and there is an attractive young lady who seems to be interested in you. You are not all that interested in her, and you do not see a long-term future with her at all. You dig into your bag of wisdom and up pops, "You only go around once in life, so go for the gusto" This tells you to fake interest in the young lady at the party because you don't want her interest to be wasted.

There are hundreds of these little bits of bad wisdom floating around in every culture. They turn us aside from righteousness and the blessings of God.

One of the things that we have to make sure that we gather is actual wisdom and not pithy slogans from our culture that are actually bad advice.

The other thing that David told Solomon was that he should acquire understanding or insight. This is the Hebrew word *bin*. The word means to discern between and to grasp the connections. I am amazed at the number of times people miss the obvious connections between things and then are baffled why they have problems.

Let me give you a few examples:

- There is a connection between what you eat and what you look like and weigh. All kinds of people do not see the connections between the amount of food they are consuming and the way they look, feel, and perform. There are only a few people who can eat everything and not gain weight. These people have different connections and problems, but we want to make them the norm.

- There is an absolute connection between what we say to people and whether we are close friends and they like us. But I watch people say the rudest things to their spouse, their children, their colleagues and expect to have a good relationship with these people. I watch people treat clients, customers, and strangers with kinder words and better manners than the people closest to them. The people closest to you should receive the kindest words from you.

It is entirely possible that David is saying to Solomon to memorize these pithy sayings in which is contained the collected wisdom of our civilization and culture and those of other cultures. For this is clearly what Solomon did. He collected the wisdom literature, committed it to memory, and even himself wrote and spoke thousands of proverbs – some of which were inspired by God.

David, the father of Solomon and the prophet of God, was telling Solomon that one does not have to learn by experience; one can grow beyond his peers – and even the leaders – by committing to memory the counterintuitive directives of life.

PROVERBS 4:6 - *Do not forsake her, and she will guard you; love her, and she will watch over you.*

This proverb takes the collective actions, statements, and choices of wisdom and groups them together as if they were a person. This collective wisdom is then seen as a woman. Solomon is trying to get us to realize that like a spouse, there are two specific actions that we can take toward wisdom that will be very positive and beneficial to our life. In a sense he is saying that we should act like we are married to this collective body of wisdom, and that we want a growing relationship with her.

There are two actions we must take, and there are two benefits that will come from the growing relationship with wisdom.

The first action is to stay faithful or not to forsake her. *Forsake* is the Hebrew word *azab* which means to depart, to abandon, to lose. Wisdom is not to be something that we date occasionally, but the greatest benefit will come to our lives if we make a permanent commitment to go after the triple-win solution all the time. To, in a sense, say "I will make sure wisdom is pleased with my choices and actions." In the same way that a great marriage has two people who really seek to please each other in how they act and how they live, so with wisdom. Business marriages ask the question what do I want to do or what will she/he allow me to get away with. This kind of thinking sees the other person as a restrictor on your life instead of one of the center energizers of your life.

Great marriages do not try and get away with selfishness that their spouse will allow; they try and please their spouse and find their connection to joy and pleasure through their spouse.

Too many people treat wisdom as an occasional date. This time I will date wisdom and make a wise choice, but I want my freedom to be selfish anytime I want. This type of thinking is what Solomon is trying to rule out. In one sense Solomon is saying, "Before you ever get married to a person, get married to wisdom!!" And do not cheat on her.

The benefit of staying faithful to wisdom is that she will guard you. The word *guard* means exercise great care over. It is this idea that is a mirror image of the marital relationship that seems to be in view here. The benefit of faithfulness is greater connection and attention from wisdom. There is an idea here – and in other places in Proverbs and in the Old Testament – that wisdom has a cumulative effect in which a safe zone is built around you where some level of the accumulating problems of life and civilization, in general, will not reach you. The idea is that if you consistently make the wise choice which promotes the good for God, others, and yourself, you will have strong allies and people who will want you to succeed. The sum total of the wisdom that you have done over time will rise up and protect you. This is not true if you only occasionally date wisdom. In other words, if you occasionally do a wise thing but do not adopt a wise lifestyle, you will not see this cumulative "force field" of wisdom protecting you.

love her, and she will watch over you
This is a second action and benefit, but it is really a mirror image of the first. Solomon is not just saying, "Stay committed to wisdom and don't be unfaithful." He is saying, "Find your joy in serving wisdom. Go after wisdom as the center of your life. Seek to please wisdom with your choices and actions."

Great marriages are produced when both parties think through the decisions they are about to make and/or actions they are about to do and ask themselves: Will this please my spouse? Will this meet the needs of my spouse? Does this allow me to connect more closely to my spouse? Regular marriages and okay marriages do not have this focus.

It is this kind of thinking that Solomon is asking us to engage in with wisdom. It is like looking over at this person called wisdom and seeing if she would be pleased before you make a decision. Would she be delighted with what you are about to do?

When you act selfishly and, therefore, foolishly, you are being unfaithful to wisdom and trampling on the growing relationship with wisdom.

The Hebrew word translated *watch over* is the word *nasar* which means watch, guard, keep. It is very similar to the word guard from the first part of this proverb. The idea is that when a strong relationship is built between wisdom and the individual – wisdom as a growing accumulation in the individual's life attends to the person, interacts with the individual, and keeps them out of trouble. Wisdom provides a buffer around them so that trouble does not reach them.

I see one type of this result regularly in the news. A shooting occurs at a night club – if the person had not been at the night club, they would not have been shot. There is an altercation at a bar or other undesirable place – if they had not been at that place, it would not have occurred. There is usually a choice to be selfish or foolish at some earlier point that got them to the place where harm could come to them. Now it is not that the wise person sits in a locked, protected room all the time; but their thoughts are oriented to wisdom, to pleasing others, to pleasing God, and not just themselves. The places they go and the things that they do are different.

PROVERBS 4:7 - *The beginning of wisdom is: acquire wisdom; and with all your acquiring, get understanding.*

The beginning of being wise is the realization that you need to acquire more applied knowledge. Knowledge is not sufficient in itself. Notice that the writer of the book of Proverbs wants you to understand that you need wisdom and not wealth, not fame, nor power, or any of the things that people traditionally want. You want wisdom.

Wisdom is the triple-win. It is applied knowledge. It is understanding the goal of life – relationships that God has told us are the point of our existence and the purpose of our existence is to love God and to love others. This makes relationships the most important. We are truly searching for depth of relationships. That is why it takes wisdom to achieve the goals of life. If you have wisdom, then you have the applied choices and information necessary to maintain great relationships. You understand the connections between seemingly random and disconnected events and circumstances.

Solomon yells at us: Understand what the point of life is – go after strong relationships! You can take shortcuts to other activities and goals but when you get there without relationships, then it is empty and hollow. But if you gain the deep connection and love of God and others and also the other things, then you are truly rich.

The beginning of wisdom is to understand what knowledge should be applied to produce. Strong relationships – not who is right in a particular situation; not who was funnier; not more money, power, fame, pleasure, etc; but stronger righteous relationships.

PROVERBS 4:8 - *Prize her, and she will exalt you; she will honor you if you embrace her.*

This proverb is further incentive to walk the path of wisdom. The path of wisdom is not as bombastic as the path of foolishness, but it is worth it. You will be exalted and you will have high value if you choose to walk this path.

prize

This is the Hebrew word *salal* which means to lift up, to exalt, to prize, to cast up. Clearly the idea in this proverb is that one should lift up wisdom as the sought-after commodity. Wisdom is not something that you hope you stumble across, but instead it is the highest prized thing at each decision point.

If people will not treat their decisions as little things and will not just do what comes easy or natural, they will be fulfilling this verse. At every decision point it becomes easy to settle for what feels right instead of looking hard for the triple-win solution. Don't fall for this. Keep digging, keep thinking, keep talking to others until it is clear what wisdom would do.

How valuable you treat wisdom is how valuable you will become.

exalt

This is the Hebrew word *rum* which means lofty, be lifted high, rise up. In other words, when you lift up wisdom, wisdom will lift you up. There is a payoff for being wise. It only makes sense that when you work hard at doing what brings God glory, what causes others to win, and what brings you a win that God and others will lift you up. This is what Solomon is pointing out.

The opposite is also true, but it does not seem true at the time. If you take the fool's road and go after what you want but it costs other people or uses other people and violates God's standards, then those two groups will bring you down. You may seem like you get ahead for the short term, but long term you are digging your own grave.

Let's talk about how you actually prize wisdom. It means that you take the time before you make a final decision or action and list out all the options that could be done in a given situation. You most likely – with big decisions – will ask for counsel of others; what options and possibilities do they see that you don't see. You will also spend time praying about it, seeking God's face and asking Him to make it clear what you should do. Over a process of time it will become really clear what you should do if you were to be wise. Then you should do it. This process slows decisions down, but your mistakes go down and you begin to build trust in other people's eyes and favor in the eyes of God.

honor

This is the standard Hebrew word for honor – *kabed* – which means to be heavy, great, glorious, rich. The idea is that the person is substantial and highly valuable and that that value is clearly known.

We, in our culture, have settled for being known instead of being honored. Much of our culture clamors for being famous and not for any contribution they would make but just because they want to be popular. Fame is not honor and is a cheap inadequate substitute for honor. So what if lots of people know you. In fact, to be famous is a prison where you cannot go out without being accosted and followed. But to be honored is to have it be known the significant contribution that you have made through your choices and actions. It is this that Solomon is directing us toward. Push hard to make a significant contribution to the lives of those closest to you and you will be highly valued. Don't strive to be known by people you will never meet. Constantly ask yourself how you can bring about a win for the various relationships in your life while building a win for yourself. When you have your answer, then you have wisdom and your honor is on its way.

embrace

This is the Hebrew word *habaq* which means embrace or fold. This is a word used to express a high level of love and affection. Solomon is saying that you have to begin a love relationship with wisdom. You cannot just occasionally interact with wisdom – its nuances and insights will escape you. Embrace wisdom as you would the perfect woman/man who is offering themselves to you. Begin a long-term relationship with wisdom. It will be well worth it.

I watch as young people are presented with opportunities, and they lack the grid or filter to separate the good opportunities from the bad ones. The good ones come disguised as work in submissive positions, but their upside is huge. The bad ones offer pleasure, power, and ease right away. Please add the wisdom filter and process to your decision making. Does God win here, do others I care about win here, do I win here? This wisdom filter will be your friend if you embrace it.

PROVERBS 4:9 - *She will place on your head a garland of grace; she will present you with a crown of beauty.*

Solomon continues here with the benefits of wisdom. Following God's will and wisdom is not just for celebrating in heaven. It has practical benefits here in this life.

garland of grace

The Hebrew word for garland is *livyah* which means wreath or garland. It clearly refers to a crown or decoration about the head.

crown of beauty

The Hebrew word for crown is *atarah*. It also means wreath. It is clear that both of these references are to the same thing – a decoration about the head which suggests honor, privilege, prestige.

Everyone in every culture has a picture of what success looks like to them. In our culture if you are an athlete, it may be a championship ring or it may be being able to dress a certain way or have a certain look. In Solomon's day – as in many cultures – there were crowns or wreaths of privilege, position, and wealth. These laurel crowns signified that a person had made it to the pinnacle of this life. They were enjoying the success that everyone wanted. Solomon borrows from this imagery and says that it is wisdom that will gain you this "look." If you want to be successful and have the look of the one who has arrived enjoying all the perks of success, then push hard to grasp wisdom.

It may seem like being selfish and going after what you want is the ticket to gaining success in this life; it is not. It is wisdom that will surround your life with the look of a champion.

PROVERBS 4:10 - *Hear, my son, and accept my sayings and the years of your life will be many.*

Solomon is declaring what sounds like a supermarket tabloid promise: LONG LIFE. What he is saying is that there are numerous roads of foolishness that will present themselves through the course of your life. Each one of these in some way shortens your life. If you allow yourself to be seduced to follow your selfishness, then to some measure your life will be shortened. Your choices matter - embrace wisdom. Dig for the triple-win choice and action, and then you will have extended your life to the longest possible for it will not be shortened by moral foolishness.

Solomon is selling us on why we should embrace wisdom as a way of life. Its rewards are more long-term and more hidden than the immediate promises of the fool's choices. He is telling us, in various ways, that it will pay off to go this way. He is saying that this is the secret rule from the one who made the universe. If you go for the win that gives everyone else a win as well, then you will have a myriad of rewards – one of which is longer life.

How is it possible for our life to lengthen when God knows everything about our life from its beginning to its end? The biblical understanding is that God knows the day you will die and everything you will do. He also knows the day you will die if you take any one of the thousand choices that will be available to you this month. In Matthew 12, Jesus tells us that God knows the possibilities that flow from every possibility. From our end there is variability to the length, blessing, and honor of our life. From God's end He knows what will happen if we take any one of the millions of different paths we will have the opportunity to live out. If we choose wisely we, in essence, lengthen our life. We have changed our destiny from our point of view by our choice even though God knew that before you chose it. It is a real choice for us; it is foreknown by God. So choose wisely and bring rewards to yourself, your family, your community of faith, and your society.

PROVERBS 4:11 ~ *I have directed you in the way of wisdom; I have led you in upright paths.*

There are, in this verse, two keys to effective teaching and parenting. First, Solomon says that he directed his son and mentors in the way of wisdom. He was there, pointing out the right way. He did not just leave it to others to point out the choices of wisdom. He made it clear that wisdom would do this or that, rather than what the fool would do.

We all need a good mentor or parent who will actually show us how the world works. We need someone who will direct us in the right way. It is a sad situation that this so rarely happens any more. This is what a father does or what a father figure does. He takes leadership in the young person's life and points out the right way. This direction is more than just talk; it must entail practice and communication and correction.

We must realize that none of us naturally wants to follow the path of wisdom. We all have the principle of selfishness in us that wants to gratify ourselves immediately and first. It is this tendency to foolishness that must be overcome with good mentoring and leadership so that we can see clearly that what we think we want initially is so often the fool's gold of selfishness.

PROVERB 4:12 - *When you walk, your steps will not be impeded; and if you run you will not stumble.*

This proverb is about the ways that we are stopped when we do not have wisdom. We are impeded or we stumble. Something blocks us or in some way we are tripped up.

What is blocking you from really having smooth sailing in your business or marriage or other aspects of your life? It has to do with a lack of acquisition of wisdom. Why did you stumble and fall flat on your face in some aspect of your life? It has to do with a lack of wisdom or understanding in your life. You did not choose the everybody-wins action or did not embrace the connections and relationships between things.

impeded

The word *impeded* is the Hebrew word *tsarar* which means enemy or distress or to make narrow, trouble, bind up, tie up, adversary. Notice the richness of this idea in the original Hebrew. Solomon is telling us from 3,000+ years ago under the inspiration of God that when you acquire wisdom and act out of it, you will avoid many, if not most, of the distresses or adversaries of life. He is suggesting that much of the trouble we encounter in life is because of our own foolishness. We have been selfish, impulsive, or rebellious. We have not been willing to listen or act in accordance with wisdom and understanding. We can smooth our road so much. It does not have to get so narrow constantly.

Think through the trouble, the stress, the narrowing, and the blockages in your life. Is it in your finances, in your career, in your marriage, in your family, with your friendships, with your church, in your relationship with God? Is it because you have not been wise? There is a choice out there that will open up the path in your life. It is a win for all the righteous people involved. God will win, righteous people will win, and you will win. It is not your first choice because it is not a selfish win. It is a long-term win for you. It is a faith choice for you. Usually you have to trust God that the rewards will come around to you longer term. The wise choice can feel like a giving up or giving away control. God is telling us that you have to make choices that are counter-intuitive to you at times. They may not "feel" right to you, but they are clearly wise. Everybody can see it but you, usually.

We are most often impeded, distressed, blocked, and squeezed by our own choices, actions, and lack of wisdom. Choose wisely and the world will open up for you.

stumble

The Hebrew word translated *stumble* is the word *kasal* which means stumble, totter, stagger from weariness, weakness, or even from fleeing under attackers. It can mean ruined, fall, feeble, overthrown, even decayed.

What is interesting here is that this stumbling, falling, weariness, and/or weakness takes place when you are running or trying to make lots of progress in a particular direction – either away from an adversary or toward a goal. In the first part of this proverb you were just living life; walking in the path of life and you were blocked. In this example of what happens when you have wisdom, you are beginning to make significant progress or escape the clutches of a difficult adversary. If you have wisdom and understanding, you will not be tripped up. You will not fall and be ruined. The progress will take place. You will get away. Weariness or weakness will not sabotage the pace you are developing.

I think of business leaders who are growing a business and have wisdom to understand when to hire, when to step aside, and when to let someone else handle an area or problem. I have watched too many businessmen and spouses and family members who have begun to make progress out of the chaos of their past only to be ruined or tripped by their own selfish choice in that they were not willing to listen to the help of others. The choice that felt right to them was not the right one.

Ask the question: Am I being impeded or blocked in some aspect of my life? If I am, then it is almost always a lack of wisdom or understanding. Look for the wisdom choice or action. Look for the interaction between things that you did not see before. Right when I was making real progress in my life, did I stumble? Does it keep happening at about the same place? Then my ruin is the result of a foolish choice or action that needs to be different next time.

Let's get specific here. When does the diet always fail? At what point does the budding relationship come apart? When does the interaction with the kids or your parents turn hostile? At what point do you get passed over for the promotion? At what point of the month do you run out of money consistently? At what point does your connection to God stall or get too hard? At what point do you always get tempted to drink or do drugs or wallow in pornography? At what point do you begin to get away from that bad person in your life but then give in to their pleadings to give them one more chance?

When you examine the answers to these questions, you will usually find that the answer is a choice or action that you consistently make which feels right to you but always spells your doom. Start making a different choice. Acquire wisdom. Acquire understanding.

PROVERBS 4:13 - *Take hold of instruction; do not let go. Guard her, for she is your life.*

This is an interesting proverb because it emphasizes something in the original that is lost in the translation. Solomon gives us crucial insight into how life works. If someone has the courage to correct us or punish us, we should take this in and make sure that we don't make the same mistake again.

hold

This is the Hebrew word *hazaq* which means to be strong or to strengthen. The translators felt like it would not make much sense to say, "Strengthen yourself in instruction" or "Be strong in the instruction that you received," so they translated it "Take hold of instruction."

instruction

This is the Hebrew word *musar* which means discipline, chastening, correction. This gives a different spin on the verse. It is talking about where you have been rebuked, corrected, or punished for doing something wrong. It is in these areas that you must make yourself strong. Don't ignore the lessons that people have had the courage to give you. Many people will let you make mistakes over and over again with no correction until an ultimate blow. So when you have been corrected about something, make sure that you take that in and change so that that problem is no longer a problem.

guard

This is the Hebrew word *natsar* which means to watch, guard, to keep. The idea is that you should make sure that you don't make the same mistake twice. God allowed you to be corrected for a reason. Tuck away the lessons of what you learn the hard way by messing up and do not forget them.

life

This is the Hebrew word *hayay* which means live, be alive, have life, life. The point of using this word seems to be that joy and sustained prosperity lie in paying attention to what you were corrected for, not in ignoring it and doing what you want. The opposite of doing what this proverb suggests is rebellion, which is death.

Solomon is saying in a very positive way: Don't be a rebel. Embrace the lessons that came from making mistakes. Don't forget where you have been corrected. As you grow up you will be collecting bits of important wisdom. Some of your most important are those places where people have corrected, rebuked, disciplined, or even punished you for doing something wrong or incorrect. Don't forget those places.

This verse suggests that, at times, we will be tempted to repeat a mistake we have already made. Don't pay dumb tax twice.

PROVERBS 4:14 - *Do not enter the path of the wicked and do not proceed in the way of evil men.*

There are at least ten entrances to the path of the wicked. Each one of the Ten Commandments marks a doorway to wickedness. In each one of these cases God is saying: "Don't even start down that road."

This seems like such an obvious lesson, but it needs to be repeated and emphasized over and over again. Just to begin down the pathway of wickedness is a problem. It doesn't seem so bad when it starts: so I curse a little – it actually feels good; so I had sex before I got married – it actually was liberating; so I stole something from the store – nobody will notice; so I lied to my teacher – he wanted to know too much anyway; so I got mad and hit someone – it was the only way to get through to this person; so I spent a lot of time thinking about being with my friend's spouse – it doesn't hurt anyone;

The beginning of the path of wickedness is where selfishness becomes significantly destructive to others, God's glory, and even yourself. Realize that God gave us the Ten Commandments so that we would not destroy ourselves with our own selfishness. Each of the commandments is a societal stop for selfishness. These are the beginning of wickedness.

This proverb is trying to warn young people that there are people out there who have dedicated themselves to getting what they want and pursue their own selfishness with such reckless abandon that they will use, damage, and even destroy you if you get in their way. These evil people have a way about them – a pathway to their evil. Don't learn the art of getting what you want without rules. There are rules to the game of life. Solomon is trying to warn young people that it is radically tempting to just go after what you want and through any means, but it will not pay off in the end. It will surround you with sorrow, coldness, loneliness, and broken relationships even while you hold what you went after in the first place. So Solomon screams to us, "Don't even get started on that path!"

It is one thing to be selfish inside the boundaries of the Ten Commandments, but it another thing entirely to unleash your selfishness to go beyond the boundaries of the Commandments in the pursuit of whatever you want.

You will not find what you really want and need out there. If right this week, as you are reading this, you are facing temptation to go after something or someone you want but you have to go outside of God's boundaries of right and wrong, just stop and repeat this verse: *Do not enter the path of wicked and do not proceed in the way of evil men.* Repeat it five times.

You may be reading this today because today or later this week you will be presented with an opportunity to get something you always wanted; you just have to compromise and sin in one little small area. Stop and repeat this verse. Don't give in and grasp your dreams through the means of wickedness. They will turn into nightmares.

PROVERBS 4:15 - *Avoid it, do not pass by it; turn away from it and pass on.*

This is a foreign concept to our culture. We believe that all knowledge should be known. We believe that endless curiosity is a good thing. We cannot imagine that there are whole categories of information that we should not know anything about. But Solomon and the rest of the Bible say that there are categories of information that it is best to not understand. These are the categories of wickedness.

God suggests here that wickedness has a corrupting influence that goes beyond just those who actually do wickedness. It reaches out to those who just stand by and watch. Those who learn about it become seduced by its power and effect. It is a corruption.

avoid

This is the Hebrew word *para* which means to let alone, avoid, let go. The idea here is to give the wicked a wide berth. Those who go outside the boundaries of the Ten Commandments to accomplish their selfish purposes without remorse or retreat are wicked.

Solomon sees this as a category of behavior. It is selfishness raised to an exponential level. I want what I want and I don't care who gets hurt or what I have to do to have what I want. He says to avoid it because it is powerful. It will reach out from its place and draw you in. Avoid it.

pass by

This is the Hebrew word *abar* which means to pass over, through, by, on. The idea here is to not stop if you are near the opening to wickedness. Don't stop. When those choices that are wicked present themselves, just keep moving. Don't even stop and wonder what it would be like to do them. Don't stop and contemplate how to be wicked. Just keep going mentally, emotionally, and physically. If you spend too much time focusing on what you think you will gain on the way to be wicked, you stand a very good chance of going down this ruinous path. Remember, it starts out with lots of gain, but it is eating away at your soul and your meaning in life.

turn away

This is the Hebrew word *satah* which means to turn aside. The idea here is when you are going along in life with various choices available to you, there will come times when a wicked choice presents itself: The chance to lie and become a liar; the opportunity to enter into an adulterous relationship; the chance to steal; the chance to have the cool relationship with someone who worships another god. Solomon says while these things are tempting, turn away from these choices. You won't be making progress. You will be damaging the positive life God has planned for you.

Unfortunately I have watched people reject Solomon's counsel here and greedily go down the path of wickedness to get what they want. They lie, they steal, they blaspheme, they fornicate, they use violence, they worship false gods. It doesn't take long for a person to be held in the prison of sin when they pursue their goals through wickedness. I have watched young men throw away college educations, careers, and the respect of their family. I have watched dads and moms shatter their families, their reputation, and their careers because they thought they could gain from wickedness.

Avoid it, pass by, turn away. It is a seductive opportunity that looks like a short cut. But it is a short cut to destruction. It is climbing aboard a wild tiger. Wherever you think you are going is not where you will end up. And you will be consumed in the process.

PROVERBS 4:16 - *For they cannot sleep unless they do evil; and they are robbed of sleep unless they make someone stumble.*

This verse forms the first part of the warning Solomon has for those who come across the path of evil and those that take that path. He has said to avoid these shortcuts to the good life. They are destructive to your significance and meaning. He says that if you turn into their ways, then you will very likely be the person who they make stumble. These people see the world as a contest in which one person loses and one person wins. So, therefore, if they make you lose, they believe they have won. They do not believe in the everybody-wins philosophy. In fact, most of them would consider the win of an everybody-wins philosophy a loss .

sleep

This is the Hebrew word *yashen* which means to sleep. Their mental worldview is completely consumed with one person wins and another person loses. If they do not gain through making another person lose, then they believe that somehow they have lost.

Solomon is saying to avoid these people because even if you are on their team, they will need to make you lose so they can win. They actually stay up at night thinking of ways to harm others so they can get ahead. This is the definition of unethical practices: harming others so that personal benefit can come to me.

Evil is not just that which is emotionally reprehensible; it is any action in which I must harm others for personal gain or benefit. We do not have to be shocked to see that something is wrong. In fact, when we see evil operate enough, we will no longer be shocked by it. But it is still wrong. This is why the Lord gave us the Ten Commandments – to declare clearly where the moral boundaries of harm begin.

stumble

This is the Hebrew word *kashal* which means to stumble, to stagger. Again Solomon is pointing out the system that those who play on the evil side of the tracks have completely embraced: "I can only win if you lose. Therefore I must make you stumble or fall or lose in order for me to be a winner."

Solomon is trying to frighten you into avoiding this whole scene. You don't have to be connected to this group or this mentality. When evil presents itself as a viable alternative, don't go there. When the chance to steal from the company comes, don't. When the chance to commit adultery comes, don't. When the chance to get your way through violence or intimidation comes, walk away. When the opportunity to profit through lying comes, keep your mouth shut or tell the truth. When the chance to get ahead by forgetting or avoiding worshipping God comes, worship God and "lose" the time.

PROVERBS 4:17 - *For they eat the bread of wickedness and drink the wine of violence.*

Solomon continues with his descriptors of those who walk about in the wrong path.

wickedness

This is the Hebrew word resha which means wickedness, evil, ill-gotten. The boundaries of wickedness are the Ten Commandments. The person who begins breaking the Ten Commandments to get what they want and no longer even feels the guilt or shame or wrong of it, is wicked.

Many young people learn the power of lying, the power of stealing, the power of sex outside of marriage, the power of violence and intimidation, and they like how powerful they feel as teens and young adults. What they seldom figure out is that they are letting what they could become slip away while they feel powerful. Being great in high school only lasts four years and then you have to go on and make something of yourself. I have watched as men and women are still living for high school 20 years later.

violence

This is the Hebrew word *chamas* which means violence, wrong. No amount of force is too great if it gets them what they want. It is not that they are necessarily prone to violence; it is just that they will not rule it out. If it gets them what they want, then they are more than happy to use violence, force, and intimidation.

Do you know people who get their way through physical intimidation or actual physical violence? Begin moving away from that kind of person if it is at all possible. They are participating in wickedness rather than righteous dialogue. It is only a matter of time before their intimidation and violent ways are turned against you.

I have seen the tragedy of this in so many boyfriend and girlfriend relationships. The fellow is all cool and tough and strong. The young lady thinks that this is great because he is the meanest and most respected. But eventually he will turn his intimidating ways on her and it will no longer be cool.

Notice that Solomon sees this as the wine of violence. They become drunk on the power of violence to get what they want. It becomes so intoxicating that they act this way all the time.

Recognize the signals of undesirable people no matter what they tell you about themselves or who recommends them. If they have these characteristics, then get away from them.

PROVERBS 4:18 - *But the path of the righteous is like the light of dawn, that shines brighter and brighter until the full day.*

Solomon reminds us of the nature of wisdom – it keeps getting better in contrast to the way of selfishness which just keeps getting worse. If you give into wisdom and follow its direction, then the choices that you make will lead you in the direction of stronger relationships and a fuller life as time goes on. But if you live for yourself and maximize your pleasure in your teens and twenties, then you will increase the destruction in your life even while you are living at the edge of pleasure.

The path of wisdom takes longer to get going; but it has richer, deeper, and more long-lasting benefits. You never hear someone who has chosen the path of wisdom say, "I wish I had not chosen this path." You do hear people who chose the path of foolishness say, "I wish I had not made the choices that I made." Unfortunately we are creating a culture in which being a pleasure-seeking rebel is promoted.

like the light of dawn
Clearly the idea here is that the path of wisdom starts slowly. The light of dawn is gradual and slowly increasing, Solomon notes that through the slow creep of time the choices that you make to begin the path of wisdom begin to bring increasing amounts of light to your life. It is not instantaneous. It is not necessarily a stark contrast from one moment to the next as you begin to make wise choices instead of foolish ones. Some people expect the heavens to open and everything to change with the first wise, triple win choice. Solomon reminds us that it is not like that.

The cataclysmic changes come in the way of foolishness. You can pursue pleasure and selfishness and be overwhelmed at the raw feelings of satisfying yourself – it is cataclysmic change. Then if what you have done is illegal, there is the cataclysmic change of being caught. Or if what you did to pursue pleasure was just significantly selfish, there is the cataclysmic change in damage you have done to your relationships.

shines brighter and brighter

Solomon is trying to inject the raw truth that wisdom takes a while to really make a hugely noticeable difference to the broader outlines of your life. Your life does not change dramatically if you follow wisdom; it begins to get incrementally better. You still work where you work; you still have the same relationships that you had. Small changes all over your life begin to show up and eventually the wise choices that you make bring dramatic differences between where you are and where you would have been if you had continued to live foolishly.

There will come a day when wisdom is shining strong in your life, and it is obvious that you are in a completely different place than you were when all you thought about was what you wanted and what would make you feel good. It is that day when you can see the radical difference between the path of wisdom and the path of foolishness.

What is interesting is that many people may not realize all the significant decisions that you made to arrive at the place of full, bright wisdom; all of the choices to honor God; to cause others to win; to lower the maximum win for yourself to a much longer-term win. They may just think that you were lucky. They may believe that you were always a person who acted in this self-effacing way, but you will know the difference. It may even be helpful to think back and project what your life would be like if you had not changed to wise choices and wise acts. Then praise God for the benefits of wisdom.

PROVERBS 4:19 - *The way of the wicked is like darkness; they do not know over what they stumble.*

Solomon gives brilliant insight into what happens when people choose the shortcut called wickedness. They lose the ability to connect the dots. They no longer can admit or see that things are connected. The fact that they have a mistress should not affect their marriage. In fact, in their understanding, it should help their marriage. The fact that they are stealing from their company should not impact whether they get promoted because nobody knows or cares about the things they are stealing. The fact that they are consumed with themselves and are immoral has nothing to do with the fact that their children don't feel close to them or that their children are experimenting with drugs and alcohol.

darkness

This is the Hebrew word *aphelah* which means darkness, gloominess. Solomon is accurately pointing out that wickedness is a place of little understanding. It is a relational, spiritual, and mental darkness. Wickedness is full of impulsiveness. What do I want next? I don't care what direction it is in as long as I can satisfy my desires. It is a terrible thing to not see the bigger picture of what is happening in and around your life. It is tragic to not realize how things connect. The lousy job you have is because you did not get the training and education you needed because you dropped out to party and sleep in. The lousy marriage you have is because all you think about is what your spouse can do for you instead of what you can do for your spouse as well as the fact that any time you are not pleased, you have an affair with the first available person. The lousy house you live in is because you can't get a good job because you are so good at lying that it is easier to lie than to do the work, so you usually get fired. The wicked never make these kinds of connections. They blame their spouse, their boss, the company, God, the politicians, etc. It is never their own fault.

stumble

This is the Hebrew word *kashal* which means to stumble. It is translated by words or phrases like: bring you down, downfall, fail, overthrown. The picture that Solomon is painting is of people in a pitch-black room trying to move around. They just keep bumping into things that they cannot see and then falling over. They chase a little light over in the corner of the room because it is pretty. It doesn't give any light into the room, but you can see it; therefore, you trip over everything between you and the light. The world of wickedness is like this. You begin chasing one desire after another and cursing the world God made for getting in your way. The hallways and furniture of life are not designed to allow you to pursue your desires without limit.

It is like all of the furniture is arranged for going north or south but the light is in the west, so you bump into every chair, sofa, coffee table, and lampstand because you must get to the light rather than understanding that all the hallways run north and south. All the hallways of the world you live in keep wanting you to pursue a different goal, but you don't want to realize that; you want what you want and so you keep stumbling and tripping and falling.

One day God will turn on the light of judgment day and you will realize that you have been a fool.

PROVERBS 4:20 - *My son, give attention to my words; incline your ear to my sayings.*

Solomon is issuing a call to embrace wisdom rather than to follow what your own desires or others tell you. He has distilled the wisdom of horizontal relationships into these proverbs and on top of that, the inspiration of God is on him to do it. That which was wrong was left out and that which was right was put in. God saw to that.

This section that we enter at verse 20 switches from warning to specific instruction about each of the parts of your body that connect you to the larger world: mind, mouth, eyes, feet, body. It is as though Solomon is saying: Let me give you basic software instructions for how to use the hardware (your body) that you have received. Do this and don't do that.

Notice the "my son" portion of the proverb. He is calling the young student to make a choice. If you are going to learn from Solomon, this is not a sampler platter. It is either you become the obedient son of a wise father or walk away. Do not try and read through the proverbs and take what you like and discard what you don't. You have come to a master teacher – a spiritual father who is prepared to guide you into the most productive, impacting, wise, and alive life possible. But you must discard what is so common in our culture: the smorgasbord approach to learning – a little from over here and a little from over there. God's wisdom comes as a complete unit.

Are you prepared to accept God as your guide for all of life? In this case He is speaking through Solomon. Buy the whole package. Let the wisdom of God control every relationship in your life. Relate to God in a biblical way. Relate to your spouse in a biblical way. Relate to your family in a biblical way. Relate to your work in a biblical way. Relate to your church in a biblical way. Relate to your money in a biblical way. Relate to your friends in a biblical way. Relate to the society at large in a biblical way. Relate to your enemies in a biblical way. We have way too much of wanting to allow the Bible to control some little religious part of our lives but not guide us in the other relationships. This is what is meant by the Old and New Testament when Jesus says: "Thou shalt love the Lord thy God with all thy heart, soul, mind and strength." Every part of life is to be submitted to Him.

PROVERBS 4:21 - *Do not let them depart from your sight; keep them in the midst of your heart.*

Solomon brings up a technique for life change that our generation does not hear often. You must repeat important material over and over again, or you will forget it and will drift back to your normal selfish mode which you were born with. Our culture is into cataclysmic change and overpowering change, but we no longer want to hear that there are some things that we will need to do every day, every week, every month if we are going to live a successful life. It is true, of course, but we don't want to hear it; so the only things we repeat every day are useless jingles from commercials and ridiculous things our impulses attach to.

We need to be repeating every day things like the Ten Commandments, The Lord's Prayer, The Golden Rule, The Ladder of Virtue, The Beatitudes, The Fruit of the Spirit. These will change our life if we focus on allowing God the Holy Spirit to develop them every day in our lives.

depart

This is the Hebrew word *luz* which means to turn aside, to depart. Solomon here is exhorting his young charges that they need to focus on the words that he is saying if they are to live securely and safely.

keep

This is the Hebrew word *shamar* which means to watch, to keep, to preserve. There is a focus on watching over something with intensity. Solomon is saying you must give your attention to the meaning of the things I am saying to you if you are to build a truly abundant life.

These are not lessons that you learn once and then never review. These lessons are there constantly and need to be reviewed constantly.

heart

Notice that Solomon uses the word *heart* or *leb* which is the standard word for the soul and spirit. The inner part of a person's being must begin to be affected by the words. If there is not penetration of the words, then it will not do you any good. This book must go deeper and change the way you think and live. The words of wisdom need to be in the nerve center of your heart and directing how you speak, act, think, and even your mental mind-set called your attitude.

Are you repeating Scripture so that you can hide it in your heart? Are the power phrases of Scripture informing how you are acting or are the lyrics from the Top 40 giving you input on what you should do?

PROVERBS 4:22 - *For they are life to those who find them and health to all their body.*

life

This is the Hebrew word *chayay* which means life, alive. Solomon states that his words contained in this book called Proverbs are more than just words. They are inspired words that will bring life to the one who understands and uses them.

Life is a gift from God and life is waiting to be lived if you grab the truths in the Word of God. Too many Christians and others are waiting for some holy zap to catapult them into some new level of living. That is not how you get there. God has given us life – first in the life and death of Jesus Christ and second in the words of Scripture. If you do not take advantage of these gifts, then they do you no good. Grab the gift of Jesus Christ and Scripture and use them every day to chart your life.

health

This is the Hebrew word *marpe* which means healing, cure, health, bringing healing. God designed the universe and human life as to how it should operate. He has given us Scripture to show us how to live the way He designed life. If you live His way, then it will bring the highest form of health that is possible for human life.

PROVERBS 4:23 - *Watch over your heart with all diligence, for from it flow the springs of life.*

watch over your heart with all diligence

Be careful about what you think about; what you allow your emotions to dwell on. You will determine your life by the things your soul does. Are they righteous or selfish? You cannot lead an unrighteous soul life without it showing up in your actual life. It is the mind, will, and emotions that bring about the real life of the person.

Think and preview and meditate on a righteous life and you will have a righteous life. Too many people spend their time scheming vengeance and bitterness and immorality and anger and greed. It corrupts their soul and then they live out of the sewer of their soul.

Clean up your thoughts and jettison unrighteous emotions and you will change your destiny.

PROVERBS 4:24 - *Put away from you a deceitful mouth and put devious speech far from you.*

Solomon continues his press for wisdom with a systematic run through the action elements of your body. He starts in the previous verse with the heart or soul or what we could call the mind and unconscious. Then he speaks in this verse about the mouth. Then in the next verse about the eyes. And then the feet are mentioned. And finally the whole body. These ideas are the main elements of a wise life.

Keep close watch over what you think about. Don't let random thoughts, fantasizes, or schemes control your mind for long sections of time.

Don't deceive with what you say. If you become known as a liar, it will destroy your potential.

Look at where you are going. Know where you are going. Make sure it is where you want to go.

Where you allow yourself to stand is crucial to the success you enjoy in life. There is a level of significant blessing for those who stay on the righteous path and do not allow themselves to be in and around evil.

Your whole body should not deviate from the wise path. This can happen by either being too strict or too loose. There is a wise path in the middle; keep your life on that sweet spot.

deceitful
This is the Hebrew word *iqqeshuth* which means crookedness, deceitful. The idea is clearly that if there is one thing that you can do to make sure that you do mess up your life with your mouth, it is use your words to deceive people. This destroys everything else you can do with your mouth.

It is interesting what Solomon does not say is the most important thing you can do with your mouth. He does not say what our modern world might think to say is the most important thing to do with your mouth: to compliment people or cast vision or state your goals or speak positive things to yourself. He says that the most significant thing that you can do with your mouth is not use it to deceive people. Your words are your reputation and avoiding the reputation as a liar is absolutely crucial.

I know some people in Christian ministry who are wonderful people and could accomplish incredible things for Christ, but they are slowly gaining a reputation of being deceptive and tricky in what they say. It is clearly holding them back, but they don't see this. Behind the scenes people just take a pass on interacting with them because there is no sense that what they say can be trusted.

The United States has even had a few presidents who have used language not to communicate but to manipulate people to their way of thinking. People began to get suspicious of the words they used as they changed the meaning of words to suit their own desires. While these men were brilliant in many areas, they did not achieve the impact that their leadership could have achieved because people saw them as deceptive.

PROVERBS 4:25 - *Let your eyes look directly ahead and let your gaze be fixed straight in front of you.*

This instruction in wisdom comes in a string of others that are for a father teaching his son. He tells the son to realize what is going into his soul; what he is thinking about and allowing himself to focus on. It is the inner part of your life that will control the kind of life you experience. He tells him to not use his words in a dishonest way to get what he wants. He tells him to be careful where he goes. You can't get in trouble if you don't go to the wrong places. And he also tells him to keep moving forward on doing righteousness. That while there are lots of interesting things that he could become involved with, don't stray from the righteous path and play at the edges of sin. In fact, when you see that something is evil or clearly on its way to evil, then you should turn away from it and you will have a much better life.

let your eyes look directly ahead
This 25th verse is in that whole idea of instructions to a son. It is really a verse that tells the young man to be careful of an overactive curiosity. There are an amazing amount of things that can take a person off the path of the straight and narrow. There are money schemes, there are women, there are organizations that promise secrets, there are conspiracies, there are theories, there are friends, there are rebels, etc. All of these are available to everyone as they go down the path of life but don't be fooled. Don't be drawn aside from doing the right thing that is right in front of you.

It is not wrong to be curious – especially about that which is righteous. But we should not be curious about what is evil or wicked or outside of the Ten Commandments. It is unfortunate that much of TV, movies, and even some of academia explore the lifestyles, consequences, and pain of those who have chosen to walk in the way of the wicked. These are all trying to make you curious about those things. The Scripture says don't do that; keep focused on the righteous pathway that God has set out for you.

The righteous pathway may, at times, look boring; but it is the sure road to a stable, enjoyable, blessed, lower-stress life. When we seek out evil, we seek out trouble and pain. It is also true that when we listen to those who have turned aside to rebellion, violence, sensuality, lying, coveting, and the like, it seems that they constantly have turmoil and pain. They will seek to draw you into the limited choices of their world. "What should I do?" they will ask you. The answer is "Repent and get back on the path of righteousness; flee from the choices of sin and your life will get easier." I am amazed at how often people want me to solve the problems of wickedness and selfishness without leaving the land of wickedness and selfishness.

PROVERBS 4:26 - *Watch the path of your feet and all you ways will be established.*

watch

This is the Hebrew word *palas* which means to weigh, to make level, to ponder, watch. The idea is that you are really thinking about where you are going to be. Start contemplating where you are going to be, not just whether you want to do some part of it.

There is an amazing number of teens who want to be with their friends at a party but do not contemplate the fact that class bullies will be there or drugs will be there or alcohol will be there or people that hate them will be there. If you only follow your desires without thinking through the whole situation, you will surely get caught in a trap that could change or end your life.

path

This is the Hebrew word *magal* or *magalah* which means the circle of the camp, the course, the path. This is not just a place that you move through; but it is the place that you pitch your tent, a place that you frequent or reside at. The environment does affect you. If it is a bad, evil, immoral environment, then you must break away or you will begin to assimilate that environment.

feet

This is the Hebrew word *regel* which means foot or feet or footsteps. The idea is if you watch where your body is, then you will be in good shape with your life. The point is that you are encased in a physical body in which your feet are the usual contact point with the planet, the circumstance, the situation, etc. If your actual individual feet are not in bad places, then neither will you be.

I am amazed at how many people want to believe that they can be in a bad place and not have it affect the real them. This is nonsense.

ways

This is the Hebrew word *derek* which means way, road, journey. This is the word that was expected previously for path. It means the journey you are on. It is literally the path through life. You and I have a choice which path we take. If we choose to avoid pitching our tent in immoral, evil, or compromising situations, then our journey through life will be much different than if we make the mistake of believing that we are not affected by our immediate environment.

established

This is the Hebrew word *kun* which means to be firm. Some have come to see this as a word which carries the idea of provision. God will provide for those who make sure that they do not pitch their tent with those who are evil. He will make sure that your journey is fully supplied.

Hebrews 12:1-3 talks about running the race that is set before us. God has a prescribed path through life that we are to run. It is a race. It is particular to us. It has difficulties and obstacles. It has opportunities for impact and significance. It is God who decides how much fame, wealth, and distance is involved in our race.

This proverb tells us not to deviate from the race that God has for us. Do not set up camp with those who are evil.

PROVERBS 4:27 - *Do not turn to the right nor to the left; turn your foot from evil.*

Every time your pathway could stray outside of the boundaries of the Ten Commandments, turn away and go a different route. It is always destruction to wander outside of those boundaries.

We always have an excuse why it is important to take the name of the Lord in vain or lie or steal or be physically violent or commit adultery or covet. But it always leads to trouble and deep damage to our relationships.

Life is about relationships – as the two great commandments proclaim: LOVE GOD and LOVE OTHERS.

Proverbs 5

PROVERBS 5:1 - *My son, give attention to my wisdom, incline your ear to my understanding;*

Solomon again emphasizes a crucial point to the man or woman who is willing to let him be their spiritual father. He has brought us various points of the wise life up to this point. Much of it has been positive in its orientation: honor the Lord; hang on to loving-kindness and truth, etc. But in this section of the proverb, Solomon – under the direction of the inspiration of the Holy Spirit – tells us one of the more difficult temptations that will come every man's way: the temptation to live a fool's life through illicit sexual activity. This particular temptation gets a lot of play in the Proverbs because it remains such a strong and lasting need and weak point – with men especially.

Men want and need physical intimacy. They also want and need emotional, mental, and spiritual intimacy. For many men, physical intimacy seems like the quickest path to have all of one's needs met. This is not true, but it seems that way especially to young men. Fornication, adultery, pornography, etc., seem like a great way to meet their need; but in reality they are get-rich-quick schemes for their soul which will bring ruin and destruction to their relationships and their soul. One does not build a great life by pursuing easy sexual relations. One builds a great life by developing discipline and sexual control and by pursuing a woman in righteousness and encouragement.

God, through Solomon, screams at us: Get ready for this temptation! It will come strong and will come often throughout your life. You must be ready for it. You must expect that the pull of this fool's pathway will seem like the right thing to do a number of times in your life. IT NEVER IS.

I have worked with a number of men and women who have committed adultery to try and meet some need in their life. It never does. It only seems like it will when you are under the cloud of emotion in the affair. Sexual foolishness and a lack of sexual discipline destroy relationships; it does not build up anyone.

God gives a whole section of advice to young people about this temptation. He details what will be said. He details what you will feel.

He details what you will feel like after it is over. He details the thinking of your unfaithful partner. All of this was written over 3,000 years ago, and it is dead-on accurate.

To pretend that this temptation will not come your way at some point in your life is naive. Get ready because it is coming. Realize just as there will be numerous schemes to separate us from our hard-earned income, so there will be schemes to separate us from faithfulness to our spouse.

It is important to say that even if one is not married – maybe never having been married – one needs to abstain from sexual unfaithfulness because you will be staying faithful to the Lord and potentially your future spouse. When you hold back from these temptations, you are demonstrating faith in God that He will find you a partner and that He has a superior life for you even if it does not include sexual relations at present.

I have had the great privilege of performing a number of weddings in which the person who is getting married presents to their beloved a purity ring that represents a pledge to save themselves for this day.

Notice that Solomon says you need to lean over and look hard at the connections that go on in this temptation. You need to understand how sexuality reaches into all areas of life and connects with men and women, with you, and with those around you.

Are you ready for these temptations – especially in the light of our culture? Are you ready for a seductive tone directed in your direction? Are you ready for someone to express real interest in you whom you know you cannot marry or cannot spend time with without restriction? Are you ready for increased pornography coming into your computer, coming across your path? How will you guard yourself against this?

PROVERBS 5:2 - *That you may observe discretion and your lips may reserve knowledge.*

observe

This is the Hebrew word *samar* which means to keep guard, observe, give heed to. This is a fascinating insight that Solomon shares in this verse. He is saying that young people can flush their ability to make their own choices and plans through sin. How many times have I watched as men and women have made idiotic decisions that don't make any sense until you factor in some relationship, some sin, some addiction, some illicit activity. They were protecting or guarding the foolish thing, the sinful thing, and flushing their own life.

Solomon is screaming at us: DON'T BE SUCKED INTO FOOLISHNESS (especially sexual foolishness)! YOU WILL FLUSH YOUR ABILITY TO CHOOSE WISELY.

discretion

This is the Hebrew word *mezimma* which means purpose or plot. This is the ability to make plans, to set goals, to make decisions both in the short term and long range. Solomon is saying that if you do not embrace wisdom, you will lose your ability to plan and make decisions. You will be robbed of your ability to make a wise decision by other factors.

The translators have chosen the word *discretion* because the English word means the ability to make responsible decisions and the power to make free decisions within an acceptable range. The idea here is that when one gives up their discretion, they no longer have the ability to make a free choice. There is someone or something that is influencing their choice so that it is no longer really free and uncoerced. In this case it means that getting involved in adultery robs one of this crucial ability.

You are no longer free because you have been hooked. You are asked to make decisions that you shouldn't even face. You feel pulls in directions that you shouldn't even be considering. You are conflicted and stretched in ways that will clearly distort your ability to make a wise decision.

Watch what you allow into your life; it may rob you of the ability to have a life – your ability to choose. Most people think they are still the captain of their ship, the king of their life; but many give away the ability to make wise choices to the vices they invite to live with them. They are held by the cords of their own sin as Solomon says at another point.

and your lips reserve knowledge

reserve

This is the Hebrew word *nasar* which means to watch, guard, keep. Solomon is saying that you will not be able to retain the knowledge you have gained or need if you continue to give in to sin. You will begin to shape the truth to fit the world you are living in – the world of self-indulgence.

knowledge

This is the Hebrew word *daat* which means information and skills. Solomon is saying that it is possible to let information and skills slip through your fingers if you get involved in adultery and other forms of foolishness.

PROVERBS 5:3 - *For the lips of an adulteress drip honey and smoother than oil is her speech;*

The key word is the word *For* – Solomon has just been telling us that one has to be careful that wisdom doesn't slip through your fingers. It is possible to be disoriented and to miss the plan that God has for you. And then he tells us the source of the disorientation: the lips of the adulteress. When you are in the midst of adulterous love, you believe the words that you are being told. They have no basis in long-term reality, but you believe them.

What is interesting is that God tells us through Solomon's words that the only antidote to those words is not to hear them and to stay far away from the door of her house. Verse 8 Even if you know all the bad things that will happen to the person who commits adultery, the promised affection is so intoxicating and disorienting that you may do it anyway if you allow yourself to be captured by the words, beauty, or touch.

It is the lips or words of the adulteress or adulterer that carry the great drawing power. The words of the adulteress always suggest that you are wanted, you are admired, you are fascinating, I enjoy listening to you talk, I could listen to you talk for hours. The fact that the adulteress has such drawing power through her words and listening ability says that these areas are huge needs for men and women. Men especially are drawn toward the person who admires them, wants them, listens attentively to them, and follows those conversations with sex. Solomon says that the power of those needs in men is so strong that it will draw men out of their marriage vows, so it is best if they never hear those words. Notice that later Solomon says to find a way to increase the depth of your relationship with your spouse. He is counseling that you find a way to have those needs met by your spouse.

It is too disorienting to have someone even pretend to meet your deepest needs. The drawing power of these needs is so strong that all your moral training can be overcome in a short period under the wonder of these needs. If one looks at the top needs of a man, six of the seven could be met in these encounters: Respect, Adaptation, Intimacy, Companionship, Attractive, Listening. These six pull too hard at the fiber of a man to resist if he has been caught by the power of her words. It is better not to even listen to the words. Stay away; you can't resist. Go home and strengthen the ties to your wife.

PROVERBS 5:4 ~ *But in the end she is bitter as wormwood, sharp as a two edged sword.*

This is the part about adultery and lust that very few men take time to think about – the end. What kind of life do any of the parties end with? It is a dismal, guilty, diseased, alienated life. Adultery always promises to bring relationship intimacy and meet a deep need, but it doesn't. It is like drinking salt water; you are only more thirsty and it begins poisoning you.

The dire consequences of adultery need to be regularly repeated. It usually causes divorce; it siphons away financial resources; it distracts attention and focus on other crucial areas thereby reducing potential and success; it usually results in diseases – in some cases sterility; it results in the background radiation of guilt and a general angst; it offers a shortcut to intimacy but instead builds a pathway around true intimacy so it is never attained; it fractures friendships; it destroys the safety of the home for spouse and children; it often damages children, significantly limiting their potential; it often throws one or both parties into poverty; it weakens moral resolve in other areas of life; etc.

Some may dismiss these consequences as "not going to happen to me," but it is clear that these consequences cluster around those who commit adultery.

It is always wise when planning your life to picture where you want to be at the end of some part of the journey. How do you get there? Well, you have to take a serious look at what each pathway will entail.

There are limitations on the pathway of righteousness, but there is also great reward. There are limitations on the pathway of sin and there is a great consequence also.

Solomon says that the affair with an adulteress woman – while she may seem very exciting and enticing at the early stages of the affair – will turn into a deeply bitter pill staining and souring your whole life. Don't go there.

bitter as wormwood

The Hebrew word for bitter is *mar* and the Hebrew word for wormwood is *laana*. The wormwood plant is known for its intense bitterness. It is referred to as hemlock in Amos 6:12 and in Revelation 8:10,11. It is represented as a star falling on the waters of the earth turning them poisonous. In Greece the people think of water with this plant in it as undrinkable.

Therefore, what Solomon is saying is that your whole life will be impacted by this act of adultery. It has a much greater impact than its actual size and duration would suggest.

I can remember talking with a woman who had grown tired of her marriage to a nice, contented, hard-working man. He still loved her, but she just wanted to experience the thrills and chills of life. She wanted to return the looks and attention of the men that noticed her. They came in for counseling and after talking to both of them at length about how to save their marriage, it became clear that she was not interested. I told her that in five or so years she would be used up and tired of the lifestyle that looked so appealing right now. She would forever break the heart of her husband and do untold damage to her two daughters. I remember telling her that there would be an awful price to pay, and she would pay a huge portion of it. She dismissed what I said, confident that her looks and her smarts would allow her to escape what I was saying. About four years later she moved back to the town where I pastored; she looked weathered and much older. I heard reports that she had been beaten by a number of the men she had taken up with. She moved back to town to be near her two girls whom she had abandoned. They wanted to have nothing to do with her. She was now stuck in a low-wage job with no husband and no prospect to trade on the looks she had used in the past.

The end of adultery is a difficult ride on a picket fence. The crop that you sowed with unfaithfulness will be reaped.

PROVERBS 5:5 - *Her feet go down to death, her steps take hold of Sheol.*

Solomon says delicately, but clearly, that spending time with an adulterous person is a sure way to shorten your lifespan. You will be dead much quicker than you would have if you had not been sexually unfaithful.

It is amazing that people are trying to be quiet about the real danger of sexually transmitted diseases. These are real problems that really will destroy you and that is not even dealing with divorce, financial ruin, reputation, and violence.

The following is a partial list of the various sexually transmitted diseases. Some of these will kill you. Some will leave you sterile, some produce great pain, some cause cervical cancer, some allow for a higher infection rate of HIV/AIDS. Do not be a fool and give into the prompting of temptation.

- Bacterial Vaginosis (BV)
- Chlamydia
- Genital Herpes
- Gonorrhea
- Hepatitis B
- HIV/AIDS
- Human Papillomavirus (HPV)
- Pubic Lice
- Syphilis
- Trichomoniasis
- Pelvic inflammatory disease (PID)

In Solomon's time the various diseases and their differences and biological footprint would have been unknown. But because of his powers of observation, he and most were aware that playing around with a morally loose man or woman would cause you to get sick and potentially to die.

He is saying that no matter how strong the impulses are, don't do it because it will change your life.

What is also nice is that Solomon does not become vulgar in his depiction of the whole process of adultery. Those who commit adultery want to glorify the details of the sinful act. Those who want to get a real picture of adultery look at the whole life.

PROVERBS 5:6 - *She does not ponder the path of life; her ways are unstable, she does not know it.*

These truths are spoken about the adulterous woman but are also true of every person who gives themselves to a form of selfishness. They have stopped pondering the path of life. Where does it end up? What is the point of life? Why am I here? What contribution am I supposed to make? Their whole focus is what they want and the particular form of foolishness that they have embraced.

ponder

This is the Hebrew word *palas* which means to weigh, balance, or make level. Clearly the translators wanted to bring out the idea of thinking and contemplation. This idea is a part of this word, but there is also the idea of action which brings balance. This woman does not balance her life. She knows that what she is doing, by committing adultery, is bringing an instability to her life. It leans her life over so that it cannot sustain itself. One cannot sustain a life in which unfaithfulness is involved. It is fundamentally unbalanced. It is like riding a car on just two wheels. This word carries the idea that this woman's life is not balanced, sustainable, level, and she likes it that way – careening from one impulsive encounter to the other and following one lustful impulse after another.

This word also suggests that there is a balance to life: a way that it is supposed to operate for long-term survival. There is supposed to be balance in the path of life. It cannot all be passion. It cannot all be sadness. It cannot all be war. It cannot all be love. As Ecclesiastes says, *there is a time for each thing under the sun...* This person who commits adultery runs after the feelings that come from lust, passion, and romance. Those are meant to be enjoyed within a long-term, committed relationship between a man and a woman called marriage.

path of life

This Hebrew phrase is more than the sum of its parts. It seems to refer to at least three ideas: One, the general way that a person should live their life; a trail marked by the boundaries of the Ten Commandments. Second, the specific destiny, good works, and plan that each individual is to do with their life. Third, the pathway that connects a person to the life that is in God. Psalm 139:24; Matthew 7:14; Psalm 16:11.

God is life. He is the source of life, and He knows the path we need to take to obtain a constant flow of life towards us. He talks about a path which you should not get off of. He talks about a balance which you should not put too much on one side or the other. In our day and age and in our culture, people have the idea that they should be able to do anything that they want to do. If I want to do it, then it is okay. They do not think about a small, narrow path that they should stay on, refusing to be drawn off that path to a phony better time.

Solomon is trying to get us to see inside the world of the person who follows their lusts. They don't see the big picture of life. They have given over control of their life to the impulses they feel. They do not think through what will happen if they commit unfaithfulness. They do not run out the consequences of their decisions. Later they are shocked by the diseases, divorce, loneliness, destruction, and lack of fulfillment that is all over their life.

There is a path that your life should take in order to maximize the gifts, talents, abilities, and dreams you have. That path is a moral path. That path leads to humility before God. That path includes impulse control and refusal to stray from God's righteous boundaries.

unstable

This is the Hebrew word *nua* which means to shake, stagger, quiver, totter, swing to and fro, etc. She is at the mercy of the latest impulse that comes her way. There is no firmness of purpose. There are no commitments that she will not do. This is the kind of person who regularly says, "It seemed like the right thing to do at the time."

The stability that Solomon does not see in this woman is what is supplied by the Ten Commandments. I will not do this or that. I can do lots of things within these boundaries, but I will not do that. This level of stability is what we need in business, in government, in the home, in Hollywood, in schools, etc. Now we have all types of people who will do what is expedient for them rather than steadfastly do what is best for the common good.

If you are willing to do just about anything that strikes you as interesting, pleasurable, or profitable, then you are unstable. In fact a great question for people is, "What won't you do?"

she does not know it

This is the most tragic part of this person's life. She is living her life based upon impulses and feelings and temptations. She has no sense that her life is out of balance or headed for trouble. She is headed for trouble and is not aware of it. It is like the person who is talking on their cell phone while driving and is headed right into another car but is too distracted by the phone.

She will be completely blindsided by the eventual breakup, by the diseases, by the lonely feelings, by the financial consequences, by the alienation of her husband's affections, by the disconnect of spiritual power and life, by the swirling emotional tornado that will come as this affair progresses and ends, by the impact of her affair in her children, by the change in her reputation, by the ease of the next affair, by other temptations that will come calling, by the need to dull the pain that is coming, by the guilt she will feel, by the stain on her soul.

There are a number of lessons here in this verse. Do not repeat the folly of this woman by being unfaithful. Do not embrace a form of selfishness which blinds you to the whole of life. Make sure that you are balancing and pondering your life. Are you fulfilling the unique calling and mission that God has given you or have you thrown it away pursuing some pleasure or pain-avoidance technique? If you are sitting in a pile of consequences from your own choices, then it is time to humble yourself before God and repent. Cry out to Him to forgive you and give you a new perspective and an ability to not give into the impulses and temptations around you.

PROVERBS 5:7 - *Now then, my sons, listen to me and do not depart from the words of my mouth.*

Solomon is practically screaming through the page: DO NOT FOLLOW YOUR IMPULSES TO LUST! It will seem like the right thing to do, but it isn't.

listen

This is the Hebrew word *shama* which means hear. This is really important, is what Solomon is saying. Just like when Christ says, "Truly, Truly..." the word *shama* is the same word used in Deuteronomy 6:4 in the great *shama*: "Hear O Israel the Lord your God is One! You shall love the Lord your God with all your heart and with all your soul and with all your might."

depart

This is the Hebrew word *sur* which means to turn aside. The idea is that you will feel an incredible pull to be taken off the straight and narrow. This will be a major struggle, but you just can't listen and turn aside to follow the impulses of lust.

Solomon is screaming verbally because he knows that your body is screaming at you to give in. When we are young - and even when we are old - it is very easy to listen to what our physical body is telling us. EAT... SIT... LUST... NAP... DRINK MORE... VENT YOUR FRUSTRATION... If we always act on what our body tells us, we will often not be moving in a spiritual direction. Your body can and will betray you. Now I know that our bodies can give us some healthy impulses like eat healthy food and get the right amount of rest. The impulses that Solomon is warning us about are those impulses that arise out of our physical bodies and our selfishness. I am talking about the impulses that come from your body to move to excess; to move to indulgence of what we know is not healthy. When you are young especially, it is very tempting to just go with what "feels" right. But that road will lead to separation from deep love and relationships. This is why Solomon always calls it death. Death is always separation.

Solomon is trying to get us to understand that there are "shortcuts" to intimacy and "cheaty" ways to what seems like love, but those workarounds never really work long term. They are like building a rocket ship with duct tape and bailing wire. The road to indulgence always leads to loneliness and despair. It is not the highway to blessing and joy that it promises. It does not matter whether the indulgence is drugs, alcohol, greed, fame, sex, or whatever; it will lead to the death of love and relationships in your life.

Solomon screams that all of us will be offered or have available opportunities to indulge. These will seem like they are the pathway to success and what you really want. They are not. Do not turn aside to these "shortcuts." Stay on the righteous road and live a truly deep and loving life. It is so worth it.

Whenever temptation comes, there is always something positive or righteous to do instead of being sexually permissive or unfaithful. Do the positive or righteous thing. It may be walking the dog or doing the dishes or writing a letter or a hundred other small but faithful things. It may seem mundane stacked up next to the "thrill" of illicit sexual pleasure but being righteous is worth it.

I have sat in my office with too many men and women who gave into the temptations of the exciting affair and came to realize too late how much they destroyed in those few moments of pleasure. In many cases they have destroyed trust that will never be rebuilt. In some cases they have destroyed the relationships with their children. In a number of cases they have picked up diseases. In many cases they have destroyed themselves financially and socially through divorce. I completely agree with Solomon - don't go down this road.

Now I have to say that God is full of grace, and He offers hope and restoration to those who have unfortunately taken this mis-step. If that is you, then embrace the grace of Christ and turn away from indulgence and lust. But if you have not done it yet, back away and do not go down that path. It is a ride on a picket fence.

PROVERBS 5:8 - *Keep your way far from her and do not go near the door of her house,*

This one verse is the command in this whole section on dealing with lust, adultery, fornication, and prostitution. Don't be anywhere near her or her dwelling place. Lust is a sin of proximity. All young men will feel it, but they must not act upon the opportunities or they will destroy their future. The next few verses of Proverbs 5 discuss the consequences of giving in to the momentary delight of unbridled lust.

This is not a sin which you get strong enough to resist. Get away from her. Don't go near to her door. What is really clear is that one doesn't beat lust, one flees from it. 2 Timothy 2:22 A young man is supposed to be somewhere else doing something else.

This verse is the sum total of the commanded action to beat lust and its many helpers. Don't think that this is not significant. The battle with lust is won or lost long before one even feels the battle intensively. It is won when you plan out your day. It is won when you choose the route you will take home. It is won when you decide where to spend your free time. It is won or lost when you decide if you will go by her house.

The next few verses of the Proverb discuss the ultimate future of those who cannot control their lust; there is a groaning at the latter end. One is trying to satisfy the fire of lust and these young men think they have succeeded, but they are destroying their potential future. They are following the impulses of lust rather than strengthening the wonder of married love and family. There will be a time when the fires of lust will burn lower, and the connection with family will be what sustains and gives life meaning.

PROVERBS 5:9 - *Or you will give your vigor to others and your years to the cruel one;*

What is interesting about this proverb is that it rips the covers off of what happens when you chase after sexual pleasure. It is what you think you want. You think that you will be getting what you truly desire, but instead you will begin giving your energy and desire to others but not in a good sense – in a parasitic sense – until you realize that everything that you really wanted will not have happened. You will have wasted your years in service to the devil and your own lusts. Going after what you thought you really wanted has meant a completely different life than you wanted and that your potential suggested.

Young men, do not give in to lust. Don't chase it or let it catch you. Sexual desire is a prison that will hold you tight and not let you out. It will demand that you think its thoughts and obey its impulses even when to do so will jeopardize your job, your marriage, your family, your reputation, your freedom. If you begin to give in to the ideas and urges of sexual lust, it will redirect your life from its destiny to a different path.

vigor

This is the Hebrew word *hod* which means splendor, majesty, vigor, glory, honor. This is an interesting word to use here because it suggests that God has a plan for each person which includes their having dignity and honor and a level of majesty. Those who follow after lust, however, give away their dignity and splendor to others. The life that was to be yours becomes a sickening search for the next sexual pleasure. Sexual discipline is essential to the attainment of your fullest potential. If you want to enjoy the abundant life and plan God has for you, then learn to exercise discipline in this area. Save yourself for the lifetime commitment of marriage.

cruel one

This is the Hebrew word *akzari* which means cruel, cruelty, completely without mercy. Some would see this as a reference to the husband of the spouse you are committing adultery with. It would seem to be much more than this and refers to the being we would call the devil – the one who rejoices with each sin and seeks to increase wickedness. He seeks to own people ever more thoroughly through their addictions to sin. He has no mercy and does not let up. He continues to press the temptation until it is devoid of any meaning and you are his prisoner.

PROVERBS 5:10 - *And strangers will be filled with your strength and your hard-earned goods will go to the house of an alien;*

strangers

This is the Hebrew word *zur* which is the word stranger but also the word adulteresses. It is important to note that Solomon uses the plural form of the word to suggest that the result of the giving in to one harlot is chasing after many. Solomon is saying here – in a much more literal form – that your energy, money, and time will go in chasing after adulteresses. A man never just has one. It starts a chain of these sexual escapades that keeps you running after them like a donkey after the carrot. It always seems like the next one will be one who will really make you happy, but after awhile it will grow boring or filled with problems.

strength

This is the Hebrew word *koach* which means strength, power, ability, might, even wealth. Solomon means here that if you give into the lures of an adulteress, then it will become a convenient pathway to deal with troubles and pain. You will spend your time, energy, money, and abilities chasing sexual pleasure. One day you will wake up without anything to show for large sections of your life.

goods

This is the word *etseb* and really is the word translated by three words: hard earned goods. It means hurt, pain, toil, labor. Solomon is trying to point out the cost of what you will be giving up to go after a few moments of pleasure. He is saying that you will work hard and go through great pain to get paid and get a little ahead only to have it flow away from you to someone else after your 15 seconds of pleasure are over. Don't do it.

alien

Nokri is the Hebrew word which means foreign, alien, adulteress. The idea is of someone whom you are with that you should not be with. This person is alien to you in terms of what you are doing with her. This type of behavior is reserved for your spouse and yet you are seeking it from an alien, a stranger. If you are not married to this person, then that person is strange to you.

Solomon has said it every way he can in one verse. This person is one of many adulteresses that you will end up chasing if you go down that road. This person(s) will end up with the fruit of your hard labor. You will end up with nothing. This is nothing more than a path that promises a rich life but does not deliver

PROVERBS 5:11 - *And you groan at your final end, when your flesh and your body are consumed;*

This is the final point of the consequences that are suffered from wanton promiscuity. It all feels so right when it starts and so wrong when it comes to a conclusion. This verse points out the health consequences that are a part of this foolishness.

Your flesh and body are consumed. Solomon and others saw the devastating effects of sexually-transmitted diseases ravaging those who had played fast and loose with God's boundaries on selfishness.

In our modern world we have grown complacent to the effects of these diseases because of penicillin and other drugs, but the effects of these diseases still take a toll. And as these diseases become resistant to our drugs, they take an increasing toll.

Young people must be warned and constantly reminded that there are diseases out there that are specifically targeted to infect those who are promiscuous: Gonorrhea, Pelvic Inflammatory Disease, Syphilis, Herpes, AIDS. These, and many other diseases, will do exactly what this verse says they will do – they will consume your body and flesh. Some will make you insane; some will give you cancer; some will render you barren; some will cause you to break out with painful lesions; some will ooze and rupture parts of your body. These are not to be treated as nothing; there is a price for promiscuity. Save yourself; it is the wise thing to do.

I remember knowing a man who was in the final stages of insanity from syphilis. It was not a pretty site. He had taken the comfort of prostitutes in his younger years and was unable to obtain the drugs required to slow the advance of the disease early enough. He walked around mumbling, swinging at imaginary enemies, bumping into the walls, drooling, and being almost completely incoherent All the while his sticklike body was wasting away.

The answer is clearly lifelong commitment to one partner for sexual pleasure in a union called marriage. Sexuality is a pleasure that God gave to humanity, but he clearly states that the only container powerful enough to contain this pleasure without damaging the users is the marriage of one man and one woman.

Multiple partners open the door for flesh-consuming diseases. Do not be reduced to groaning near the end of your life, wishing you had held back from the fifteen seconds of intense illicit pleasure. Live your life fully, enjoying all the pleasure and joy that life brings using each blessing, gift, treasure, and pleasure in its God-ordained way. God is not trying to hold back on us. He is trying to have us enjoy the wonder of life without the pain.

Sexuality is like a fire and needs to be placed within the right container. Just because you are cold doesn't mean that you start a fire in the middle of the room. There would be just too much damage, and it would almost certainly get out of control and you would not be able to stop what it consumes. In the same way sexuality was meant to be contained within a lifetime commitment between a man and a woman. That is the proper fireplace to contain the fire of sexuality safely.

Any other form of sexuality is foolishness and a form of selfishness. And that selfishness – started outside of the proper fireplace or using different fuels – will damage and destroy.

It is for your protection and benefit that God puts boundaries around sexual expression. He is not trying to rain on your parade. He is saying this is how to enjoy this intense pleasure safely. Enjoy it.

PROVERBS 5:12 - *And you say, "How I have hated instruction! And my heart spurned reproof!"*

Solomon is reminding us that there will come a day when you look back at your life and notice the significant choice points. There will be a time when you will regret the shortcuts of lust or greed or violence or lying or magic. The context around this proverb is the shortcut of lust, fornication, and adultery. But all of the shortcuts to success that wander off the path of righteousness end up in the same place – the place of regret; the place of missed opportunities; the place of emotional, spiritual, mental, and even physical consequences.

Solomon is trying to paint a vivid picture of a day five to ten to twenty years in the future when you are mired in your problems and at a place you didn't expect to be. It is then that you will think how stupid you were to do what you did. Solomon is trying to get you to see yourself in the future, either rejoicing and enjoying life or hurting and reeling from the problems.

instruction

This is the Hebrew word *musar* which means discipline, chastisement, correction, punishment, warning. It has the idea of instruction but instruction after having done something incorrectly. Nobody likes to mess up and even more unpleasant is the process of being punished or corrected for messing up. But if we are to grow into maturity, we must learn how to handle correction well. You can't become successful in this life without messing up from time to time. It is crucial that you learn from those mistakes. We all have to be willing to receive correction if we are going to reach our full potential. The teenager is crippled if they cannot receive correction well. We all think we are right, and yet some of those things that seemed right will be wrong. The ability to receive the chastisement, the correction, and the punishment is the key to not making the same kind of mistake the second time.

At any age we must not be closed to correction or we will be open to huge mistakes that severely wound our lives.

reproof

This is the Hebrew word *tokechah* which means rebuke, reproof, punishment, correction. It is a synonym for *musar* which Solomon uses earlier in this verse. This word seems to be more often used for verbal rebuke and correction if a distinction can be made.

The clear import of this proverb is that one should listen to those little warnings that bring you up short from what you were thinking about doing that would have been wrong because there will come a day when you will deeply regret your actions if you ignore your mentors and the boundaries of morality that you were taught.

PROVERBS 5:13 - *I have not listened to the voice of my teachers, nor inclined my ear to my instructors!*

Everyone has those who tell them that they should not get involved with adultery and fornication. There will come a time when the person who gets involved in casual sex will regret the decisions that they have made.

Every teen has this rebel orientation to throw off the advice of their teachers, instructors, parents, and authorities. They want to believe that somehow the world is different for them. Somehow the same rules do not apply and passion really will be enough for all of life. It will not be enough.

Everyone has opportunities to betray the Lord and righteousness by slipping into a sexual relationship with someone who is not your spouse. This is always a mistake. It just feels right at the time. The few moments of passion and excitement will not recompense for the problems that are created.

There are some things that seem right but are not. Listen to the voice of God when it declares where the boundaries go. Unfortunately our society has decided to allow crossing the line of sexual faithfulness seem like no big deal. It is even promoted as something that you should do if you haven't. This is all a part of the world system that wants to blind your mind to the reality of God and His rules for a blessed life.

This proverb points to the conclusion that the old man who has pursued numerous pleasurable sexual encounters comes to – that real relationships are hard to come by and pleasure is not the same as intimacy. Caring and giving to those who you can trust is soooooo much better than selfish pleasure seeking. It does take discipline to say no to yourself and to your willing accomplice, but it is essential that you discipline yourself for a wise life – one in which your relationships are vital and real and not plastic and selfish.

PROVERBS 5:14 - *I was almost in utter ruin in the midst of the assembly and congregation.*

ruin

This is the Hebrew word *ra* which means evil, distress, misery. The idea here is the calamity and misery that comes from violating God's moral boundaries. There are consequences to violating God's law. When we are tempted to follow our impulses into the land of selfishness and harm to others, there will be misery and distress.

I have had the unwelcome assignment of interacting with pastors after they have been found out to be involved in adultery. When the truth of their actions becomes known, the devastation is immense. The few moments of pleasure never are worth the destruction. Their reputation, their marriage, their family, their career, their walk with the Lord, their finances, their friendships – all of these are significantly damaged and will take years to repair, if they are repairable. So when Solomon has the person who is the adulterer say *I was almost completely ruined,* it is so true.

midst

This is the Hebrew word *tavek* which means midst. The idea is that we live our lives in the view of a whole host of relationships. Other people surround us and make up our lives. To destroy trust with these various elements that make up our lives is incredibly short-sighted and stupid. **Life is Relationships**. The shame, guilt, distrust, etc., that will now be a part of the fabric of your life should scream to you: Don't violate the sacred trust you gave to your spouse!

assembly

This is the Hebrew word *qahal* which means assembly, group, congregation.

congregation

This is the Hebrew word *edah* which means congregation.

In the above two words Solomon goes out of his way to emphasize the shame and exposure that you will feel after adultery. He is seeing the web of relationships that make up your life and the ruin that your breaking trust in the one area means to all of the relationships. He is also seeing that you are a part of a synagogue or church that binds you to God and God's moral structure. In the midst of that group there is ruin, condemnation, and destruction.

One of the things people who commit adultery never do, before their plunge into this temptation, is to count the cost of their actions. If a person keeps the consequences of breaking trust firmly before them, they cannot do this sin. This is what Solomon is trying to do with this section of proverbs. DON'T FORGET THERE ARE IMMENSE CONSEQUENCES TO ADULTERY. No matter how alluring it seems, remember the consequences.

PROVERBS 5:15 - *Drink water from your own cistern and fresh water from your own well.*

The next nine verses are a metaphorical picture of sexual enjoyment between a testosterone-laden young man and his wife. This picture is highly erotic but also deeply poetic rather than vulgar. The sexual imagery and beauty of the interaction between a man and his wife are all captured here without being lascivious and vulgar. This poetic and stylized description of the connection between a man and his wife is important because sexual love ceases to be love – especially for the woman – when it becomes a technical description of how the various parts interact or when vulgar, aggressive, and rapacious descriptions are used to describe the action.

The phrase d*rink water* goes in a number of directions but is clearly a reference to the need and pleasure of sexual interaction with one's wife. It is important for a wife to realize that a man has a need for sexual connection that is as strong as his need to drink water. It is his job to control it, but it is her privilege to help fulfill it. Many, if not most, women do not have the strong need for sexual fulfillment that the typical man has; but it is important for women to understand that their husbands do. If she turns him away repeatedly because she does not have the need or interest, then she is not being sensitive to the difference between men and women and is potentially destabilizing her marriage.

One drinks water to quench a deep thirst. So a husband engages in sexual relations with his wife to quench a thirst. The burning fire that is sexual passion should be put out by your companion of covenant not by streams in the street. The allusion here to drinking is to putting out the burning fire of sexual passion. Even as the Apostle Paul connects in 1 Corinthians 7:9 when he talks about the ability to be single or the burning with passion precluding that privilege. If you are burning with passion, then get married and quench that burning.

In the Song of Solomon 4:15 the bride is called a stream and a garden spring – in a sense a river quenching the passion of the sexual impulse.

A wife and the satisfaction of married love are referred to a cistern and a fountain. Both were high treasures for a people dwelling in the Middle East. The cistern collected the water that ran off from the rains. A cistern was usually an underground storage facility where rain water was directed and protected from evaporation by being underground or sealed in some fashion – stored water for drinking later in the summer when all the streams had run dry. A fountain was called living water – fresh and life sustaining. So a wife's sexual satisfaction is a stored provision that is deeply satisfying; and she is also a life-giving, fresh, and new experience. All of this takes place without guilt in the context of marriage as well as the quenching of the fires of passion that burn within the heart of a young man.

It is the wise wife who figures out the cycle of her husband's needs to have the fire quenched and the nutrients of love carried by a willing woman wanting her husband.

PROVERBS 5:16 - *Should your springs be dispersed abroad, streams of water in the streets?*

springs

This is the Hebrew word *mayan* which means spring.

The idea here in this verse is subtle motivation to avoid adultery because of the various results it will cause. Most have seen, in this verse, the consequence of diluting one's sexual intimacy through repeated adultery. It is no longer special and unique to be with your spouse.

There are two other possible interpretations and/or applications to this verse. Springs in the Song of Solomon – which Solomon also wrote – refer to a wife's sexual interest and intimate anatomy. It is possible that Solomon is warning that if the husband commits adultery, he runs the risk of pushing his wife out of the house through divorce and neglect.

Some have also suggested that *springs* here means the husband's issue from sexual intimacy. In this idea Solomon is stating that one is scattering oneself all over and allowing it to run in the street and be common.

In each case the idea is that there are consequences to adultery so don't do it. The overarching theme in all these possible interpretations is that God has given a man a gift in his wife and the specialness of their relationship should not be diluted by sexual encounters with others outside the marriage relationship.

PROVERBS 5:17 - *Let them be yours alone and not for strangers with you.*

Solomon continues the exhortation that your power, seed, and blessing should not be scattered around where you cannot claim it or use it. Solomon's argument here will seem strange to our ears because we do not see the family as he saw it. In Solomon's day, the family was the basic economic unit. You did not hire people to work in your company; instead you were operating a family business that relied upon your children for its very existence. The more children you had, the better your family business thrived. It has been estimated that in a farm economy, each child that a family produced created approximately $10,000 of profit for the family over and against what they consumed. So Solomon's point of view is that a father is creating employees for his family business.

Solomon is saying, why would you want to be involved in adultery where you do not in any way gain from the joy, strength, and leadership of children. He is exhorting young men to not manufacture a work force that you have no claim on or control over. Your children should support your family, not just be scattered abroad for strangers to gain control over and blessings from. The family was the basic economic unit of the nation. Each family was a small business. Every father was looking for more good employees. Solomon says to young men with this mindset: Think about what you are doing if you commit adultery. It doesn't make any sense to create people that are blessings and production for others and not for you.

Most of those who read this devotion are not living in a farm economy where the direct application of this argument makes sense. But the idea of children being a blessing and arrows of impact sent into the next generation still does apply. Even in an industrial or service economy, the family is the basic unit of life and a father and society as a whole gains immeasurably by actually parenting the children they produce. Every social measure has been applied to fatherless children and it is frightening. Fatherless children are more 70+ percent of those who are prone to gun violence, teen pregnancy, violent acts, prison, etc. It is a terribly destructive force in society for a man to father a child he does not parent.

The culture of the Old Testament saw children as a blessing. It was terrible to produce a blessing that one could not claim or enjoy. The father is the head of the home and yet because of his lack of discipline, he spreads his blessings and strength to where he gains no joy or advantage from them.

On a more philosophical note, Solomon is reinforcing that biblical idea that the family is the basic unit of society and that which disperses or destroys the family destroys the society, whether that is the lack of sexual discipline on the part of the father or laws or programs which encourage a lack of participation in the family by the father. We, in our culture, have unwittingly created a society in which fathers are encouraged to procreate but not to be a part of the family they start. We reward women stipends for having babies out of wedlock. If the father stays around and marries the child, then the stipend goes away. So we have created an incentive for young men to be driven off and act irresponsibly.

The family is also under attack by those who would want to define the family and a marriage not based upon its procreative and blood lines but around other more selfish definitions. If pleasure becomes the definition of a family – whether emotional pleasure, sexual pleasure, relational pleasure, or psychological pleasure – then it is only a matter of time before the culture is shattered. Usually it takes only one generation for there is no one to carry the culture into the next generation.

Our culture is also at a turning point where large sections of the culture do not see children as a blessing but as a curse or an unwanted by-product of sexual relations. If we as a culture continue moving in this direction until we tip completely into the selfish point of view that all things must be justified by whether they give us immediate pleasure, our culture cannot survive. We have seen this type of thinking manifest itself in other cultures and those cultures have descended into debauchery and destruction. A completely selfish culture – where every individual is out for himself with no thought about family or the collective society – cannot long survive.

PROVERBS 5:18 - *Let your fountain be blessed and rejoice in the wife of your youth.*

The wisdom tucked into this verse is so incredibly deep that most men completely miss its truth. The fountain in this proverb is one's wife – the source of children that will be born to this union.

Solomon is saying if one's wife is blessed, treasured, cherished, and rejoiced in, then the prospect of sexual fulfillment for you and her will be heightened. A woman is a totally different sexual being than her husband. She needs to sense that she is valuable and treasured as a person, not just a sexual object. She needs to sense and see that her husband values the relationship with her above the sexual fulfillment that he can get out of her.

rejoice in the wife of your youth

Notice the word *rejoice*. To rejoice means to re - joy and the word *joy* is always associated with depth, harmony, and connectedness of relationship. Solomon is imploring young men to invest new energies in the wife they have, and that reconnecting with her will bring a level of blessing and encouragement to her that will allow her to respond to him. Solomon is rightly saying to married men that if you want a lively and enjoyable sexual relationship, start treasuring and filling up your wife in her needs and she will respond to you.

Does your wife feel blessed to be married to you? Does she feel neglected or abandoned as you pursue work and hobbies, only approaching her for your own selfish ends? What could you have done over the last three months for your wife to really honestly say that being married to you is one of the greatest blessings of her life?

With incredible insight Solomon – moved by the Holy Spirit of God – gets it right that a husband who focuses his attention on his wife's needs will develop a dynamite relationship in which the physical relationship will be a delicious frosting to the substance of their relationship.

Gentlemen, the secret to a great sex life is: Let your fountain (wife) be blessed and rejoice (reconnect deeply) with the wife of your youth. It is the depth of the relationship that creates the wonder and pleasure of a sexual relationship.

It is interesting that this advice is coming from a man who just kept adding wives and concubines to meet his own sexual pleasures. I would submit that this verse is an admission that that method of satisfying his sexual need did not satisfy his soul. It is possible that Solomon actually went back and began to develop a relationship with these women who he just kept adding to his harem, and that he found that developing a relationship with these treaty wives was deeply rewarding.

What often happens in marriage is that a man becomes consumed with his own sexual fulfillment. This drives him to try and meet this consuming impulse in his life outside of the boundaries of marriage. He will eventually run into the consequences of this behavior either financially, martially, physically, emotionally, etc. If he had been willing to invest in his wife and renew their relationship, he would have found a renewed woman ready to interact with him physically.

The New Testament is right when a man honors his wife, understands his wife, gives her security in the relationship, builds a dynamic unity, develops a system of agreement in which the two can live and make decisions as one, nurtures his wife as his number one relationship, and defends his wife from internal and external foes, he will create a dynamic marriage in which his soul, spirit, and body will be satisfied in and with this woman. Too few men have been willing to put in the time to really allow their wives to be blessed.

PROVERBS 5:19 - *As a loving hind and a graceful doe, let her breasts satisfy you at all times; be exhilarated always with her love.*

This is a hidden verse about the work of married love. This chapter of Proverbs is so often thought to be about avoiding adultery and, it is, but it also is a primer about how to stay in love with your spouse. Solomon uses the imagery of a deer and speaks of mental images and the mental work involved in staying in love with your wife instead of being enamored with the cheap new thrills of an adulteress.

let her breasts satisfy you at all times
This phrase is either a statement utilitarian direction or this phrase deals with the mental sexual work of staying in love. The context of the verse is how to stay in love with your wife and not need the services of an adulteress. Therefore the directions are not just how to have your needs met but how to stay in love. Also the words, at all times, would suggest far more than whenever you are sexually interested. These suggest that at the odd moments that you are faced with sexual temptation, think of the real thing with your wife. Instead of dreaming about some strange woman, dream about that which you can experience. The strongest sexual organ in the body is the mind, and this must be kept focused on the right people – your spouse. If a man allows himself to wander mentally or in reality to enjoying the breasts of another woman, then he has committed adultery. Jesus says this in Matthew 5, and Solomon says it here from the positive side. Solomon is saying that you must use your mind to keep you interested in your wife.

This practice of mental discipline in which a man does not let his mind wander to whatever it wants but instead trains it to think about what is good and right and beneficial has been lost in our culture. We often think that any thought that we might have is okay to think about. This is not true. We must bring some level of discipline to our minds, or we are not going to have a great life. There are some things we should think about and some things we should not think about.

Fascinatingly enough, one of the good things to think about is sexual relations with your wife. Solomon is saying to think about that whenever you need to – it's a good thing.

It is interesting that Solomon can speak from experience of doing this wrong. He allowed himself to lust after any beautiful woman he saw and multiples of wives and concubines that he had eventually turned his heart away from the Lord. Most likely when he wrote this under the inspiration of the Holy Spirit, he was realizing the mistakes that he had made by not focusing on his wife and he had not yet been turned aside to pagan gods. It important to realize that he is saying: Don't let your mind fantasize about other women; it will get you in trouble – even if you are like Solomon and can just add her to your endless harem. Fantasize instead about your wife and the joy of physical intimacy with her.

as a loving hind and a graceful doe

These are images that Solomon chooses to describe sexual love in the mind of a man. This is the imagery of intimacy, physical tenderness, and the desire to touch.

These animals suggest softness, curves, tenderness, and sensuality. Solomon wants the man to be fantasizing but about his wife, not about some other woman. He is suggesting that the images of his wife in the man's mind are important.

be exhilarated always with her love

Because of our unique dating and engagement culture, we enjoy the true meaning of this verse before we are married – when we cannot stop thinking about her and when she intrudes into every activity and constantly brings pleasure into our life. In the life of Israel with arranged marriages and little or no interaction before marriage is begun, this exhilaration takes place after the wedding. But it is this contemplation of what it feels like to be loved by this woman that is being mentioned here.

A note to young ladies at this point: You can significantly increase the occurrence of this exhilaration your husband experiences by loving him deeply in the areas of his primary needs. The primary needs of a man that can be met by his wife are respect, adaptation to him, domestic leadership, intimacy sexually, companionship, attractiveness, listening. A woman can largely control how much her husband thinks about her by meeting these needs he has. She does not do them because he meets her needs but because she wants to meet his needs and wants to maximally fill him up to fulfill his God-given potential. It is his job to fill her up and meet her needs. Her needs are different and she is filled up in a different way.

There will be those times when you and your wife do not agree or that you are experiencing some distance. Don't let that become an opening for an adulteress. Instead, men, focus on what it is like to be in love with this woman in the good times. Go back there mentally and then ask yourself what would it take to get back to those wonderful times.

PROVERBS 5:20 - *For why should you, my son, be exhilarated with an adulteress and embrace the bosom of a foreigner?*

This proverb is a question of reasons for going to the arms of an adulteress when you can get all you want and need from the wife of your youth.

The term *my son* is an interesting insertion here. It suggests that you have been trained and mentored by Solomon's teaching and, therefore, know better than to be led astray by a mistress.

Remember that a mistress actually does what a wife can and should do, and she aims her attention in a lazer-like focus on a man until he is drawn almost irresistibly to her.

My wife and I were commenting the other day on the exploits of a Hollywood starlet who has been very good at breaking up marriages and drawing any man she wanted into her clutches. She focuses her attention on him and meets his top seven relational needs until he is completely hers, and then after a while she just seems to get bored with him and discards him to go after another man.

exhilarated

This is the Hebrew word *shagah* which means to go astray, err, to commit error. It is something of a mistranslation to use the word exhilarated when all of its meanings are to err or to go astray. The import of this verse seems to be Solomon's probing question. Why would you go astray with a strange woman? You have a wife at home that can supply all that you need.

The power of what Solomon is saying is in the words *go astray*. No man wants to be said to be going astray. These words alone will bring him up short and cause him to look at what he is doing. Remember that a man who is beginning to be with an adulteress thinks that he is doing the right thing because it feels so right to him. He finally has a woman who is giving him focused attention on his top seven relational needs.

adulteress

This is the Hebrew word *zur* which means to be a stranger. It is regularly used of a person who is not your spouse. This person is strange to you because it is not the person who you are supposed to be with. This idea of a strange person can also apply to the unmarried. When you are dating or spending time with a person that you know will not be or should not be your marriage partner, then this is a strange person. The more you try and make it work with this person, the more convoluted and involved your life becomes. Do not spend time with a person who is "good for now" but clearly not someone you would marry. Sometimes singles will stay in a relationship with someone who they know and will admit is strange to them just because they don't want to be lonely. They don't want to give up this one person until they can see the next person. This is short-sighted. If they are strange to you then, do not stay in a relationship with them. It will take you astray.

embrace

This is the word *habaq* which means embrace or fold. The idea is of an expression of love and affection. When you allow your relational needs to be met by a person who clearly is not or should not become your spouse, then you are playing with fire and you will get burned.

Solomon is screaming at us: Don't let your emotional and relational needs be met by someone other than your spouse; it is the way of error! It may be exhilarating. They may meet your needs at a deeply emotional level, but it is wrong. It is the way of error and it will break you.

PROVERBS 5:21 - *For the ways of a man are before the eyes of the Lord, and He watches all his paths.*

This seemingly small verse tucked away in a section warning against adultery is a lesson in theology. When understood properly, it is shattering and unnerving.

God created the universe by having a 4+ dimensional space-time entity spring to life out of eternity from no pre-existent matter. This dimensional space is what we call our universe with its stars, space, planets, comets, etc. God is completely outside of our universe, understanding everything about it. He is not limited to being in the universe or limited by any of the universe's laws. He is outside, beyond, above – in a word – transcending the universe. He can see immediately every part of it. For He dwells outside of it. We inhabit one little habitable planet in one galaxy. Remember, He is beyond our dimensionality and can see, know, and understand more about us than we can know about ourselves. He sees everything about us – even our thoughts and internal struggles – before anything becomes words or actions.

The best analogy I have been able to use to explain this is the movie, *The Truman Show,* which is the fictional story about a baby that is adopted by a television corporation so that it can film everything about its life. They build a huge dome in which they create a city called Sea Haven where this baby grows up and lives. They have cameras everywhere, capturing everything about his life. It is the concept of always being watched that I want to draw from the movie. He can't go anywhere where he is not watched. We cannot go anywhere from God seeing all we do.

The Bible declares that we are being watched – by God and by angels. Even when we are behind closed doors in the dark, we are being watched. The following verses are just a few that show this idea: Psalm 139:1-6, 7-12f; 1 Peter 1:12; Luke 15:10; Ephesians 3:10; Colossians 2:15; Job 7:20; Daniel 4:13,17, 23; Matthew 18:10; Genesis 6:11; Proverbs 3:4; Luke 1:6; 2 Corinthians 2:17; 2 Corinthians 4:2; 7:12; 12:19; 1 Timothy 2:3; 1 Peter 3:4; Acts 24:16.

Understand that you are living your life in front of God. He and, at some level, angelic creatures can see into your life, into your actions, and into the private places. God actually sees into your thoughts as they are forming and the whys of your motives.

Solomon is declaring a forgotten truth. God sees everything you are doing. That is why Solomon is arguing so strongly to stay away from adultery. Because it is not hidden; it is not secret. It is being watched as you are doing it.

This makes me think of what we would do differently if everything we did was caught on tape. If a film crew was following us around capturing everything we said (even the grumbling) and everything we did (even the hidden stuff), we would live different lives. What we need to understand is that this is exactly what is happening. We are being watched all the time – by God and other angelic beings.

PROVERBS 5:22 - *His own inequities will capture the wicked, and he will be held with the cords of his sin.*

This is the equivalent of the New Testament verse: *You reap what you sow.*

It is important to realize that what looks alluring and wonderful as a young person is actually a straightjacket of pain. The pathway that leads through adultery and free physical intimacy without marriage does not end up where you think it ends up.

What you are tempted by is what you will be captured by. You can be captured by good temptations or wicked temptations – they end up in very different places.

his own iniquities will capture the wicked

The word *iniquities* is the Hebrew word *awon* which means iniquity, guilt, punishment, and is related to the word which means twisting, distorting, or warping. The way a person warps the people and opportunities around them to serve their own selfish purposes will capture those who continue to practice them. These practices become addictions.

Remember that iniquity is a synonym of wickedness which is anything done repeatedly that is outside the boundaries of the Ten Commandments. An iniquity is one type or form or act of twisting a good gift of God into a selfish, morally destructive thing to serve your desires. When a person persists with these actions, then they can be labeled wicked. They no longer have regard for God's boundary structure.

We become enslaved to our habits. Many people will say that God is against me and that is why I have all these problems. No, God has built into the universe consequences for immoral actions. In the beginning it is these consequences that immoral people are feeling as their lives begin to be a dead-end. In fact, God – in the book of Romans – says that one of His punishments for people who persist in wicked behavior is to stop trying to hold them back and release them to the full measure of their lifestyle.

People do not escape from God's consequences or God's wrath. It is being revealed right now against all ungodliness and unrighteousness. It will also be revealed against all form of wickedness on judgment day.

he will be held with the cords of his sin

Like Gulliver in the famous tale, so the sinner is bound by small strands that individually might not enslave him but collectively hold him in a place he does not want to be. When we sin with a high hand and begin living in rebellion to God's moral boundaries given in the Ten Commandments, we begin to weave our own straightjacket that will keep us from enjoying life as it was meant to be lived.

Remember, young men and young ladies, if you give yourself to illicit romance and sexual license, you will become bound to it. Stop selling yourself so cheaply; hold out for the one whom God has selected for you. Remain pure; it is worth it.

The person who commits sexual sins throws spiritual, mental, emotional, physical, and relational ropes over themselves for the Devil to pull on and keep from God's best. Don't do this. It doesn't matter how much you think you love this person or how much you "need" to make love, don't trash your purity. If you have already given in, then stop now and begin to build purity in your life from this point forward.

Some of you will understand when you are much older that this was not all it was cracked up to be, and you changed the trajectory of your lives for a short romp. Use the power of Christ's forgiveness to break free of the cords that have held you since your teen years. Break free.

I have watched people who, after years of guilt and shame, have finally experienced God's love and forgiveness by confessing these sins to God and proclaiming to the Devil that you are, through Christ's death on the cross, canceling out any power he has in your life through those sinful acts.

PROVERBS 5:23 - *He will die for lack of instruction, and in the greatness of his folly he will go astray.*

die

This is the Hebrew word *muth* which means to die or bring about death. The idea that Solomon is teaching is that the wicked who pursue their own selfish desires with reckless abandon – without regard to who gets hurt in the process – refuses to learn either from their mistakes or the lessons others try and share with them. They just keep pushing to get the object of their selfish focus and end up destroying relationships, their body, and eventually their life because of it.

instruction

This is the Hebrew word *musar* which is discipline or chastening or correction. The idea is that they will not receive correction. Those who are focused on their selfish desire and will harm others to get it are not willing to evaluate their mistakes. They are not willing to have others point out where they should have done something different. This is one of the clear characteristics of those who are confirmed in their wickedness. They will not listen to correction or redirection about the object of their sinful or selfish fascination. They have decided that they will make power or sex or money or fame the goal of their life and nothing will keep them from obtaining it.

What is also true in this insight from Solomon is that the only way back from wickedness is repentance about the focus of your selfish behavior. You must receive correction about why your life is so messed up. You must confess with God that what you have been doing and how you have been living is wrong.

If your life is really in a mess with lots of trouble and consequences, you may want to see if it is because you are living outside of the Ten Commandments: idols, cursing, lying, abortion, violence, multiple sexual partners, stealing, etc. Wake up and realize lots of your troubles are because of your pursuit of these things. Repent and listen to a different way of life.

folly

This is the Hebrew word *ivveleth* which means folly or foolishness. This is selfishness which is on display in this person's life. Notice that Solomon says that the wicked person is involved in a high level or great amount of selfishness. Their life is built around themselves in some colossal way. We have all seen this with the alcoholic or the womanizer or the braggart. There is a greatness of selfishness about the wicked.

That means if it is all about you all the time, then you are headed in the wicked direction. If you do not regularly think about blessing and caring for others and sacrificing for other's benefit, then your life is headed in the wrong direction. If thinking about yourself and what you want and what would please you is all you do, then welcome to follyland.

astray

This is the Hebrew word *shagah* which means to go astray to commit error. In the English it means to get off the right path. Solomon is saying that the wicked person who gets captured by illicit sex, illegal wealth, or abusive power or pride is off the right path and just keeps going deeper into the jungle. They will seriously damage their potential in life and their ability to perceive what is happening to them.

Proverbs 6

PROVERBS 6:1 - *My son, if you have become surety for a neighbor, have given a pledge for a stranger,*

This is the classic passage against co-signing a note for someone, so that your financial health is in the hands of another person. Its application can also be stretched to be against borrowing in general, or striking surety, or making a pledge even for yourself.

One should not be involved in promising to pay the debts of another. If a person is not able to secure the necessary financing on their own, it is because they are a bad risk. It is this type of risk or exposure that leaves you completely at the whim, foolishness, or sloth of another.

PROVERBS 6:2 - *If you have been snared with the words of your mouth, have been caught with the words of your mouth,*

This verse is the continuation of the idea developed in verse one – namely, that you have promised to pay the debts of another person. But it also carries a nugget of wisdom about the use of the tongue that is surely independent of co-signing and borrowing. Namely, that one can be put into a snare by what they say.

if you have been snared with the words of your mouth

The word *snare* is the Hebrew word *yaqosh* and appears first in the sentence. This emphasizes the word and the importance of the concept in the sentence. The writer is trying to emphasize that promising certain things is a trap or a snare which you make yourself. This is foolish talk.

The second word in the Hebrew sentence is *speech* or *words*. And the third word is *mouth*. In other words, the sentence reads: *A trap built with words out of your mouth*. This is the definition of foolishness. Who would build their own trap? Who would build a trap for themselves using their own words that everyone knew came out of their own mouth? Who would walk into a trap to be caught? Who would walk into their own trap that they themselves designed? The answer to each of these questions is A FOOL.

In trying to appear big and generous, the fool has built and stepped into a trap. How impulsive and lacking sense.

Let's expand the application of this idea a little further. How many of us have used our mouth to spin a tale that is really not true but makes us look good? This is also a trap built with our own words. We then are forced to openly admit our fabrication or to protect our tale with greater fabrications. Don't build a trap with your own words. Tell the truth. Don't try and have people be impressed with you because of what you say or what you do. Just do the right thing and the appropriate praise will come to you. When we try and make ourselves look better, through loaning people money or stretching the truth, it is a trap that will be an uncomfortable prison.

If you have built one of these traps, before it springs closed verse 4 tells us to get out by telling the truth and canceling the contract. Don't allow yourself to be caught.

have been caught with the words of your mouth

There is a difference between the first phrase and the second phrase. The first is a snare that has been built but it has not been sprung. The second is the trap that has been closed and caught someone – namely, you. The first phrase refers to before the problem has occurred and the second is after you have been caught by what you said and made to pay for another.

In either case the person must do the same thing: seek deliverance from the trap. It is obviously better to be delivered before the trap has sprung shut.

The picture is of a person who is walking down the path of life and stops to build a steel cage on the side of the road to impress his friends. Instead of making progress on the path, he is busy building this cage. Then he walks into the cage and waits for the door to be thrown closed and locked. It is the friends that you have been trying to impress who will throw the door closed and imprison you. Don't let this happen. Keep moving on the path of life.

When we make a pledge to cover the debts of others, this is a fool's trap. Only a fool needs us to cover their debts, and the goods purchased by such an arrangement did not need to be purchased.

I have watched as people have derailed their marriages, families, and even careers to help out a friend, relative, or boss. Often these include bailing a person out of prison or co-signing for a car or starting a business. When the debt becomes due, it totally destabilizes the helper's life while the person who needed the help moves forward without them.

Do not do this...

PROVERBS 6:3 - *Do this then, my son, and deliver yourself; since you have come into the hand of your neighbor, go, humble yourself, and importune your neighbor.*

deliver

This is the Hebrew word *nasal* which means deliver, rescue, even save. Solomon here acknowledges that, at times, everyone will make mistakes. We all need to know how to undo something that we should not have done. How can we rescue ourselves before our mistake becomes permanent or complete?

Too often we have this idea that we must finish what we know is a mistake. If you discover something is a mistake, then stop and seek to deliver yourself from the problem. It takes humility – which is hard on our pride – and a willingness to be vulnerable in the admission of our mistake and request for a change.

humble

This is the Hebrew word *raphas* which means to stamp, tread down, humble, trampling under foot. It is a word of lowness and submission. In this instance Solomon suggests that you do this to yourself. Make yourself low and under the level of the person you are approaching. It is a shame that many in our day do not know how to approach another person from this position. Even children are taught to power up and try and connect with people through a power position. When you have made a mistake, take the humble route. Don't try and justify how you were tricked into the problem. Don't try and blame others. Don't try and threaten what you will do if you are not let out of the problem. Just humble yourself. Step down on your pride, admitting that you made a mistake when you said what you said or when you did what you did. This will not be easy and your pride will give your suggestions on how to stand up and be powerful. Refuse to listen to the impulses of your pride. They will not help you; they will only make matters worse.

importune

This Hebrew word is a surprise and the strength of the word is shocking and fascinating. The word is *rahab* which means storm, boisterously or strongly or boldly. The idea is that this is a request that will not go away. It comes on strong and will not take no for an answer.

From a very humble position Solomon is saying that you strongly ask to be let out of your mistake. This is not a *could you please if it is not any trouble for you*. It is a *please, I need to be released from the mistake I made. I should not have agreed to do that; I just cannot do that*.

In one sense the idea is that you become a storm upon the person until he/she releases you from your mistake. You are open and humble about your mistake, but you must be released from your own stupidity. This word importune is a strong word.

When you make a mistake either through what you do, what you say, or what you sign, then be willing to admit that you made a mistake; but go after being released and stay humble but stay after it. Just like the unrighteous judge says about the woman who importuned him. She was like a relentless storm at his court until she received justice. So persistent, humble relentlessness has its place in the arsenal of the wise person. They need it to get themselves out of the stuff they do when they are not wise.

PROVERBS 6:4 - *Give no sleep to your eyes, nor slumber to your eyelids;*

This proverb is a word against the still common practice of being the guarantee for other's debts. Strictly speaking, this section means it is incredibly foolish to co-sign for a loan for others. It is ridiculously foolish to put your own goods at risk based on the behavior of others.

If you find yourself in this case, then go to the person who owes the debt and plead with them to repay the debt. Do not let yourself treat this as though it were nothing.

If one cannot secure a loan on the strength of their own pledges and work, then they are clearly a bad credit risk. And we do not help them by allowing them to borrow past their ability to pay back. We actually cripple them.

The appropriate response to the person who wants us to co-sign a loan for them is to look at our resources and see if we can spare the money. If we can and it seems especially helpful, then we should give it to them, telling them it is not a loan but a gift and the only repayment they must make is to someone else in need in the future.

Notice the unrelenting focus of this proverb's advice. Don't go to sleep; don't take a nap. In other words, do not procrastinate this problem. It will not go away. It is a serious problem. Your goods are at risk because of another's behavior. This is not good.

PROVERBS 6:5 - *Deliver yourself like a gazelle from the hunter's hand and like a bird from the hand of the fowler.*

This is the application of this whole section on making pledges, going surety, or even getting into debt. Just like a gazelle who had been caught would struggle with all its life to become free, so should the person who is in this unwise position.

You need to fight like your life depends on it to be free from the debt of this loan. This also means work hard; show that you want out of this arrangement. You may not realize it, but this is a life-and-death struggle. If you get on the wrong side of the credit struggle, it will destroy you.

One Christian financial guru suggests that a person get a second job until the debt is paid off. He takes the admonition of verse 4 seriously. Give no sleep to your eyes. His thinking is that until you are free of the debt, emergency measures are needed. Deliver pizza, sell something – with a guaranteed paycheck that can get the debt snowball rolling in the right direction.

PROVERBS 6:6 ~ *Go to the ant, O Sluggard, observe her ways and be wise,*

The sluggard is the habitually lazy person who does not put out maximum energy.

One of the dangers of foolishness is that "I will only try when I feel like it or when I want to."

This quickly becomes "I will not put out when it is needed" which becomes "I cannot put out maximum effort when others are counting on me."

The sluggard becomes a sluggard by a slow easy-choice process.

It is important to do your best even when you don't feel like it so that when your best is really needed, you will be able to give it.

The sluggard ends up in poverty while hoping for instant riches.

They need to watch those who work hard. They need to be around people who work hard. They need to be in a context in which the minimum is still a lot. This is the only way to speed up a person with sluggard tendencies.

Do not give in to the tendencies of laziness. The television is a big help to sluggishness. Also, it is true that attitude is the key to combating sluggishness. A willing attitude to try what those in authority tell me keeps sluggishness from more deeply affecting my life.

I find that I must fight the tendency to be sluggish. It is not enough to just be active and busy. Sluggishness is also when you spend time doing what is not the most productive use of your time; it is just the easiest or most convenient at that moment.

PROVERBS 6:7 ~ *Which, having no chief, officer or ruler, prepares her food in the summer and gathers her provision in the harvest.*

The key idea that is being communicated in this couplet is that the ant does not need a supervisor or boss to be productive and to get the right things accomplished. If you will not be productive unless someone is riding you all the time about it, then you are a sluggard.

I think many parents develop slothfulness in their children by always riding them and not asking enough questions. What do you think you should do right now? How do you think you should do it?

Make a list of the things that you should be working on this week or this month. Are you able to work on those things by yourself or do you need a person to tell you to do them? Can you give yourself permission to act in these areas?

Can you be your own boss by prioritizing your work and then doing it according to priority?

PROVERBS 6:8 - *Prepares her food in the summer and gathers her provision in the harvest.*

Prepares is the Hebrew word *kun* which means at its root to bring something into being with the result that its existence is a certainty. Clearly the idea here is that the ant should be studied because it collects its resources over the summertime and then has the provisions to exist when there is not provision.

Notice that we are to study this process and realize that we must work hard at bringing into existence that which does not now exist, so that it will be there when we need it. This would refer to financial resources as well as skill development, information, and relationships.

Many times – especially in this culture – we want things instantly with no preparation on their parts, but all the above take time and skill to collect and or make. If we continue with the instant orientation of the culture around us, we become completely dependent upon others and will never get ahead or be really able to see a growing pile of resources from which to demonstrate generosity and enjoy stability.

This series of proverbs is directed at the sluggard who dreams and craves and lusts after things that they have no inclination to work for. This is what defines a person who is a sluggard. The biblical answer for laziness is hard work with the payoff at the end of the hard work. Understand that laziness and procrastination is a temptation. It is subtle, but it will slowly rob you of your potential and dreams. There are things that you must do this day and this week and this season of your life to be in the place you need to be later. If you do not put in the work now, it will be lost later.

When one of our daughters was young, we were forcing her to memorize her math facts: addition and subtraction. Were we cruel and inhuman because we made her go over and over it every day? No. We love her and were preparing her for achievement later. Our oldest daughter was forced to practice piano because she wanted to be able to play piano someday. If we never had her practice, then she would never develop that skill and be able to enjoy the piano. The same is true of life. I have forced myself to set aside part of my paycheck into a pension fund even though we could really use the money now. There are times to go to school even when you would rather be doing something else. There are times to save money when you would rather spend it. There are times when you have to learn a new skill so you will not be passed over for promotion later. There are times when you need to start a new friendship so that relationship will be available later.

I regularly hear people who are bored with the sameness of their lives. This means that there is some missing preparation of "food" in their lives. Look at what potential God has given you and focus on maximizing it. Put in the time now to hone, to collect, to prepare, and to develop what will be needed then.

Laziness is a form of selfishness that afflicts all of us. It is a temptation to be less than we can be. Now I am not talking about workaholism and franticness. We have too much of that in our world also. But I am talking about the subtle putting off things that we should do. There are many things that we should put off or not do at all, but we must not allow laziness to keep us from accomplishing our high-priority items.

Ask yourself every day, every week, and every season: What are the top two or three things I need to get done in this period in order to be adequately prepared for the next season? Then make sure that you do those things. Do not put them off. They will not scream at you until you need them, and it will be too late.

PROVERBS 6:9 ~ *How long will you lie down, O sluggard? When will you arise from your sleep?*

There is a danger in seeing sleep as a refuge. It steals the life of its adherents. Obviously everyone needs a regular and healthy amount of sleep; but there is a temptation to use sleep to battle fear, anxiety, and a host of other ailments.

Sleep can become a temptation as well as a refresher. It is like most temptations – we need it in moderation and it can become our undoing when we take the blessing of moderation and try and make it our main course. We need money; but if we make it our goal, we will pierce ourselves with many a pang. We need intimate physical relations; but if we focus on the pleasure of that, then we will wander into affairs and destroy ourselves. We need authority and power; but if we pursue these without restraint, we will forget God and abuse people.

There are times when you must push yourself past where you are comfortable. You need to not give into the impulse to sleep and take it easy – not in a workaholic pursuit of activity but a regular declaration of the superiority of the soul over the body. You will not sleep every time the impulse comes.

PROVERBS 6:10 - *"A little sleep, a little slumber, a little folding of the hands to rest"*

Notice that the translators have put this proverb in quotation marks. That is because they understand that this is what the sluggard says to others and, more importantly, to themselves. The core of the lie that the sluggard tells himself is that he is only resting a little. The truth is that the sluggards are resting all the time.

Solomon wants us to avoid lying to ourselves and becoming world-class procrastinators. We tell ourselves that we are only resting a little, that we are only sleeping a little longer, that we are only needing a little more deep sleep. All the while the opportunities that God has for us are streaming past us, and eventually all this "little" sleep will cause us to miss it.

It is possible for you and me to miss the plan that God has for us; to not be a part of the good plan and the potential that God built into us. One of the ways that we can miss His wonderful plan for our life is by being lazy and procrastinating about everything; just putting off the important stuff that needs to be done today.

This is especially a strong temptation for young people whom Solomon is addressing in this section of the proverb. When we are in the teen years, we are eager to do the things that sound fun and exciting; and we discover a need for more sleep and rest before the things that sound like work. Don't let this sluggard disease infect you.

If you find yourself trying to put off doing something that should be done because you want to sleep a little more, realize that you are beginning down the fool's pathway. Do the thing and then you can rest.

Notice that this is not a question of whether the person gets enough rest; it is that they put off doing important things because they need a little more. Don't become addicted to sleep. Don't allow your body to dictate to you when you will work hard or when you will begin projects or complete them. If you are not careful, your body will become king and your potential will slip away.

Do what you need to do now. This does not mean that there is anything wrong with taking a nap. Solomon is trying to get us to recognize if we are beginning to lie to ourselves about our little nap which really is laziness, procrastination, and sloth.

Some of the most dangerous lies we tell are the ones we tell ourselves. Don't let this be one of the ones you tell yourself. I have watched young people with lots of potential sleep in and miss job interviews which would launch their life in whole new directions. I have watched young people who have overslept and missed tests that they needed to take in order to get into a particular college. If you have a tendency to put things off or to love sleep, realize that Solomon is talking to you. Watch out for the temptation to take the sloth's path. It is a fool's diversion. It promises what you want, but it does not go where your life could go.

If you have given in to sloth on too many occasions, choose to stop. The way to fight back against procrastination, laziness, and sloth is to do the thing that needs to be done right away. If there is something that needs to be written, write it now. If there is a phone call that needs to be made, make it now. If there is a meeting that needs to be had, make the call and schedule the meeting. Deal with things. Put off sleeping and rest until the end of the day.

PROVERBS 6:11 ~ *Your poverty will come in like a vagabond and your need like an armed man.*

Remember that this verse is about the sluggard, the sloth, or the lazy person – the person who, like electricity, follows the path of least resistance. Whatever way is easiest is what this person wants to do. This kind of person will face the natural consequences of their easy choices. It is the hard choices that result in abundance, joy, and love. We have to be prepared to turn away from the quick, easy choice when it is presented, knowing that what comes with that choice is not good.

The end result of easy choices is poverty, lack of funds, need, and, thereby, really hard choices.

Only when you make the hard choices to do your best and work hard do you eventually get the opportunity to enjoy the easy choices.

When you give in regularly to the easy choices, you will be forced by a strong authority to do something you don't want to do.

The result could be the reposition of the desired item, jail, fines, creditors, etc. Don't give into the easy choice. Go after the righteous cause even though it may be much harder.

PROVERBS 6:12 - *A worthless person, a wicked man is one who walks with a perverse mouth,*

This proverb is interesting by trying to get us to comprehend the signs that we are in the presence of a person who is wicked. What is the tell-tale evidence that a person cannot be trusted? The answer, according to this series of verses, is that the person can be discerned by the twisted corrupt form of speech they use. The word is *perverse* which means twisted, crooked. It is used for the braiding of the hair where one strand is very difficult to follow through all the twists and turns it takes.

When a person must cover what they really mean by twisting words to make them sound nice or to mean something they don't mean, then you are in the presence of a wicked person – a person who lives outside of the boundaries of the Ten Commandments.

The designation of *worthless* and *wicked* is a connection that is not usual. So it bears some attention. *Worthless* is Belial or Son of Belial. This is connected directly to the Devil as the Lord of the Flies. All who are worthless are ruled by the lord of the worthless. They have become refuse and are destined for the refuse pile to be ruled by the king of the refuse pile. We, in our day, tend to see wickedness as active evil of an extreme sort and worthlessness as harmless slothfulness. There is a stronger connection between the two. The worthless person does not only contribute nothing to the society, they are a parasite on it as well as surely becoming a wicked person who lives outside of the moral boundary structure of God. They cannot survive inside of God's boundary structure, and so they live in the world of iniquity in order to avoid work as much as possible.

The bum on the street who refuses to participate in the economy of the society is not just a harmless derelict but also a wicked person who must survive by a willingness to do whatever it takes to make a living. There are high-class worthless people who survive at a higher income range by doing the sewer work of the wicked.

Notice what this proverb is saying. Can a person say what they mean and mean what they say? If they cannot, then they are possessors of a perverse mouth. This means that they are not only twisted in speech but in actions wicked. Don't miss this relational connection. The better you are at twisting your words, the deeper you are beyond God's moral boundary structure.

This section goes on to give other clues that signal the presence of a wicked person – one who will cheat you: winking with the eyes; scraping or signaling with the feet; pointing with the finger.

PROVERBS 6:13 ~ *Who winks with his eyes, who signals with his feet, who points with his fingers;*

This verse is in the middle of a section of verses that runs from verse 12 to19 which deals with the worthless and/or wicked person. The idea is that there are characteristics that point out the person who is wicked. We should be alert to this kind of person so that we can avoid entanglements with this person whether business, romantic, or social. It is also a warning not to become this person.

winks

This is the Hebrew word *qaras* which means to nip, pinch, wink. It might also be what we see as squinting. It is the clear indication that there is a way that the wicked person uses his eyes or looks that gives away an orientation to worthlessness or wickedness. This action or look signals that the person is being deceptive or radically selfish. Some have seen in this the wink that lets the gang know that they are going to deceive the potential victim. Others have seen in this expression the squinting of those who are unaccustomed to the light and do their work in the dark. Some have thought that this is more of a nervous twitch.

What is interesting about each of these signs of a wicked person is that they do not communicate openly but through shadowy signals and behind-the-back means. Only those in the know would understand what these things meant.

signals

This is the word *malal* which means to rub, to scrape. It has been translated signal, scrape. There are two ideas that could be conveyed here: 1) that this person is actually trying to communicate to their friends with their feet; 2) that they are shuffling their feet signifying that they don't really have anything to do and are waiting to do harm or some nefarious activity.

points

This is the Hebrew word *yara* which means to throw, to shoot. It has been translated as point, shoot, instruct, teach. The idea is that some form of communication is taking place through hand signals.

In each case, in this verse the people are using secretive means of communication. Winking, scraping, and pointing are all forms of communication that must have been agreed upon ahead of time as to their meaning and/or are designed to hide communication to some or all of those that are around.

The sense that Solomon is trying to convey is that if you are around a person who is very given to secretive and hidden communication because they do not want everybody to have all the communication, something is wrong and most likely you are in the presence of a person who is, at best, worthless and could be wicked. For each of these forms of communication is for getting a message across while hiding that message to some in the group.

This happens in high school and junior high when the "in" crowd has all these signals to exclude the "out" crowd. They can, at times, fake including them only to ridicule them or use them. This happens in business as people in the office will exclude some from the real info. This happens as some businesses have hidden parts to a contract or agreement that they don't want others to know about. This happens in almost every group or organization as a person with selfish motives wants to put one over on others. Watch out for this – winking, feet signals, hand signals. Don't become like this. If you have to get your message across secretively rather than openly, is there a problem with the message or the goal?

PROVERBS 6:14 - *Who with perversity in his heart continually devises evil, who spreads strife.*

Remember that this section opens with the statement that we are talking about the person who is worthless and wicked. The person who provides no productive service for the society, but instead is a parasite on the society. The person who continually uses the benefits and people of a community to meet their needs.

The word *perversity* is the Hebrew word *hepek* which means contrariness, twisted, distorted.

The word *devises* is the Hebrew word *haras* which means engrave, plow, devise.

The word *evil* is the Hebrew word *ra* which means evil, distress, badness, misery.

At the risk of repeating myself over and over again... The wicked person is the one who continues to do and say things that are beyond the Ten Commandments with little regard for those moral boundaries. This is the type of person that Solomon is trying to give us insight into – the person who lives outside of God's moral boundary structures.

He says that this person has a twisted contrariness in their soul. Their inner life develops strategies of selfishness that knows no boundaries. There is nothing that causes this person to go: "We shouldn't do that."

It is important to spend some time talking about evil. Let me aim at a simple definition of its root. Evil is selfishness pushed to the place where its accomplishment is destructive to the individual and the society and, therefore, must be outlawed. We must not make this category of actions called evil that is so different from "normal" actions that it seems that we could never commit them. God says that evil is that level of selfishness that pushes past the boundaries of the Ten Commandments. Murder, rebellion, sexual sins, stealing, fraud and lying, coveting another's goods -- these are God's revealed boundaries for selfishness. When a person allows their own natural tendencies for what they want to move them to these actions and behaviors, they have begun to commit evil actions. If they do not repent and come back to righteous living, they become evil.

One of the dangers of our culture is we are encouraging – through our movies, books, magazines, television, and other media outlets – a life of the mind that devotes itself to accomplishing and contemplating evil. This proverb warns us that this is the thought patterns of the wicked and worthless. If we are always thinking about how we could steal something or how we could get rid of an opponent or rebel from God-given authority, we have allowed our mind to pursue twisted thoughts about evil.

We can choose to think about anything we want. Let's think about what we should be doing, not what we shouldn't be doing.

who spreads strife
Another telltale sign of a person who is worthless and wicked is that they spread strife. This almost appears to be a throw-away line in this proverb, but it is in reality a well-placed insight into the actual lifestyle of those who are wicked. Notice that this is no more what the person thinks about but instead it is what the person does even if it does not seem like they are the cause of the discord between people. Everywhere they go, people begin to be at one another; there is discord. This is a sure sign that someone is pursuing a level of selfishness that is beyond the "normal" selfish inclinations.

It is entirely possible that Solomon is pointing out the outward evidence of a person who is like this; lots of strife being spread by them. We cannot know what a person thinks about; but if someone is constantly surrounded by strife and spreads its contagion, then there is perversity in their heart – devising evil.

Look for these signs and do not allow your own mind to move in these directions. Also make sure that you are not pursuing your own selfish ends at work, in the church, or the community that you will not let disagreements die down.

I have watched people in the work place and in ministry continually point out their selfish perspective and gather support until there are distinct camps. This causes division over usually what started out as a personal issue.

PROVERBS 6:15 ~ *Therefore his calamity will come suddenly; instantly he will be broken and there will be no healing.*

Solomon spends four verses on describing the wicked, morally degenerate person. In this verse he describes the nature and speed of his demise.

therefore

This is two Hebrew words *al* and *can* which both mean results and can both be translated as therefore. It is clear through the use of both words that Solomon is trying to direct us to the consequences of this type of person. They do not just go merrily along without incident. God brings results into their lives based upon the moral wickedness they have been involved in.

It is important to realize that we live in a moral universe where moral choices bring consequences. Some have tried to hide that under scientific nonsense, but choices make a big difference. It does make a difference whether you choose to swear; whether you choose to be faithful to your spouse; whether you choose to steal, embezzle, lie, and plot to take other peoples' possessions.

calamity

This is the Hebrew word *ed* which means destruction, ruin, disaster, calamity, vengeance, trouble. It is regularly used as the time or day of reckoning or time of payback for their behavior. Unfortunately we have developed a society that has forgotten that what goes around comes around; that whatever a man sows that shall he also reap. We have abandoned the idea of consequences for a random universe in which if no one stops you, you have gotten away with it. And if you can get away with it, then it is okay and even right. This is a far cry from the universe that God actually built, and we are fooling ourselves and storing up wrath and destruction for ourselves.

We must return again to a more accurate understanding of the interactions and reactions of the whole fabric of the universe that we live in – that morality and our choices count significantly and that it pays to stay within the boundaries.

The idea here is of trouble and paybacks that are so severe that there will be no rebuilding. There will be no ability, desire, or raw material to start again.

Now it is important to say that there is always room for repentance even after the consequences have landed and broken the person, company, and organization. In fact, repentance is one of the reasons that God has directed the calamity to fall.

Now some have been troubled that they do not always see the wicked receive their calamity and so, therefore, there is no God or justice in this world. The consequences of sin and the moral payback may be hidden from your view, or it may be to some degree at Judgment Day when there will certainly be no healing. But there will be moral balance obtained. It is much like a science experiment where a vacuum is created. It may be maintained for a period at great trouble and even expense; but if there is one mistake, air will rush in and balance this imbalance and destroy your experiment. Nature abhors a vacuum. In the same way, some have built and maintained a morally bankrupt life in which profits and pleasures flow toward themselves. This is maintained at great cost and energy. If a mistake is made in the system of elaborate involvements, then moral order will be restored – often violently.

suddenly

This is the Hebrew word *pithom* which means sudden, suddenly, surprisingly. The proverb in the original reads: *Therefore - Therefore suddenly*. Which puts a huge emphasis upon the results and the swiftness of the results. It was not expected.

The idea seems to be that the morally wicked person is living their life of shortcuts and bad moral choices and then without warning, something happens and it is all over. The Bible does not spell out particular judgments but instead just says calamities or destruction. The emphasis is upon it coming out of the blue. There is not a long, slow lead-up. It just nails them.

broken

This is the Hebrew word *sabar* which means to break, to break into pieces. The idea here is the pieces and the breaking. It is not just a stopping or consequences that causes the person to go another way. This idea is that the mechanism or life that they have used to accomplish the evil they are guilty of is shattered. We have seen this kind of shattering with businesses that were corrupt to the core: cheating employees, shareholders, government. There have been a number of these types of investigations in the early parts of 2000. One only has to look at the Enron scandal.

I have seen the same devastation on a personal level in some divorces where a person's whole life is shattered. I have seen this level of destruction in criminal investigations and incarcerations. I have seen this level of shattering with bankruptcies. This, at times, ends in murder.

no healing

This is the Hebrew word *marpe* with a negative in front of it. It means healing and restoration. What the wicked have done brings a level of shattering in which healing, restoration, rebuilding is not possible. Their former life is shattered and unrecoverable. The level of their selfishness demands an end to their activities.

The lesson here: Do not become one of these people for the profits and pleasure you reap are only for a season, and then you will be shattered in an unrecoverable way.

Another lesson would seem, obviously, to not associate or get entangled with this type of person for their destruction may very well be your destruction.

A third lesson is to understand this type of person and the breaking that is coming; to spot this type of person and give them a wide berth.

PROVERBS 6:16 - *There are six things which the Lord hates, yes, seven which are an abomination to Him:*

Solomon condenses that which disgusts the Lord into an easy-to-remember list. It all has to do with your putting yourself above or before others.

It is interesting to let the power of this verse speak to us in a modern culture that has been force-fed a theology that God is only love and kindness. He also hates certain things which destroy the order that He created. He hates that which promotes the self above others or at the expense of others.

hates

This is the Hebrew word *sane* which means to be hated or to be full of hate. Hatred is intense hostility towards someone.

Think this through: God actually has intense hostility toward certain actions. This is the Supreme Being who dwells outside of our space time universe in a dimensionality that is called eternity, whose properties we do not completely understand. This Supreme Being is multi-personal, all-powerful, infinite in wisdom and knowledge. He used His infinite wisdom, knowledge, and power to create the world. This Almighty Being declares, through His chosen mouthpiece, that He has intense hostility to certain actions that we can take. Imagine that one day you will be evaluated by this Supreme Being for everything you ever said, did, or thought. You do not want to have done the things that He feels intense hostility toward.

Look at the list: Pride, Lying, Murder, Coveting, Quickness to evil, Lying, Strife. Don't do these things. What is interesting is that this would not have been the list that we would have thought God should hate – from our perspective. We would have gotten murder, but we would have suggested that physical harm to another is what causes God to be nauseated. Each of these things directly affects relationships between people. When a relationship is killed, it is not how God wired the world to work.

abomination

This is the Hebrew word *toeba* which means abominable or deeply loathed, repugnant. There are some things that should not be done. They destroy the fabric of life. Notice that God finds abominable that which destroys the way that the world was supposed to work. When a person commits an action that destroys the way God designed the universe to operate, then it is abominable. It is interesting that God gave us the ability to do things that He found abominable, but He did. We have been given the ability to do things that totally gum up the works that God set up. Do not use your power to choose for things that God finds repugnant.

PROVERBS 6:17 - *Haughty eyes, a lying tongue, and hands that shed innocent blood,*

God begins to detail, through the mouth of Solomon, those actions and attitudes that He hates. It is a different list than we might expect it would be. What is interesting and foreign to our thinking is that God has strong emotions about some actions that we can take. Think this through. God is emotionally angry when you do any one of these seven things. We are not used to thinking about God in an emotional state. You could be doing something that God hates.

haughty

This is the Hebrew word "rum" which means high, lofty, haughty. Clearly the idea is pride, superiority, a condescending attitude toward others. When people look at others as beneath them or inferior to them, this is "haughty eyes." When it is clear in how people act or evaluate others that they believe that they are better than the others – either because of something they have done, something they have, something they are – then this qualifies as what God hates.

Now what is important here is that this is a natural tendency in all of us, and we have to choose to treat people with respect and dignity and internally not put ourselves above them in some way.

lying

This is the Hebrew word "seqer" which means lie, breaking a promise, deception, betrayal, denying a truth, leading astray. The original idea seems to be a spring that is intermittent in that one could not count on it to supply water or that it was bitter water.

Think this through. God hates when you act like something you are not; when you make a promise to a person that you don't keep; when you lead a person or group astray; when you deceive or lie to someone. He hates this type of action.

Now lying is always selfishly motivated. We believe that we can benefit personally by a lie more than the truth, but what we fail to realize is that the lie has to be supported. The lie takes us somewhere.

There is no such thing as one lie just like there is no such thing as eating one potato chip. Lying is not a one-time thing; it leads to somewhere and something.

An important question is: Is any part of your life a lie right now? Are you having to prop up and support that which is not true about yourself? If you begin to live your own lie, then you dwell in an imaginary world and you will eventually lie to yourself.

shed

This is the Hebrew word *"sapak"* which means pour or pour out. Clearly this is the idea of pouring out a person's blood in terms of killing them. The Hebrew idea of the body was that the blood was the active agent and when the blood was poured out, then the life was gone. The life was in the blood. So pouring out the blood of a person was a poetic way of saying to kill them.

Notice that Solomon notes that it is innocent blood being spilt that brings out God's hatred. The guilty being punished does not cause His anger or hatred. This is an important qualification that some have not made in our day.

It does not matter whether it is an individual or a group or a government which pours out a person's life. If a decision was made or action taken that caused the death of an innocent person, then it is wrong and God hates that. Note that while these actions and attitudes cause God to have a strong emotional reaction, it does not demand His action to stop this action from occurring. God has given us a limited freedom of choice; and He will allow us to play out, to a certain degree, the power and responsibility that comes from those choices. We then have to live in the wreckage of our lives.

In our day and age, we have begun to blame those in authority over us for every problem or difficulty that they could have prevented. We blame government for not preventing us from doing things we shouldn't have done. We blame our parents for not raising us in a perfect way. We blame God for not keeping every problem, difficulty, or evil out of our lives. We have embraced a lack of personal responsibility. It is always someone else's fault who should have stopped it or moved us out of the way. The problem is that this kind of thinking does not correspond to the world as it is. God has said we are responsible for the choices that we make. They have consequences – some of which is to agitate God and destroy our relationship with Him.

You can choose to repent of lying, murder, pride, and bigotry. If you do not, then you will face an angry God come judgment day. You will also live in a selfish sewer of negative consequences.

innocent

This is the word "naqi" which means innocent, clean. This is not the idea of absolute innocence because even Solomon states that no one has that. But this is innocence in terms of having nothing that is deserving of punishment or death in relation to a particular incident. It would be safe to assume that it means in ancient Hebraic civilization what it means today. There are people who are minding their own business and not doing anything wrong; and yet wicked people hurt them through greed, violence, power, oppression, or in some other selfish way. They do not deserve what happens to them for it does not fit the life they have lived.

It is instructive that God states that innocent people do suffer and have their blood shed. While He is Sovereign, He allows this for some reason. The choices of the wicked are allowed to stand. The unthinking choices of the selfish are allowed to reverberate through time, destroying lives. God provides grace where sin abounds and offers to bring good out of the evil of man's choices, but in many cases He allows the choices.

God emotionally reacts to these choices of evil men to pervert righteousness for their own purposes. He hates those who do these things. It is also true that these men's wicked choices serve His larger purpose or He would have stopped them. None of God's ultimate purposes can fail, but He does not stop all wicked choices in this life. Just because God allowed it or you had support in doing it, doesn't mean that it has God's backing.

Do not do these selfish things that wound, hurt, or steal the life of someone else just for you to have more. Yes, the naive can be taken advantage of and if you don't, someone else will; but it matters that you don't. God hates the people who take advantage of the naiveté of people.

PROVERBS 6:18 - *A heart that devises wicked plans, feet that run rapidly to evil,*

One of the things that God hates is a mind that plans ways to go deeper into the jungle of sin.

Each of us was designed to grow a beautiful garden for the glory of the Lord. But because of sin we constantly want to wander into the jungle of sin. When we give our mind to the planning and devising and plotting of ways to move deeper into the jungle of sin, we become one that God hates.

Remember that the jungle begins at the edge of the Ten Commandments: Other gods; Idols; Cursing; No worship; Rebellion; Murder; Adultery; Stealing; Lying; Coveting.

There are no solutions to your problems in the jungle of sin. It may seem like that is where all the fun is and where all the solutions are, but you trade small problems for huge ones if you go out in the jungle to meet your needs.

PROVERBS 6:19 - *A false witness who utters lies, and one who spreads strife among brothers.*

This is the final piece in the list of six things – yeah seven – that the Lord finds to be an abomination.

The sixth thing that the Lord hates is a false witness who utters lies.

We, as a society, do not tend to see this as a big deal; but God says that it is a big deal. It strikes at the foundation of a free and secure society to have people bear false witness against their neighbors.

Whatever God says is important is different from what your culture says is important. God is right and the culture is wrong. We, as a culture, continue to try and slide away from God's clear instruction about what should be allowed and what should be penalized. Christians must realize that they have a prior commitment to Scripture even over what their birth culture tells them. We need to learn what God says and reconfigure our values and priorities to coincide with His views.

witness

This is the Hebrew word *ed* which means witness, evidence. It is preceded by the Hebrew word *sheqer* which means deception, disappointment, falsehood. Do not underestimate the significance of God's hatred of liars. You can't have an intimate relationship if it is not built on trust.

Do not follow the easy, selfish method of getting ahead: lying. The seventh thing that is an abomination to the Lord in human conduct is spreading strife among brothers.

spreads

This is the Hebrew word *shalach* which means to send. The translators used the word *spread* to cover the idea of sending strife out to others.

strife

This is the Hebrew word *medan* which means strife.

Notice that he does say that strife can be spread by some people. There are people who specialize in getting others stirred up rather than getting people to cooperate and get along. Do not become the person who uses their life to get people to hate each other, to divide, to be stirred up against each other.

brothers

This is the Hebrew word *ach* which means brother, brethren, countrymen, kinsman. Brothers are those who should get along and not be mixed up in disagreement and strife.

PROVERBS 6:20 - *My son, observe the commandment of your father and do not forsake the teaching of your mother;*

It is my hope that my girls will learn the proverbs and use these as their guide for life. If they will use the precepts of wisdom as their guide, then they will enjoy their life and be pleasing to God.

I am writing this annotated Proverbs account to be a guide to them and to my grandchildren and great-grandchildren.

Love God and *love your neighbor as yourself* are the two key commands that this father would give his girls.

They must overcome the foolishness in their heart. Foolishness will destroy them. Foolishness is the urge within every person to be selfish, to be impulsive, and to be in charge of themselves or rebellious.

my son observe the commandment of your father

It is important to realize that this message is for the children and for the parents. Who really makes a child listen to the commands and wisdom of a father? It is the father and the mother. If a parent does not insist that their children pay attention when they say something, they will be raising a fool. Those parents will know no end of grief when the little selfish child grows up. Dads and moms must cause their children to act when they give a direct order. It is this type of training that is essential for the driving out of foolishness from the child. If the parents do not stop the child from being selfish and to do what the parents want them to, they are imprisoning the child in a world where all their impulses feel right and everybody else's ideas and suggestions seem wrong. If this is taken to extreme, then love is not possible.

PROVERBS 6:21 - *Bind them continually on your heart; tie them around your neck.*

This is the what-do-you-find-yourself-thinking-about proverb; the what-are-you-meditating-on proverb. In our day and age we have the ability to not think but to have lies pumped into our minds constantly so that we never have to face the way life really works. When we meditate through popular songs, movies, radio, TV, or magazines on the idea that whatever would make us happy should be what we receive, we find ourselves absolutely appalled when God does not give us everything that would make us happy.

Solomon – like Paul, Jesus, and other prophets of the Scripture – declares that we should meditate on what the Bible says our thoughts and ways ought to be. We can expect to find our desires not being accomplished when those desires disagree with the Lord Jesus.

continually

This is the Hebrew word *"tamia"* which means continuity. The meaning is that it must be done constantly. There is an element in which wisdom must be constantly retied to our thinking. It slips off in the normal course of events. God requires us to fill our mind with the right stuff, or we will not act in the right way. Biblical meditation is about saturating your mind with key biblical ideas.

tie

This is the Hebrew word *"anad"* which means to bind around. The idea clearly is that you must keep the wisdom that you need, close to you. Keep filling your mind with these ideas.

The early church memorized five documents and said them every day: The Ten Commandments; The Lord's Prayer; The Fruit of the Spirit; The Apostle's Creed; The Beatitudes. These passages were committed to memory and repeated as the major instruction manuals of Christianity. We would do well to memorize these kinds of documents and squeeze all the life of the Lord out of them.

PROVERBS 6:22 ~ *When you walk about, they will guide you. When you sleep, they will watch over you; and when you awake, they will talk to you.*

Solomon is making the necessary assumption that the parents of the people he is addressing are seeking their children's best and protecting the children with their advice and instructions. There is the natural tendency to rebel from our parents' advice and think that it is a new day, and they are only trying to restrict us from having fun.

Your parents gave you certain instruction for a reason. They are older and wiser and have seen more of what the world will do to people. They understand how small and seemingly innocent things lead to bigger things. They have insights into how to navigate through the world into which they are birthing you.

walk

This is the Hebrew word *halik* which means step. The idea is wherever life is taking you.

guide

This is the Hebrew word *naha* which means lead or guide. Your parents' wisdom will direct you through the maze of tough decisions that you will face in life. If you have rebelled from them, you will not pay attention to the small, little directions that are so crucial to building a good life. Go back and think through what they told you to do and start paying attention. Let what they said guide you; they know what they are talking about.

sleep

This is the Hebrew word *sakab* which means to lie down. There is the possibility that Solomon is also suggesting the idea of whom you marry and have sexual relations with as the word *sekobet* is a related word and it means physical intimacy.

watch

This is the Hebrew word *samar* which means to keep, guard, observe. The idea here is that if you listen to the direction of your parents' commands, then you will be much more secure when and where you sleep at night. Also, their commands will help you find a good mate.

awake

This is the Hebrew word *qits* which means to awake. Solomon is saying that when you get started in the day, the things that your parents said will rule out certain activity and rule in certain activity that will really help.

talk

This is the Hebrew word *siha* which means meditate, muse, speak. Clearly we are the product of many of the things that our parents said to us and directed us into. If we would be willing to listen to the righteous declarations of our parents by not rebelling from their restrictions, then our ability to make better choices would improve. This is the idea of standing on their shoulders and being able to see more clearly.

Too many kids feel the need to reinvent everything themselves and mess up their lives in the process. This does remind us parents that we can have a huge impact in our kids' lives by the direction we give them and the way that we approach them. If we can keep them in a relationship with us, then they will listen to our direction; and it will save them from a lot of problems later.

PROVERBS 6:23 - *For the commandment is a lamp and the teaching is a light; and reproofs for discipline are the way of life*

God is giving us a metaphor to understand why He has given us commandments, teachings, and rebukes.

for the commandment is a lamp
He tells us that the commandment is a lamp or that which contains the light and holds the light. It can, in some cases, focus the light but not usually in Ancient Israel.

the teaching is a light
The teaching is the light. This is the explanation of the commandments that come following God's moral boundaries. There is far more contained in each commandment than just the surface words of the commandment. There is its meaning in different situations. There are the exceptions implied through the use of the words in the commandment. There are the specific places where one crosses from good to evil in their conduct because of the commandment. There are the various places that the commandment applies and the various ways that it applies. There is also the opposite of the negative commandment – the positive action that is also commanded in the commandment.

and reproofs for discipline are the way of life
The reproofs for discipline are a way of life. The idea is that the rebukes that God has built into life through laws of nature, laws of civilization, social rules, etc., mark the edges of the path of righteousness. You have to blow through all the rebukes in your life to outside of the path of righteousness. This proverb is saying: don't do it.

God is marking out the edges of the path of life for you with the rebukes that He is sending your way. They could be physical rebukes, financial rebukes, vocational rebukes, marital rebukes, social rebukes, etc. Stop resenting these rebukes but welcome them as the only way God could clearly mark out the edges of the right path.

This is much like what James tells us in James 1:2-4. God is for us and He has given us the lamp, the light, and the markings for the edge of the path. Right now are you trying to push past a rebuke in a particular area? Stop and think.

Now it is also instructive that God says that it is only those reproofs that are for discipline that mark the edge of the path of life. There are all kinds of people who want to rebuke us when we don't do things their way. These rebukes do not mark anything except the little box that others want to keep us in. We should push through those. The word *discipline* is the word for instruction or we would say, in this context, constructive criticism. God has rebukes that do these, society has these, our friends have these. All these together mark out the edges of our particular path of righteousness or life.

It is amazing but with all of these together, it is an individual path for each one of us.

God sends reproofs or spankings into our life to let us know that something is wrong and needs to be changed.

- The reproofs could be relationally: marital problems, friendship difficulties.

- They could be financial problems: not enough money, lawsuits, defective merchandise.

- They could be spiritual: spirits, distance from God, guilt.

- They could be mental: confusion.

The problem with our society is that we don't recognize the reproofs as spankings. We think of them as just normal life because everybody else is having the reproof also.

PROVERBS 6:24 - *To keep you from the evil woman, from the smooth tongue of the adulteress.*

Solomon is warning his young student – who wants to learn wisdom – to listen to the commandments of the Scriptures for they will form a protective wall between you and the serious sin of adultery.

Just recently I was interviewing a man who got involved in adultery and he said what they all say. He allowed this person who was not his spouse to meet relational needs that only his spouse should have been meeting and eventually the relationship grew until it became sexual. This is how it always happens in long-term affairs. There are one-night stands that are just stupid decisions to give into lust; but they are usually encouraged by alcohol, drugs, loneliness, depression, wrong friends, pornography, etc.

Once you have begun to connect with an adulterer or adulteress, relationally it is too late. The time to stop is way before you ever meet this person. Do not allow yourself to have your relational needs met by someone who is not your spouse. If you are single, then do not allow your relational needs to be met by someone who could not or will not be your spouse someday.

What are your relational needs? Well if your are a man, they are usually: Respect, Adaptation, Domestic Leadership, Intimacy, Companionship, Attractive Soul and Body, and Listening. If you are a woman, they are usually: Honor, Understanding, Security, Building Unity, Agreement, Nurture, Defender. When someone meets these needs, we are drawn toward them. Do not underestimate the power of these relational needs. We are drawn towards anyone who will meet these needs, but we get to choose who we let meet these needs. Unfortunately many people in marriage have decided to no longer meet the needs of their partner, and this puts greater tension on the individual to find someone who will meet these needs. It is always a mistake to look to someone other than your spouse to meet these needs even if for a period of time your spouse is not meeting your needs.

PROVERBS 6:25 - *Do not desire her beauty in your heart, nor let her capture you with her eyelids.*

A man can be captured by the look of a woman, how she acts, and the way she relates to him. She can make it seem as though she really wants him and that he is a desirable man. She can, through her listening and focused interest, propel him to a world of love, respect, and importance. It is this orientation that often fools men into sexual unfaithfulness.

One cannot be too careful. Notice what Solomon says: "Do not desire her beauty in your heart." You win or lose the battle in your mind, not in your actions. Do you allow yourself to fantasize about this person? If you do, you are already losing the battle. There are significant battles you must win after this; but if you embrace the idea of sexual fantasies, then you are losing and have lost some significant battles.

Stop thinking about this. Think about something else. Think about your spouse, about your job, about hobbies that you love, about the Lord and your seeing Him face-to-face one day.

I hear about men being captured by the beauty of their secretary or a neighbor or a colleague instead of realizing that they are interested and tempted by this person's beauty and steering a wide path around this person. Some think nothing of their mental flirtations and move right on ahead. Pay attention to your own temptations enough to realize that if you are interested in that person or they strike you a certain way, you should realize that they represent fire to you. Move away. Move back. Change the approach to that person. They cannot be treated like everybody else; something else is in play here. You must be careful.

Solomon describes accurately that no marital unfaithfulness begins with the unfaithfulness itself. It always begins as a mental fantasy first. There are lots of stages and phases before actual adultery is committed. It is even possible that some of you reading this right now are in some of the early phases of a flirtation or fantasy situation with someone who is not your spouse. You need to stop and go in the opposite direction. Break off contact with that person. If you have to seek a transfer or have them transferred, then do it. There is not a pot of gold at the end of this adultery game – just diseases, loneliness, depression, broken hearts, half the money, and mistrust.

Recognize that it begins with a desire of beauty in your soul and in your mind. It begins with the mind, and it needs to be beaten in your mind. While it promises life and excitement and love and joy, it separates you from life. It brings broken relationships and a series of lies and problems. Don't go down this road. Get off this path before you begin.

This proverb talks about beauty, but it does not mean just physical beauty. It is sexual beauty. It is the allure of a woman who knows how to treat a man. A woman of average physical beauty can transform herself into a woman of great beauty by learning the top ten needs of a man and developing the skills to meet them. A man is attracted to a woman who displays the skills and meets the needs of a man. It is a woman's clear ability to meet a man's needs that makes her beautiful. Often it is not her physical beauty but her ways of showing respect that is alluring, her willingness to listen to him, or her ability to "enjoy" his hobby or interests.

How does an adulteress capture a married man by her beauty? A number of studies have suggested that it is respect and listening as much as physical attractiveness and sex. Men, be careful that you do not begin to let another woman meet needs that your wife should be meeting. If you do, you have begun to move down the road to an affair.

Now on the other side, it is important that a man's wife know how to capture her husband's heart through her beauty – through her respect, listening, companionship, leadership, etc. (1 Peter 3:3,4) It is these areas that bring out the beautiful woman on the inside. She should also keep herself physically attractive and be willing to accommodate him sexually; but those are not the only, or in many cases, the primary ways to captivate him with your beauty.

PROVERBS 6:26 - *For on account of a harlot one is reduced to a loaf of bread, and an adulteress hunts for the precious life.*

harlot

This is the Hebrew word *zanah* which means to commit fornication, to be a harlot, to commit adultery. Solomon is trying to get you to see this temptation for the economic bad deal it is. Look at what you are trading. You are giving up all you have and all you have worked for to chase after a few minutes of pleasure in the arms of someone that you don't even know.

Solomon is trying to frame the discussion of giving into adultery as an economic equation and to allow you to evaluate its merits before the power of the temptation is on you. Sexual temptation is a very powerful force and can make you do things that you would not normally do. So it is best to evaluate this temptation that is surely coming – when you have a clear head. It is a bad economic deal.

Once the adulteress has got you, then it is never without entanglements. There are relational, financial, medical, emotional, spiritual, and moral entanglements.

loaf of bread

This is the Hebrew word *lechem* which is bread, food. There will be nothing left after you have started to pursue sexual unfaithfulness – only the bare minimum to survive: a loaf of bread. Solomon is pointing out to us: Look at what happens to people who go down this road. They have two houses to maintain; two relationships to maintain. There will be nothing left for you. You think this is an answer; it is not. It is a financial and emotional prison cell that you can avoid by being faithful to your spouse.

adulteress

This is the Hebrew word *ishshah* which means woman, wife, female, adulteress. The idea here is that Solomon notices that the adulteress is doing some calculating and is going after the deeper pockets, so you should calculate yourself out of this mess entirely by never entering into it.

precious

This is the Hebrew word *yaqar* which means precious, rare, splendid. The idea here is that the more valuable your life is, the more the sexually unfaithful people will make themselves available to you. They are parasites looking for a rich place to hook on. Those who are sexually unfaithful are selfish and looking for what is best for them. They do not love you. They are using their techniques to hook deep into your life and drain it dry.

Solomon is really saying: Before you get under the spell of a temptation you should examine it under the bright light of day. Let me give you a few examples:

- "I will feel a pull to steal something that isn't mine and that I haven't paid for." No matter what I feel at the time, it is wrong and will make me a thief. I could get caught and have those penalties. I will resist this because it is a stupid idea, even though it may present itself as the coolest thing to do at the time.

- "I will feel a pull to be sexually unfaithful at some point in my life." It will expose me to disease, guilt, shame, unwanted relationships, other sins, and lies." No matter how good it may seem at the time, it will be a bad deal. "Avoid it.

- "I will someday feel like trumpeting how wonderful I am and believing, because of something I have done, that I am better than some people that I know." This will not be true. If I allow this idea that I am somehow a more valuable person than others, I will begin to treat them differently and this will damage my relationships. No matter how significant what I have done, it does not make me a better person than someone else; it allows me to fulfill the personhood that I am.

PROVERBS 6:27 - *Can a man take fire in his bosom and his clothes not be burned?*

Solomon is trying to tell young men especially that the urge they have to meet their sexual needs cannot ever be allowed to flow outside the boundaries of marriage. It is like taking a hot ember and putting it into your very heart.

Everything about you will change if you go outside of marriage and have an affair. Your affections and your focus – as well as your conscience and sensitivity – will be changed. Sexual unfaithfulness is a fire. It seems, at the beginning, that it is a fire that cannot be denied; but then it becomes a fire that cannot be quenched, burning up everything that is most precious to you.

I have watched what happens to men who want to add this "extra" to their lives. It is like adding a fire to the middle of your living room. It will not add just the little benefit that you think it will add. It will go way beyond where you think you can contain it.

Solomon is saying to think about what will happen, not just what you want. The problem with most adultery is that the people involved did not consider the wreckage that their infidelity would cause.

Yes, you will miss out on a few moments of stolen passion; but you will also miss out on a ton of misery, destruction, and pain.

PROVERBS 6:28 - *Or can a man walk on hot coals and his feet not be scorched?*

This verse is the second verse dealing with fire in regards to adultery. The previous verse compares being involved with an adulteress to taking hot coals inside one's clothing or near one's bosom. This verse compares being involved with an adulteress to a person who would walk over hot coals.

The two pictures deal with the passions that an adulterous relationship excites. I have worked with a number of people involved in this sin, and they have testified to the all-consuming nature of the passion in this type of relationship – for a little while. It is like an out-of-control fire threatening to consume one's heart and become the preoccupation of one's whole day.

If it is more than just a one-night stand, an adulterous relationship is white-hot with passion for between two weeks and six months and then it cools. The problem is that many of the decisions that this "couple" make are during the white-hot fire of passion. They think that it will stay this passionate; it will not. They have never felt anything like this before and want it to continue, but it will not. It will consume their emotional energy, financial resources, and other relationships and then die out only when all the fuel is gone.

One of the things that Solomon is saying here in this verse is that committing adultery is full of passion, but it is like throwing hot coals on the path that you must walk every day. It will scorch you. If you give in to this immoral passion, all the rest of your life will be burned along with your soul. One does not just add adultery to the mix of one's life. It comes in to take over; it spreads itself in every area of life. You cannot keep this kind of passion contained in a little pot in the closet.

Solomon is saying that adultery will burn your heart; it will burn your whole life. Don't go near it. You can't control it. You can't contain it. It will scar you in ways that you can't imagine, so avoid it just the same way that you would avoid a walkway that was strewn with hot coals.

PROVERBS 6:29 - *So is the one who goes into his neighbor's wife; whoever touches her will not go unpunished.*

Solomon has just listed two impossible scenarios to demonstrate the danger and sure punishment that comes with adultery. He asks if a person can have a piece of wood that is on fire inside next to his skin and not have his clothing catch on fire. The obvious answer is: "No, it is not possible." The second scenario that he sets up is: Is it possible to walk across hot coals and not scorch your feet? The answer is: "No."

This proverb in verse 29 is the conclusion to this line of instruction about adultery. DO NOT THINK YOU WILL GET AWAY WITH IT. I have had the unfortunate assignment of dealing with a number of people who were caught in adultery. It is always exposed. It always causes significant damage to everybody connected to the affair. It was exciting for a short period of time, but let me tell you the consequences and punishments last a whole lot longer than the pleasure.

touches

This is the Hebrew word *naga* which means touch or reach. The word touch clearly means reach out for in a sexual or intimate way. This is very similar to the Apostle Paul's admonition in 1 Corinthians 7:1 It is good for a man not to touch a woman. It is not that he is saying that physical touch of someone else's wife is outlawed, but touch that has any sensual or erotic connection is outside of the boundaries of moral behavior.

unpunished

This is the Hebrew word *naqah* which means to be clear, empty, clean, innocent. The word is preceded by the word *not* or *no* and reads they will not be innocent or free. Solomon is forcing the would-be adulterer to see what they never think about. You will be caught and there will be significant consequences. I can't tell you how many people I have talked to who have committed this sin and when the consequences start piling up, they all want to go back to before they did this thing.

There are financial punishments, relational punishments, marital punishments, vocational punishments, spiritual punishments, mental punishments, and many others.

If you are in a place right now where you are tempted to commit adultery, get out of that relationship in any way you can. Do not go through with it. If you are in an adulterous relationship, then stop it. Every day you don't allow it to continue reduces the amount of the pain and consequences that are coming. I know that this person has become dear to you and you do not know what you will do without this person, but it is a mistake. There is not an easy way to stop these relationships. Jesus said you just need to cut them off cold turkey. Call the person and say that it is over and you no longer want to see them, talk with them, or have any contact with them anymore. I have found that this is the only way. There is no way to make the other party in adultery understand. It just has to end and now is better than later. The less time the adultery continues, the less the consequences and punishments will be. If you are in one, get out. If you are moving in that direction, stop it. Get away emotionally and physically from that person. If you are attracted to someone who is not your spouse, don't say anything to anyone; just move away from contact of any sort with that person and let those feelings die. There are feelings that should not see the light of day. If you do not act upon them, they will eventually go away. Do not betray yourself and God for some feelings. It is not worth it.

PROVERBS 6:30 ~ *Men do not despise a thief if he steals to satisfy himself when he is hungry;*

Solomon changes the argument to talk about the deep loathing that surrounds the person who breaks another person's marriage to fulfill his own self desires.

Solomon is painting a vivid picture of a destroyed reputation. A man's pride is at stake. He needs to realize that this is not a secret sin. He needs to think about the destruction of his reputation way before he gets anywhere near that kind of sin. It is too late when you are under the pull of temptation. The place to contemplate this is when you are putting out the plan of your life. This is when you plan out what kind of reputation you want. If you do not want it to have a stain that will not wash out, then build proper boundaries around you and another person's spouse and/or any sexual sin.

I have seen this sin up close too many times as I have had to confront men, and even pastors, about immorality. It is always the same devastation when it comes out. It is always a deep stain where others cannot trust them in the same way after this comes out. I have recently watched as a young man caught in adultery struck me as just wandering in a daze, being reproached by all sides. Even when he was offered help he didn't know whether he wanted it. Now your spouse doesn't know if he/she can trust you. Your friends don't know if they can trust you. Your kids don't know how to treat you. Your colleagues don't know how to deal with you.

Solomon is saying this is not the same kind of sin as even stealing. There is at least some explanation for stealing if you are desperate. You have to pay it back, but it is redeemable. But adultery is a permanent stain – a permanent weakness that only in the grace of God can a person overcome. Do not go down this road, Solomon instructs. I am discouraged that our culture – through the magazines, the television, the movies, the books – all want to downplay the significance of fornication and adultery. It is not a big deal they say; everybody cheats on their spouse. Don't listen to them. Everybody does not cheat on their spouse. And it is a ride on a picket fence for those who do.

PROVERBS 6:31 - *But when he is found he must repay sevenfold; he must give all the substance of his house.*

Solomon is reminding the Jewish listener of the laws of restitution in the Old Testament. If a thief were to steal something from you, then depending upon the condition that you found out who did it and whether they still had it with them, the thief would have to repay you twice, four times, or seven times the value of the item that they stole as well as what they stole.

In this system of justice there is real opportunity for forgiveness and restoration because the person who had their property stolen actually benefits if they have their possessions stolen. So they are happy that you stole from them.

I have used this idea of multiplied restitution to reconcile former friends. If someone stole something or cheated or in some other way didn't pay, I have suggested that people pay double in order to restore the relationship.

Solomon is using this idea of godly justice to point out that there is no amount of restitution that will make the sin of adultery restored. The adulterer steals something that cannot be restored. They steal trust. They steal oneness. They steal affection. They steal respect. All of these things do not have an amount associated with them.

Solomon goes on to say that for the kind of violation that adultery brings, there is no adequate restoration that can make the other person happy. God's justice system is designed to be restorative if at all possible. These provisions about stealing are designed to cause people not to steal but also to bring about the restoration of the relation broken by the theft.

That is why Jesus Christ coming to earth, living the perfect life, and surrendering the perfect life for our sins was the perfect act of justice. He did that to restore our relationship with God. If we embrace the wonder of His death for us, we can interact with God without fear even though we have done many things to offend Him.

PROVERBS 6:32 - *The one who commits adultery with a woman is lacking sense; he who would destroy himself does it.*

This proverb is the plain statement of the case: adultery crosses the line of acceptable behavior. It is unwise. It is foolish. It is personally destructive.

The proverb states that the person who would go outside of the marriage boundaries is lacking sense. The word *sense* is the Hebrew word for heart or thinking capacity. It is sometimes used of the idea of understanding. The person cannot put it all together what will happen when they do this.

Let me just comment on this straightforward proverb. Adultery in our day and age is seen as no big deal. Everybody does it. The media suggests that marital infidelity is acceptable and even desirable. In fact, the modern media encourages people to think about adultery in the exact opposite way that this proverb does. In the end, one will find that God is right and the modern media and modern ideas of morality were wrong.

Because we have abandoned God's limits on behavior and embraced sexual license, we have emotional and family destruction. The moral line of *thou shalt not commit adultery* is there because society cannot continue to exist as a healthy enterprise when sexual passions are uncontained.

In our day there is a weak desire to place the limit on sexual conduct right before homosexuality. This will fail; God does not place it there. He places it at marital fidelity. In order for society to have stable families, there must be shame and societal chastisement for those who break down family bonds. The stability of the family must be preserved or the society will begin to come apart. For single people that means fidelity to someone you may not even have met yet. Does it help society when one person saves himself/herself until marriage? Yes. Does it hurt society when one individual is unfaithful to their marriage vows? Yes. The faithfulness of every individual helps the society be a stronger entity. Please do not believe the hype that adultery is no big deal. It is a big deal. It is a big deal for you personally and it is a big deal for our society as a whole.

This particular proverb is about the personal damage done to the individual when adultery takes place. You have taken your ability to think and put it on the shelf. Think through the consequences; it is not worth it.

PROVERBS 6:33 - *Wounds and disgrace he will find, and his reproach will not be blotted out.*

wounds

This is the Hebrew word *nega* which means a stroke, a plague, a mark, an affliction. It seems light to call this word a wound when it is much deeper than that in Hebrew. It means a severe mark that does not go away; a permanent affliction or mark that cannot be washed away.

Solomon is trying to warn people. You will be stained. You will be carrying an affliction that does not heal easily, if at all. This wound has physical, emotional, and mental aspects to it.

disgrace

This is the Hebrew word *qalon* which means dishonor, ignominy, disgrace, shame. Our present culture does not have the proper place for shame. Because we are so afraid of shaming a person, everything becomes permissible. The sin of destroying a marriage through sexual unfaithfulness is shameful. It needs to be discouraged, not encouraged as it is in our day.

I am deeply saddened by the fact that we have begun to attach shame to being righteous rather than being wicked. In some circles in the teen culture it is a shameful thing to be a virgin. It is a shameful thing not to have cheated on an exam.

We must bring back the concept and the practice of disgrace and shame for certain actions. There should clearly be forgiveness and restoration, but society needs to have the right thing to become shameful.

We need to be a society where people think about living their life in front of the eyes of God and others. I was telling one of my daughters the other day that we need to live our lives so that we are not ashamed of any part of our life. I let her know that we have monitors on the Internet and monitors on the car she will drive so that she can get used to the idea that an open and accountable life is the best life. Many in our society have the idea that they have a right to do hidden things – even destructive or harmful things – that others don't have the right to know about. But the problem is that they will eventually find out. I try to live my life so that anyone can look in on it and not find hidden stuff that would disgrace me or God. We all will sin. But you should avoid the hidden shameful practices that if others found out you what did, it would cause you to lose massive amounts of respect from them. If you have any of these areas of hidden sin in your life, find a way to stop doing this. Bring a new level of openness and accountability into your life.

reproach

This is the Hebrew word *cherpah* which means a reproach, contempt, scorn. Contempt is a good word here because it conveys the negative emotion that flows out of others toward those who destroy or damage the marriages of others through adultery.

Solomon is pointing out that while adultery looks enticing and pleasurable, you will have a blot on your life; and people will hold you in deep contempt because of your breaking of your marriage vows.

Those who have committed this sin also need to know that even though the blot or contempt that others feel for them may not go away, God has made a way through the death of Christ to remove the stain of this sin. Forgiveness is possible in Christ, and He will wash you thoroughly from your iniquity.

PROVERBS 6:34 *For jealousy enrages a man, and he will not spare in the day of vengeance*

jealousy

This is the Hebrew word *qinah* which means ardor, zeal, jealousy. This is a very strong emotional word. One becomes passionate or consumed by something to where its loss or its pleasure is all-important. This is that word.

"Do not forget, my young would-be adulterer," Solomon the man of wisdom reminds, "that this person you are contemplating violating is connected to another person and when that emotion is stirred up, it will not be pretty."

Solomon is walking young men especially around the whole of adultery and looking at the seduction, the aftermath for the perpetrator, the aftermath for the seduced, the aftermath for the injured parties not involved in the adultery, and so on. He is forcing you to see all the storylines that lead out from this evil action. This act will start storylines that you will wish had not been started.

enrages

This is the Hebrew word *chemah* which means heat, rage, anger. Solomon is saying that strong emotions of jealousy – which involves possession of what is precious – releases a level of action and energy that transforms a man into doing what he would not normally do.

Anger is the reaction to not getting one's expectations fulfilled. When those expectations involve having your prized possessions violated or stolen, then the energy in that anger is white hot and will impel people to do things they would normally not even think of, let alone have the energy to do.

Unfortunately we have seen this kind of energy be displayed over and over again in divorce proceedings and separation settlements. So much of what takes place in these things is spite and the desire to get back at the other person for what they have done to you.

We are, unfortunately, returning to a way of thinking and acting whereby a person who feels that they were done wrong by the legal or justice system will exact their pound of flesh out of the offending party even if it means they spend the rest of their life in jail.

spare

This is the Hebrew word *chamal* which means to spare, to have compassion, to show pity. The truth that Solomon is bringing out here is that marital infidelity seems to wipe out a person's compassionate nature. The idea of mercy to a person who violated this most sacred trust does not compute to the person who has been wronged. Solomon is right that there is little, if any, mercy once adultery has taken place. We see this in the venom in divorce cases and the murderous rage in many men whose wives have cheated on them. This does not excuse the rage or the violence that a person may do, Solomon is just pointing out to the person who is tempted to break a marriage vow that there will be little or no mercy once it is found out. So don't do this.

vengeance

This is the Hebrew word *naqam* which means vengeance. The idea in that day was that those involved in meting out justice to offending parties were often the offended. Solomon sees that consequences for adultery would come from the offended spouse and since their heart was so enraged at having their dearly beloved ripped from them, there would be no mercy when it came time to punish the offender. In our modern era there has been a more broad application of biblical principles, such as an unemotional person deciding the consequences and punishment for offenders. But I find that many are still after direct vengeance for those who wrong them. This is strong reason not to mess with adultery.

As we look at Solomon's advice here that is built on solid observation and channeled through God's inspiration, it is important to not fall for the false promises of lust and adultery. Of all the sins a person can commit this one carries levels of ongoing toxicity that others do not. You may think you are having a great time but you will be destroying your life. Do not commit adultery.

PROVERBS 6:35 - *He will not accept any ransom, nor will he be satisfied though you give many gifts.*

With this proverb Solomon finishes the 360-degree picture of adultery. He has been showing all the various actions and consequences of adultery so that potential adulterers will know that this is what happens when you do this. He is also saying: Let me force you to think about aspects of this sin that you won't think about until it is too late. What about the injured spouses? What are they going to be feeling and will their rage ever die down? The answer is, no, it will not die down and nothing you can do will restore the trust and relationship that you destroy if you commit adultery.

In the previous verses Solomon says that there is a fix for stealing (paying double the value of what you stole); but when it comes to adultery, there is no going back and making this crime whole. Solomon says there is no seven-fold amount over the price of the adultery that will cause the pain, anger, hatred, and vengeance that they feel for you to be over. They, and only they, decide to move on and reconnect with their spouse. There is no amount of goods that will tip the scale in the direction of the person saying, "I am so glad that you did this with my wife/husband."

In most cases the couples know one another. You are deeply wounding someone who you know and may be friends with.

The actual sentence in the Hebrew reads: *He will not allow any bribe to lift up his face.* In other words, there is no amount of money that will make it all go away. There is no way to say: I am so sorry, please forgive me. When it is over – and it will be over – there will be no appeasing the wounded spouse.

Solomon has been, for two chapters, building the case that adultery is a temptation that you just cannot fall into. It will twist and distort your life in a myriad of ways.

About Author

Gil Stieglitz is a catalyst for positive change both personally and organizationally. He excites, educates, and motivates audiences all over the world, through passion, humor, leadership and wisdom. He has led seminars in China, Europe, Canada, Mexico, and all over the United States.

Since founding the nonprofit ministry Principles to Live By in 1992 to help people and organizations win at life through Biblical Wisdom, Dr. Gil has been asked to repair, lead and reinvigorate numerous organizations and individuals. He successfully led a church to 1400 percent growth in a disadvantaged area. As a Denominational Superintendent in the Western United States he led 50 churches and 250 pastors to over 300% growth. As a Superintendent of Schools he oversaw a school system as it doubled in 4 years. As an executive pastor at a mega – church he rebuilt a staff and added over a 1,000 people. He injects dynamic life change as a professor at universities and graduate schools on the West Coast and through seminars, sermons and lecture series. He also partners with Courage Worldwide which rescues young girls who have been forced into sexual slavery in America.

He has a B.A. from Biola University, a Master's Degree and a Doctorate in Christian Leadership from Talbot School of Theology. He has authored over two dozen books, manuals and development courses including three best sellers. Dr. Gil's resources are available on Amazon.com as well as on www.PrinciplesToLiveBy.com.

Gil and his wife, Dana, have enjoyed over twenty-five years of marriage and reside in Roseville, California, where they raised their three precious girls.

Other Resources by Gil Stieglitz

BOOKS

Becoming Courageous
Breakfast with Solomon Volume 1
Breakfast with Solomon Volume 2
Breakfast with Solomon Volume 3
Breaking Satanic Bondage
Deep Happiness: The 8 Secrets
Delighting in God
Delighting in Jesus
Developing a Christian Worldview
God's Radical Plan for Husbands
God's Radical Plan for Wives
Going Deep In Prayer: 40 Days of In-Depth Prayer
Leading a Thriving Ministry
Marital Intelligence
Mission Possible: Winning the Battle Over Temptation
Proverbs: A Devotional Commentary Vol. 2
Satan and The Origin of Evil
Secrets of God's Armor
Spiritual Disciplines of a C.H.R.I.S.T.I.A.N
The Schemes of Satan
They Laughed When I Wrote Another Book About Prayer,
    Then They Read It
Touching the Face of God: 40 Days of Adoring God
Weapons of Righteousness Study Guides
Why There Has to Be a Hell

**If you would be interested in having Dr. Gil Stieglitz
speak to your group, you can contact him through the website
www.ptlb.com**

www.ingramcontent.com/pod-product-compliance
Lightning Source LLC
Chambersburg PA
CBHW021213090426
42740CB00006B/205